PERFORMING ARTS

Dance in CUBA

MULTIMEDIAL LINKS

The numbered links* that appear in the footnotes of this book refer the reader to films specifically selected by the Author from the resources available on the Web. For every link, there is a corresponding QR code at the top of the page that allows access to the video of interest directly from the reader's smartphone or tablet. To view the videos, just follow these simple steps:
1. On your smartphone or tablet, download one of the many free applications for reading QR codes.
2. Open the application.
3. Frame the QR code indicated at the top of the page of the book and click on the option "Open URL" (or similar).

*All of the links indicated in this book have been verified for the last time in January 2021.

Elisa Guzzo Vaccarino

Dance in CUBA

FROM CLASSICAL BALLET AND CONTEMPORARY DANCE TO TRADITIONAL AFRO-CUBAN AND POPULAR DANCES

Edited and translated from the Italian by
Sandra Eiko Tokunaga

Brief Note to Readers

■ Entities, schools and dance companies are at times indicated with the following respective acronyms:

ABT: American Ballet Theatre
AD: Acosta Danza
AIDA: Asociación de la Danza para las Américas
BNC: Ballet Nacional de Cuba
CIC: Certamen Iberoamericano de Coreografía
CNEART: Centro Nacional de Escuelas de Arte
CNDC: Compañía Nacional de Danza Contemporánea de República Dominicana
CNESex: Centro Nacional de Educación Sexual
CFNC: Conjunto Foklórico Nacional de Cuba
CQD: Ciudades Que Danzan
DCC: Danza Contemporánea de Cuba
ENB: Escuela Nacional de Ballet
ENA: Escuela Nacional de Arte
FAC: Fábrica de Arte Cubano
GEDE: Grupo de Experimentación de la Danza y el Espectáculo
GTH: Gran Teatro de La Habana
ICAIC: Instituto Cubano del Arte e Industria Cinematográficos
ISA: Instituto Superior de Arte
LASA: Laboratorio Artístico de San Agustín
LHD: Los Hijos del Director
MCB: Miami City Ballet
SFB: San Francisco Ballet
UNEAC: Unión de Escritores y Artistas de Cuba
WASA: Wifi Alternativa de San Agustín

■ Cuban names in full consist of the first name, paternal last name, and maternal last name. Officially both last names are used, but for brevity's sake the paternal last name is acceptable.

■ At times the titles of some ballets from repertories of the nineteenth and twentieth centuries may appear in Spanish, in keeping with Cuban usage.

■ Italian translations of quotes originally in Spanish have been made by the Author except when expressly indicated. The English translations of these quotes are from the Italian.

■ The Author wishes to indicate the following chronology of the Diaghilev legacy of related companies that formed after the death of Serge Diaghilev, founder of the original Ballets Russes (1909-1929):

1932-1935: Les Ballets Russes de Monte-Carlo (that included the Ballet de l'Opéra Russe de Paris). In the United States the company took the name Monte Carlo Ballets Russes (1933-1935). In London its name was Colonel de Basil's Ballets Russes (1934), and it was directed by René Blum and Colonel W. de Basil.

1935-1939: Colonel de Basil's Ballets Russes.

1936-1938: René Blum's Ballets Russes de Monte-Carlo.

1939-1948: Original Ballet Russe directed by Colonel W. de Basil.

Season 1937/1938-1963: Ballet Russe de Monte Carlo created in Monte Carlo by René Blum and directed by Léonide Massine. Names anglicized for the USA/UK tour.

1938-1963: Ballet Russe de Monte Carlo initially directed by Julius Fleischmann and Serge Denham. After 1942 Denham was sole director.

1951-1952: Original Ballet Russe directed by George Kirsta and Vsevolod Grigoriev.

Cover: Francesco Partesano

On front cover: (*from above*) Viengsay Valdés in *Carmen* (photo by © Nancy Reyes), Alicia Alonso as Kitri in *Don Quixote*, in the fifties (photo © Alex di Paola, Museo de la Danza, Havana), Carlos Acosta and Marta Ortega in *Mermaid* by Sidi Larbi Charkaoui (photo by © Johan Persson).

On back cover: (*above*) DCC in *Carmen* by Kenneth Kvamström (photo by © Alice Pennefather); (*below*) Malpaso in *24 Hours and a Dog* by Osnel Delgado (photo by © Bill Hebert).

Photo credits: see p. 220. Special thanks are expressed to Alfio Agostini, director of "Balletto Oggi/Ballet2000", for allowing access to the precious archives of the magazine. Heartfelt gratitude to the dance companies that appear in this book and to their photographers.

Edited and translated from the Italian by Sandra Eiko Tokunaga

Printed and bound in Italy by: MIG – Bologna

Copyright:
2021 © Gremese International s.r.l.s. – Rome

All rights reserved. No part of this publication may be stored, reproduced or transmitted, in any form or by any means, without the prior written permission of the Publisher.

ISBN 978-88-7301-787-5

CONTENTS

Introduction 11

CHAPTER 1
BALLET IN CUBA: THE BEGINNINGS 13

CHAPTER 2
ALICIA ALONSO AND THE BALLET NACIONAL DE CUBA 17
- Training and Success
- Alicia Alonso and *Giselle*
- *Giselle*: The Choreography by Alicia Alonso

CHAPTER 3
FOUNDERS OF CUBAN BALLET: THE ALONSO DYNASTY 31
- Fernando Alonso
- Alberto Alonso
- Laura and Iván Alonso

CHAPTER 4
BALLET NACIONAL DE CUBA: STYLES AND BNC GENERATIONS 43
- Men and Women of the BNC

CHAPTER 5
CUBAN MALE BALLET DANCERS: A SPECIAL STORY 51

CHAPTER 6
CUBAN BALLET DANCERS IN THE WORLD 57
- Miami
- Exemplary Careers: Carreño and Acosta
- To Dance *a lo cubano* in a Global World

CHAPTER 7
BNC: CHOREOGRAPHERS 65
- Alberto Méndez
- Iván Tenorio
- Gustavo Herrera
- Eduardo Blanco, *Enfant Prodige*

CHAPTER 8
BNC: REPERTORY 71
- BNC Female Choreographers
- Cult Ballet and *Cubanía*
- Alicia Alonso Gran Teatro de La Habana
- Great Choreographers: Rarity and Specific Identity
- Choreographers of the 1900s

CHAPTER 9
CUBAN MODERN DANCE: FROM RAMIRO GUERRA TO TODAY 85
- Training Abroad
- Return Home
- A National Modern Dance
- *The Decalogue of the Apocalypse*
- Modern Dance in the USA and Cuba

CONTENTS

Chapter 10
DANZA CONTEMPORÁNEA DE CUBA 101
- The DCC and Offspring

Chapter 11
**IN THE WAKE OF GUERRA:
FOR AN ETHNO-CUBAN DANCE** 119
- First Generation

Eduardo Rivero
Santiago Alfonso
Victor Cuéllar
- Second Generation

Marianela Boán and DanzAbierta
Susana Pous and DanzAbierta
Rosario Cárdenas
Narciso Medina
- Third Generation

Jorge Luis Abril
Lidice Núñez Lopez
- In Havana and Beyond: Other Companies

Chapter 12
**CUBAN CONTEMPORARY DANCE:
THE NEW MILLENNIUM** 135
- Centro de la Danza de La Habana
- New Faces
- New Dance and New Critics

Chapter 13
ACOSTA DANZA 147

Chapter 14
OTHER PATHS AND DESIRE FOR INDEPENDENCE . 157
- Isabel Bustos and Retazos
- Videodance

Chapter 15
BALLET, MODERN DANCE AND EDUCATIONAL REVOLUTION 163
- La Escuela Nacional de Ballet: From Cubanacán (ENA) to Prado (ENB)
- ENA – Escuela Nacional de Arte
- ENB – Escuela Nacional de Ballet
- Training in Modern Dance
- ISA – Instituto Superior de Arte

Chapter 16
YORUBA* DANCES: CUBA *BLANQUINEGRA 173
- Afro-Cuban Culture: The African Patrimony
- Religion and Politics
- Dance of the *Orishas*

Chapter 17
POPULAR DANCES: THE RHYTHMS OF CUBA 185
- Eras and Genres

Rumba
Trova and Bolero
Danzón
Son
Mambo
- Latin Music Today
- Women in Cuban Music

Chapter 18
THE TROPICANA 197
- The Beauties of the Tropicana

Bibliography 212
Videos and Films 217
Acknowledgments 218
Photo Credits 220

INTRODUCTION

Dance in Cuba is a universe so vast that to tell its story seems an almost titanic undertaking. It is a challenge even beyond the fascinating rhythms and moving figures "born to dance" of those who inhabit the Isla Grande of the Caribbean.

Before the advent of Fidel Castro's nationalist revolution, the focus of colonial and post-colonial governments was on *caribeño* luxury. There were the cabaret nightclubs such as the Tropicana where patrons drank, smoked, and flirted

Rumba for Alicia Alonso at Callejón de Hamel, Havana, 2016.

INTRODUCTION

all in the name of a merrily abundant and multiracial Eros. There were also the theatres that catered to the White bourgeoisie and borrowed from elitist European models to present operas, concerts and ballets.

After 1959, the new government began to direct, promote, authorize, foster, finance and manage performance events and entertainment according to a more modern concept. This also embraced the authenticity of oral cultures. *Cubanía* was a concept that suggested nation, homeland and identity. It brought unity to diversity and took pride in the sentiment of sharing as a people.

In approaching today's complexity – the fruit of so many upheavals – to grasp the pervasive centrality of dance on this island nation, an event of great significance stands out. This event united the two choreographic and dance extremities of the island's mixed-race "glocal" reality.

This happened in 2016 when the mythic classical ballerina Alicia Alonso, just as a reigning head of state, and over ninety-five years of age, attended a *toque de tambores* in her honor in Havana's Afro-Cuban quarter of Callejón de Hamel. The "illustrious child" and "prima ballerina assoluta" Alicia Alonso danced without her shoes amidst the riot of colors of the famous murals of Callejón, the capital of Afro-Cuban *rumba*. The "living legend" Alicia, overseas standard bearer in the Caribbean of White Italian-Russian-American academic dance, in all her planetary prestige, crossed the "forbidden" bridge between ballet and the slave culture of Cuba. She was given the symbolic key to Callejòn, a work by Salvador González, creator of the first of the polychromatic paintings of the quarter. The bands Rumba Morena and Los Ibeyes evoked for her the *Yoruba* divinities of death and rebirth.

A memory of ballet shoes and bare feet, elevation to the sky and percussion on earth, sacred and profane, Black and White, spontaneity and discipline, innovation and tradition. And in this memory, the invocation *"Aché!"* to the vital force in *Yoruba* rituals became the auspicious cry for Alicia Alonso at the close of the ceremony. It marked a historic moment in the embrace between the worlds of two ancestries that were considered at one time irreconcilable.

On 20th December 2020, after months of *Quédate en casa* ("Stay at home") video posts, with dance performances only on the Web because of the pandemic, there was a live gala staged at the Gran Teatro de la Habana. The occasion was the 100th Anniversary of the birth of Alicia Alonso. Meanwhile in many points in the capital the *Assoluta* danced on giant video screens. From that day on, in Alicia Alonso's honor, the 21st December would be celebrated as the *Día Iberoamericano de la Danza*.

Elisa Guzzo Vaccarino

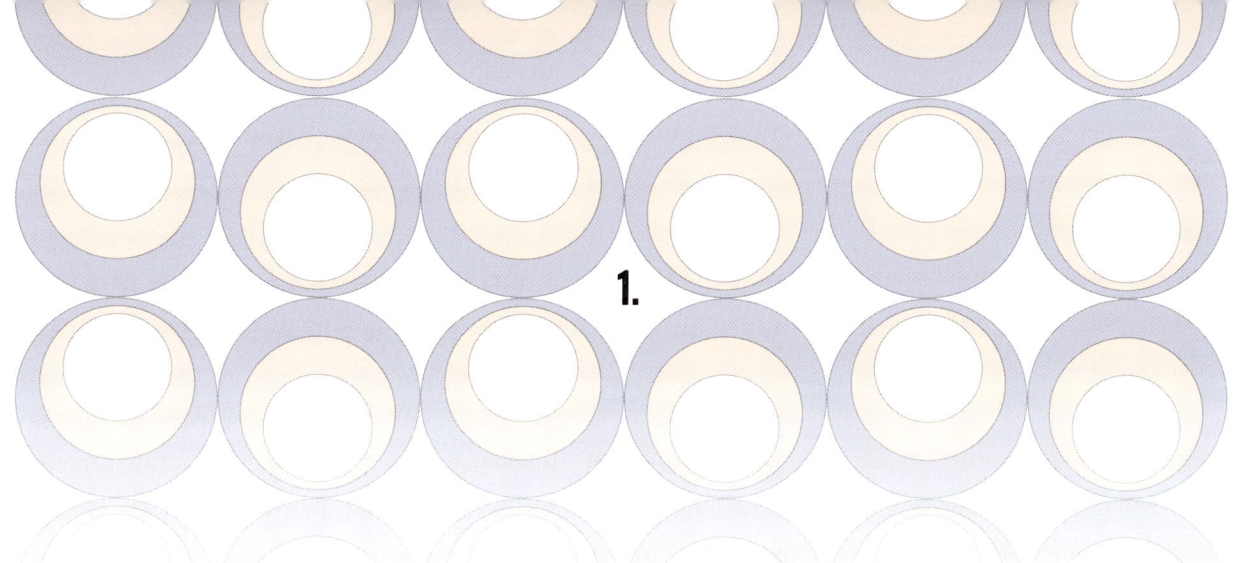

1.

BALLET IN CUBA: THE BEGINNINGS

In colonial times Cuba was considered a veritable eldorado abounding in flourishing businesses and moneymaking ventures. For the artists and dance companies touring the great "market" of Latin America, the Cuban "marketplace" was an absolute must.

In 1834 don Francisco Marty y Torrens, who had amassed a fortune as a fish merchant and slave trafficker, was approached to build a new theatre in Havana. The island was under the rule of the powerful and despotic colonial governor Miguel Tacón who offered Torrens extremely favorable conditions. The free labor of galley slaves was even included in the proposal. The new theatre, the Tacòn precisely, was inaugurated in 1838 with a grand masquerade ball.

Fanny Elssler (1810-1884), the 'divine' fiery Austrian ballerina, also considered 'the pagan' (Maria Taglioni was her 'Christian' rival), danced *La Sylphide* at the Havana Teatro Tacón in 1841. Much to her regret, as she wrote in her letters from Cuba,[1] she was obliged to work with local ballerinas whom she felt did not have the technique or appearance that corresponded to European canons. At the Tacòn, Elssler also presented *Nathalie, ou la Laitière suisse* – created in 1832 by Milanese Filippo Taglioni (1777-1871) for his daughter Maria Taglioni. Yet most notably, Elssler performed her tremendously popular *La Cachucha* on a Spanish folk song complete with castanets. The ballerina returned to Cuba the following year with her sister Teresa who specialized in male roles. A series of other ballets followed such as *La sonámbula* by Jean-Pierre Aumer, *La Gitana* by Joseph Mazilier, *La Bayadera* by Filippo Taglioni, as well as his *Robert le diable*.

In 1848, Hippolyte Monplaisir (Hippolyte George Sornet, Bordeaux, 1821 - Besana in Brianza, 1877) came to Cuba with his *Compañia francesa de bailes*. Monplaisir, a pupil of Carlo Blasis, was a dancer of La Scala and foremost figure of

---

1. Cf. Francisco Rey Alfonso, edited by, *Fanny Elssler: Cartas desde La Habana*, Editorial Boloña, Havana 2005; *Grandes momentos del ballet romántico en Cuba*, Editorial Letras Cubanas, Havana 2002.

1. BALLET IN CUBA: THE BEGINNINGS

Teatro Tacón, Havana, about 1900.

Fanny Elssler, 1841.

the Opéra de Paris. Monplaisir was accompanied by his wife Adèle Bartholomin. The couple danced the *pas de deux* of the new *Giselle* by Jean Coralli (Giovanni Coralli Peracini, whose father was an actor of the Théâtre Italien de Paris and resident choreographer at the Opéra 1779-1854)[2] and Jules Perrot (1810-1892). Perrot, among his many achievements in Europe, had been *maître de ballet* in Saint Petersburg.

A troupe of funambulists, Los Ravel, brought many works from the international dance repertory to Cuba. In 1849, there was a complete version of *Giselle* as well as *Ondina* and *El juicio de Paris* by Perrot. The group staged *Catalina o la Reina de los bandidos*, also by Perrot, *La vivandière* by Arthur Saint-Léon (Paris, 1821-1870), who was also the author of *Coppélia*), *El diablo a cuatro* and *Paquita*, both the latter by Joseph Mazilier (Giulio Mazarini, Marseilles, 1801 - Paris, 1868). Mazilier had been the leading male dancer in *La Sylphide*.

At the time, everything happening in Europe, the innovations in choreography, the latest in vogue dancers, all very soon came to Cuba. The years of the War of Independence in Spain, however, interrupted the history of ballet on the island until the beginning of the twentieth century.

The world-renowned Russian star Anna Pavlova (1881-1931)[3] came to perform at the Teatro Payret in 1915 with her most famous ballets: *The Dying Swan* and *Chopiniana* by Mikhail Fokin (Saint Petersburg, 1880 - New York, 1942), as well

---

2. Cf. José Sasportes, Patrizia Veroli, edited by, *Giovanni Coralli, l'autore di Giselle*, Aracne, Rimini 2018.
3. Cf. Francisco Rey Alfonso, *Anna Pávlova en Cuba*, Ediciones Cuba en el Ballet, Havana 1996.

1. BALLET IN CUBA: THE BEGINNINGS

as *Raymonda* by Marius Petipa (Marseilles, 1818 - Gurzuf, 1910). Petipa was the founding father of the repertory of grand tradition. Two years later, Pavlova returned with *Giselle* and *Coppélia*, and in 1918, with *The Sleeping Beauty* by Petipa.

Ernesto Lecuona, considered one of Cuba's greatest composers, dedicated the *Vals de la mariposa* ("The Butterfly") to the great ballet star, and eminent Cuban literary figures such as Dulce María Loynaz, Alejo Carpentier and Renée Méndez Capote wrote in admiration of Anna Pavlova.

Anna Pavlova as Dragonfly, 1911.

Alicia Alonso as protagonist Lizzie Borden, with Lucia Chase and Boris Romanoff in Agnes de Mille's *Fall River Legend*, 1948.

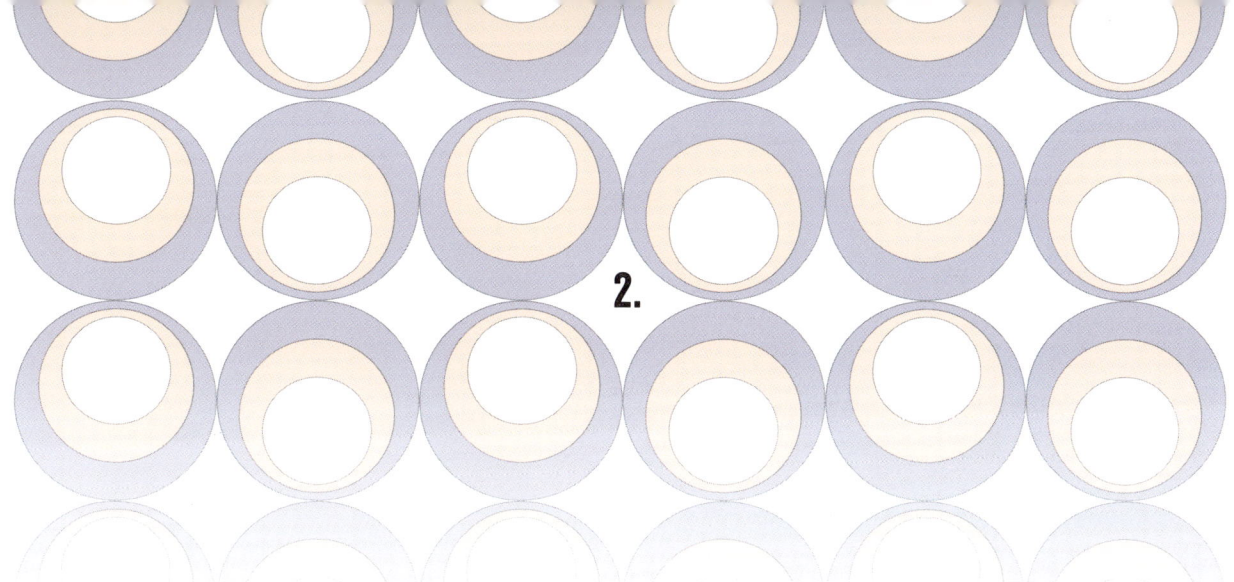

ALICIA ALONSO AND THE BALLET NACIONAL DE CUBA

The names Alicia Alonso and Ballet Nacional de Cuba (BNC) immediately evoke a series of impressions: a touch of Spain due to Cuba's status as a former colony, a touch of Russia, because of the alliance with Moscow after the Castro revolution, and a touch of the Caribbean, as the warm melting pot that Cuba is.

Yet only the vibration of the intrinsic Latin rhythm corresponds to the truest profile of the dance company founded and directed by the great ballerina – the "assoluta" – Alicia Alonso. The BNC was first created as the Ballet Alicia Alonso in 1948. In 1955, it became the Ballet de Cuba and, in 1959, the year Fidel Castro came to power, it became the Ballet Nacional de Cuba.

The Cubans inherited from Spain a fervent passion for flamenco and its rhythms. The Havana Ballet Festival, directed by Alicia Alonso from 1960 through its twentieth year in 2018, has always given flamenco a prominent place on its program. The Cuban flamenco star Irene Rodríguez is a familiar guest at the Festival with her vibrant flamenco company, and she also works in collaboration with the BNC.

In terms of the Russian ballet school, during the last century there were some émigrés ballet masters who came to Cuba. The fact that the island went through a phase of political alliance with the USSR[4] – with the famous missile crisis of '61 and the U.S. embargo, was not a determining factor for a "Cuban road" to classical ballet. The Russians did not establish a ballet school in Cuba based upon the Saint Petersburg or Moscow models. Alicia Alonso had already seen to developing the Escuela Nacional de Ballet (ENB) as we know it today, with the aim of forming national talent at home.

Alicia was invited to perform in Moscow, Saint Petersburg, Perm and Kiev. She was the first representative of the Americas to receive this honor and in Cuba she offered hospitality to Russian

---

4. See https://tatianasolovievaproducciones.com/las-raices-rusas-del-ballet-cubano-en-la-figura-de-alicia-alonso/.

2. ALICIA ALONSO AND THE BALLET NACIONAL DE CUBA

dancers and teachers. Alonso was an ambassador of her country to the world. And Barack Obama, as a politically liberal president, during his sensational visit to Cuba in 2016, was invited to the stage of the Gran Teatro, named precisely after Alonso.

Yet Italy and Russia also played a role in the story of the Alicia Alonso phenomenon. She was indeed unique, not only as a ballerina, ballet teacher and choreographer, but as the director of her own school, ballet company, festival and, moreover, founder of the *Museo Nacional de la Danza*. These she led with her sure, firm hand unfailingly through all of the complex phases of recent Cuban history, and despite the cruel inexorable personal threat of blindness.

Alicia Alonso as a child in *The Sleeping Beauty*, 1931.

TRAINING AND SUCCESS

Alicia Ernestina de la Caridad del Cobre Martínez del Hoyo (Havana, 1920-2019) was born into a family of Spanish origin. She was extremely young when she married the ballet dancer Fernando Alonso – whose name she took. Fernando's mother, Laura Raynier de Alonso, was head of Pro Arte Musical.[5] She was a fine pianist who

Alicia Alonso and sister "Cuca", 1950.

---

[5]. On educational activities and presentation of performances by the Association, including the modern works of Ted Shawn and Harald Kreutzberg, see Wendy Perron's interview of Gloria González Negreira, born in Havana in 1925 and who died in 2012 in the USA. Gloria married Leon Fokin, nephew of Mikhail, in 1949, when he was a professor in Cuba. She then followed him on tour with the Ballet de Cuba, to the Soviet Union in 1960, and then to the United States. Gloria worked with sister-in-law Irene in the latter's school, and returned to Cuba in 1998 to celebrate the BNC's fiftieth anniversary: *Gloria Fokine – A Conversation* in "Dance Magazine", Spring 2007: https://www.dancemagazine.com/gloria_fokine_a_conversation-2306899534.html.

2. ALICIA ALONSO AND THE BALLET NACIONAL DE CUBA

Alicia Alonso and Fernando Alonso in *Undertow*, 1947.

Alicia Alonso with second husband Pedro Simón.

Alicia's sister, Blanca María, nicknamed "Cuca", born in 1918, also began dancing at Pro Arte.

After Alicia completed her first Cuban studies of flamenco followed by ballet, she attended the courses of a nobleman and former officer of the Russian artillery, Nikolai Yavorsky[6] (Odessa, 1891 - Santiago de Cuba, 1947).[7] He was a soloist in the troupe created by the very wealthy Ida Rubinstein to rival the Ballets Russes. Rubinstein had come to Cuba in 1930 with the company Opéra Privée de Paris. The company was led by Maria Kuznetsova-Benois[8] and consisted of Russian émigré singers and dancers.[9] Yavorsky taught in Havana from 1931 to 1938, and in his own school in Vedado. He moved to Santiago and continued to dedicate himself to teaching until his death in 1947. He was known for imposing rigorous discipline in the study of daily exercises, and his technical knowledge was impressive.

Alicia also trained with an Italian teacher, Enrico Zanfretta (Venice, 1863 - New York, 1946). In New York in the late thirties, Zanfretta coached dancers who appeared in revues and in cinema — not to mention the multifaceted star Carmelita had undertaken to promote ballet in Cuba's capital. Alicia, known as "Hunga" because of her dark gypsy eyes, made her debut as a child at Pro Arte in 1931 in the *gran vals* of The Sleepng Beauty.

---

6. See https://www.revolvy.com/page/Nikolai-Yavorsky.
7. Cf. N. Yavorsky, *Mi biografía*, Spanish trans. from the Russian by Mirelcy García González and Pablo Batista Aja, in *Expediente 1*, Legajo 1, Nicolai Yavorsky Personal Fund, Archivo Histórico Provincial de Santiago de Cuba.
8. Maria Nikolaevna Kuznetsova-Benois-Massenet (Odessa, 1880 - Paris, 1966) was a renowned opera singer and dancer in Saint Petersburg, until the Russian revolution. She then emigrated to the West and appeared in *Jospehlegende* by Fokin for the Ballets Russes of Diaghilev, of which she was a sponsor. In 1928, she then created her Opéra privée de Paris that produced operas and ballets. Massenet performed in public until 1933, and after she retired from the stage, she taught acting and voice.
9. Cfr. M. A. Rossiysky, *Russian Emigré Community in Cuba: Chapters of History*, Veche, Moscow 2002; S. Y. Nechayev, *Russians in Latin America*, Veche, Moscow 2010; E.R. Triguero Tamayo, *Nikolai Yavorsky: un maestro ruso en la isla del ballet*, Ediciones Santiago, Santiago de Cuba 2010: http://librinsula.bnjm.cu/secciones/326/nombrar/326_nombrar_2.html.

2. ALICIA ALONSO AND THE BALLET NACIONAL DE CUBA

Chollar and Wiltzak as Colombine and Harlequin in *Le Carnaval*, about 1920.

Alicia Alonso and Anton Dolin in *Giselle*, 1943.

Maracci — with the support of the Federal Dance Project. Alonso once declared that she owed her sparkle to Zanfretta's renowned virtuosity.

Alonso studied the Russian style at the source with Alexandra Fedorova (Saint Petersburg, 1889 - Ridgewood, 1972),[10] the wife of Alexander Fokin. The latter was the brother of Mikhail, the first choreographer of Diaghilev's Ballets Russes. Leon Fokin, also a teacher, was Fedorova's son. Alexandra Fedorova had been a ballerina of the Mariinsky of Saint Petersburg and the Ballet Russe de Monte Carlo. From 1937 she was a ballet teacher and choreographer in the United States. The determined Alicia then perfected her art in the Big Apple with Anatole Vilzak (Vilnius, 1896 - San Francisco, 1998) and his wife Ludmila Schollar (Saint Petersburg, 1888 - San Francisco, 1978). They had both been ballet dancers in Diaghilev's company before they moved to America. Alonso went to London and studied with Vera Volkova (Tomsk, 1905 - Copenaghen, 1975) who had been a pupil of Agrippina Vaganova at the legendary Saint Petersburg Academy. The school had been the breeding ground

---

10. For Alexandra Fedorova, ballerina at the Mariinsky of Saint Petersburg, see https://themakingofmarkova.com/tag/alexandra-fedorova/. For the Alexandra Fedorova Papers, see http://archives.nypl.org/dan/19747.

2. ALICIA ALONSO AND THE BALLET NACIONAL DE CUBA

for artists such as Vaslav Nijinsky, Rudolf Nureyev, Mikhail Baryshnikov and Natalia Makarova, among other famous names.

Alicia continued to combine her extraordinary, inspired talent with relentless and merciless ballet training. In the meantime, she supported herself by dancing in Broadway musicals such as *Great Lady* and *Stars in Your Eyes*. She gained precious insight into effective dramaturgy and staging from this experience. As a choreographer, this helped her to render ballet accessible to her people and to all.

Alicia joined the Ballet Caravan, the precursor of the New York City Ballet that became the most important company in the United States. Although Léonide Massine would have been most happy to have had her join his company af-

Alicia Alonso and Jorge Esquivel in *Carmen*, **in the seventies.**

ter casting her in *Capricho Español*, Alicia instead made her debut in 1942 with the American Ballet Theatre. The company had been founded in 1937 by Russian Mikhail Mordkin (Moscow, 1880 - New York, 1944). He had trained at the Bolshoi of Moscow and was famous for having danced with the legendary Anna Pavlova and for Diaghilev. Alicia Alonso was asked to replace the ailing Alicia Markova (London, 1910 - Bath, 2004) – the Russianized artistic name for her real English name, Lilian Alice Marks, "the British Giselle" – opposite Anton Dolin (Patrick Kay; Slinfold, 1904 - Paris, 1983). Dolin was also English and already a member of the Ballets Russes. He became a fundamental partner-coach for the eager "Hunga" and saw her make her debut in *Giselle*, in a signature role that would be Alicia's all her life.

Alicia Alonso and Igor Youskevitch in George Balanchine's *Theme and Variations*, **ABT, 1947**

It took place on 2 November 1943, at the Metropolitan Opera House of New York. A landmark date for Alonso. She had temporarily overcome her problems of retinal detachment that had

2. ALICIA ALONSO AND THE BALLET NACIONAL DE CUBA

Alicia Alonso en pointe, in the fifties.

begun in 1941. This had forced her to be painfully bedridden and she mentally learned entire choreographies, moving her fingers across the bedsheets. The eye operations that followed turned out to be in vain and could not save the ballerina from progressively losing her sight. She fought this condition for decades with her iron will and without ever ceasing to dance the choreographies "filmed" in her mind and thus imprinted in her body.

During the period from 1955 to 1959, Alonso danced with the Ballet Russe de Monte Carlo post-Diaghilev that had been formed by René Blum.[11] Since 1938 the company had been named Ballet Russe de Monte Carlo under the direction of Léonide Massine. This experience brought her in contact with the Russian atmosphere of twentieth-century innovation that post-revolution exiles were creating and performing in the Old World and even more so in the New World.

George Balanchine (Saint Petersburg, 1904 - New York, 1983)[12] was the last of Diaghilev's great choreographers. He embodied the epitome of neoclassical ballet in America with his company, the New York City Ballet. In 1947, Balanchine created the virtuosic *Theme and Variations* for Alicia and her partner, Russian-Ukrainian Igor Youskevitch (Pyriatyn, 1912 - New York, 1994). This was a concert composition on the twelve final variations of the *Suite for Orchestra N. 3* by Tchaikovsky. Balanchine's work drew inspiration from the exceptional technical mastery and musical sensitivity of the Cuban ballerina.

It is not surprising that during the course of Alonso's extraordinary career, the two characters most representative of Alonso were Giselle and Carmen. The *estrella cubana* possessed the qualities of both: lyricism and fire, line and swiftness, emotional expressivity and complete formal control.

---

11. Cf. Judith Chazin-Bennahum, *René Blum and The Ballets Russes: in Search of a Lost Life*, Oxford University Press, Oxford 2011.

12. Cf. B. Taper, *Balanchine, a Biography*, University of California Press, Berkeley 1996; Elisa Guzzo Vaccarino, *La danza d'arte, Balanchine, Cunningham, Forsythe*, Dino Audino Editore, Rome 2015.

2. ALICIA ALONSO AND THE BALLET NACIONAL DE CUBA

Alonso's dramatic temperament also shone in exemplary American works such as *Fall River Legend* by Agnes De Mille. The latter, the niece of the epic film director Cecil B. De Mille (New York, 1905-1993), was a choreographer of intense dramatic drive.

ALICIA ALONSO AND *GISELLE*

Alicia Alonso said that the story of "her" *Giselle* all began in 1945 in Havana at the Sociedad Pro Arte Musical and the Auditorium del Vedado (today named after Cuban musician Amadeo Roldán). Alicia's partner for the ballet was Fernando Alonso, with the Native American ballerina Rosella Hightower in the role of Myrtha, the Queen of the Wilis. Hightower was an étoile of the Ballet Russe post-Diaghilev and in 1961 had founded the prestigious Ecole Supérieure de Danse de Cannes. She was later ballet director of the Opéra de Paris, and the Teatro alla Scala of Milan in 1985-1986.

Alicia later danced *Giselle* with the Ballet The- atre opposite André Eglevsky (Moscow, 1917 - New York, 1977), who was from the Ballet Russe de Monte Carlo directed by Colonel W. de Basil.[13] The role of Myrtha was again danced by a ballerina of Native American descent, Marjorie Tallchief, who had been married to Balanchine. This was the same cast that went on tour to Europe.

During the 1946/1947 season Alicia's dance partner was Igor Youskevitch (Pyriatyn, 1912 - New York, 1994). The Russian-Ukrainian dancer had first studied with Elena Poliakova. He continued his training with Olga Preobrajenska (Saint Petersburg, 1912 - Paris, 1962) who for decades was a greatly admired teacher in France. Youskevitch studied with Lithuanian dancer Anatole Vilzak and Alexandra Fedorova. He was a first-class dancer in the Ballet Russe de Monte Carlo under the direction of Léonide Massine.

In 1948, the Ballet Theatre of New York faced financial difficulties that forced it to cease activity. Alicia once more looked to Cuba and her *Giselle*. This time her partner in the role of Albrecht was the American dancer, born to Czech émigrés, John Kriza (Berwyn, 1919 - Collier County, 1975). He was also from the Ballet Theatre.

Alicia now undertook to personally stage *Giselle* in Havana. She would not only dance the title role, but she also created the choreography

---

13. In 1934, Colonel de Basil decided to go his own way without René Blum, with whom he had co-founded and co-directed a first company. Cf. Vicente García-Marquez, *The Ballets Russes: Colonel de Basil's Ballets Russes de Monte Carlo 1932-1952*, Knopf, New York 1990.

2. ALICIA ALONSO AND THE BALLET NACIONAL DE CUBA

for the ballet. She appeared with Youskevitch, as Albrecht, and Alberto Alonso as Hilarion (Alberto Alonso, her husband Fernando's younger brother, was also a choreographer and famous for his tremendously successful *Carmen*, created for Maya Plisetskaya). Alicia's *Giselle* was performed by her newborn company the Ballet Alicia Alonso. She had created her ballet company in Cuba in the fervent hope that national talent could now develop at home and not "in the airplane" as she had been obliged to do, a Latin dancer in the United States.

The *Giselle* presented by Alicia Alonso was unique in every way. Alicia was not only the sublime dancer of the title character, but she was also the ballet's penetrating, intelligent, and forward-thinking choreographer and – if that were not impressive enough – she was also its artistic director responsible for the impeccable presentation of the ballet by the company. The fact that a classical ballet in the repertory of the grand tradition was directed by a woman, when all of the great ballets of the nineteenth century were – and are – notoriously the choreographic domain of men, made Alicia's *Giselle* all the more extraordinary.

The Cuban *Giselle* was so incisive, bold, moving and essential that Alicia was invited by the Opéra de Paris in 1972 as ballerina and choreographer to present her version. Here this was precisely where the ballet *Giselle* had been created by Coralli-Perrot-Adam in 1841. The Cuban

Ballet Nacional de Cuba in *Giselle*, 2007.

Giselle then migrated for long periods in Russia under the direction of Marius Petipa. It then returned to Paris during the first decade of the last century with the divine Anna Pavlova. Another extraordinary fact: Alonso danced the leading role of *Giselle* from 1943 to 1993. She performed a short part of the ballet during a gala celebration commemorating her fifty years in the role.[14]

14. **Link:** Alicia Alonso in Act 2 of *Giselle*. In 1963 with Russian

2. ALICIA ALONSO AND THE BALLET NACIONAL DE CUBA

Thus the world was witness to a unique longevity in the history of ballet, despite Alicia's problems of sight. She compensated for this handicap by perfectly mastering all aspects of the reperto-ry's choreographies, and of this one in particular, whether spatial, musical, choreographic, or technical, physical, and psychic.

Alicia Alonso danced *Giselle* with the world's greatest partners, whose talent equalled her own: in 1955 with the Danish *danseur noble* Erik Bruhn at Jacob's Pillow, at only two months from his debut as Albrecht; in 1958 with Vladilen Semionov at the Kirov-Mariinsky in then Leningrad; in 1963 with Azari Plisetsky for the making of a film about her; in 1969 with Flemming Flindt, as guest star of the Danish Royal Ballet;

Azari Plisetsky, brother of Maya Plisetskaya; in 1978 with Cuban Jorge Esquivel, in 1980 with Vladimir Vasiliev étoile of the Moscow Bolshoi; in 1984 again with Esquivel; in 1988 with Rafael Padilla, Cuban; in 1991, and again in 1993, at seventy-two years of age, with Chinese Cuban Lienz Chang. The latter had an impressive international dance career that included, among others, with Roland Petit, then ballet master also at La Scala of Milan and at the San Carlo of Naples. See also *Giselle eres tu/You are Giselle* by Roberto Ferguson, Televisión Educativa Cubana, 1988.

2. ALICIA ALONSO AND THE BALLET NACIONAL DE CUBA

in 1972 with Cuban Jorge Esquivel, a dancer of extraordinary presence. Esquivel was Alicia's trustworthy partner who would accompany her during the years of her declining sight. And her performances of *Giselle* continued: in 1978 in Washington and New York, for the U.S. debut of the Ballet de Cuba; with friend and great innovator of flamenco for the stage Antonio Gades,[15] as Hilarion; and in 1980, with Vladimir Vasiliev for the Festival de Ballet of Havana.

An impressive performance in 1981 of Alicia Alonso's choreography was danced at the San Carlo di Napoli by Carla Fracci (Milan, 1936), "the Italian Giselle", opposite Paolo Bortoluzzi (Genoa, 1938 - Brussels, 1993). In 1960, Bortoluzzi had attracted the attention of Maurice Béjart (Marseilles, 1927 - Lausanne, 2007) and was a principal dancer in Bejart's Ballet du XXᵉ siècle.

Alonso later created *Desnuda luz del amor*, a work specially conceived for the gifts of the dancer and actress Carla Fracci (Havana, 2006).

GISELLE: THE CHOREOGRAPHY BY ALICIA ALONSO

Alicia's unparalleled success as the veritable embodiment of the spirit of Giselle was due to her qualities as an extraordinary ballerina, but also to the choreography that she personally created for this ballet. Her choreography worked like perfect clockwork and it was executed by a corps de ballet just as perfect and compact.

Alonso's *entrechats* that were high, feathery, elastic, and executed with "expressive" feet were famous, yet no less famous were the impeccable lines of her Wilis. The lines of their arms and feet were just as precise, hypnotic, and terrifying as their merciless rigor for the men condemned to death for having betrayed them.

"Great works never die, they can sleep, but they reawaken with great artists",[16] Alonso once said, "they don them each evening, as if they were reborn at that very moment". These are the words of a complete artist, one who was both protagonist and director, which was so rare for a woman in the world of ballet.

While Alicia was in the United States, she was influenced by the expressive training of choreographer Antony Tudor. He had developed what was called the "psychological ballet" and was instrumental in the shaping of Alicia's perception of drama. During the forties he created a role for Alicia in his Freudian ballet *Undertow*. This dealt with the frustration of an unloved young man who plunges into a spiral of transgression that inevitably drives him to commit a murder.[17]

As an indication of the great universal appeal of Alicia Alonso's choreography we might consider that her *Giselle* was performed at the Colón di Buenos Aires in 1958, at the Opéra de Paris in 1972, where she later brought *The Sleeping Beauty* in 1974; and at the Staatsoper of Vienna in 1980. During the 1982/1983 season, at the Teatro alla Scala in Milan Alicia's choreography of *The Sleeping Beauty* was also staged and she danced in the ballet opposite Jorge Esquivel.

---

15. **Link:** Video of *Bodas de sangre* by Antonio Gades, performed by the Ballet Nacional de Cuba.

16. Many statements on *Giselle* appear in texts and documentaries, Cf.: Alicia Alonso, *Diálogos con la danza*, Letras Cubanas, Havana 1986 and later editions; Ediciones Oceano, Mexico 2004, with DVD included; Mayda Bustamante, *Alicia Alonso o la eternidad de Giselle*, Ediciones Cumbres, Madrid 2013.

17. Cf. George Amberg, *Ballet in America – The Emergence of an American Art*, Duell, Sloan and Pearce, New York 1949.

2. ALICIA ALONSO AND THE BALLET NACIONAL DE CUBA

Alicia Alonso received many awards for her qualities as choreographer. All of the important works of the classical repertory of grand tradition staged by the national Cuban ballet company were honored, including *Coppelia*, *La Fille mal gardée*, *The Nutcracker* and *Don Quixote*. These works reflected the different yet equally enthralling sides of the Cuban heart, whether light or fiery, playful or sensuous. If there may have been some reticence sometimes concerning taste in props or decors, the choreographies were always considered effective and functional. They worked in terms of the abilities and qualities of dancers everywhere.

Alicia Alonso "*eterna*" in the title role of *Giselle*.

From left, above, Hugh Laing, John Kriza, Igor Youskevitch; standing, Muriel Bentley, Alicia Alonso, Antony Tudor, Dimitri Romanoff, Nora Kaye, Max Gobermann; seated, Oliver Smith and Lucia Chase, 1948.

Alicia Alonso and Fernando Alonso in *Dioné*, 1940.

3.

FOUNDERS OF CUBAN BALLET: THE ALONSO DYNASTY

The extraordinary phenomenon behind the emergence out of nowhere – so to speak – of a distinctly Cuban ballet was the "Alonso triad": ballerina Alicia, ballet master Fernando, and choreographer Alberto.

It is said that Fidel Castro himself once made a secret visit to the Alonsos. Indeed, they were a team that could ensure the highest standards, whether in directing a ballet school or a dance company or creating artistic works. The Comandante came offering the means to develop ballet on the island. In exchange, they would make Cuban ballet a beacon of culture and art for all the world and bring fame and prestige to their country. And this is precisely what came to be, despite all of the material and artistic obstacles that had to be overcome.

There was some dissidence, but it was short-lived. In 1985 Caridad Martínez, the first mixed race ballerina[18] to have made a career at the BNC, dared to co-sign a letter with colleagues Rosario Suárez, Amparo Brito and Mirtha García to Alicia Alonso. This demand for more freedom in the artistic choices of the company resulted in the creation of the Ballet Teatro de La Habana in 1987. The company existed until the end of the *periodo especial* when dwindling resources, even from the USSR, forced many Cuban artists to emigrate.

Alicia Alonso from then on reigned supreme, not only as a ballerina of the highest level, but as the director of ballet for the entire island. Her will would always prevail on any issue. There was no obstacle too formidable, and she had Fidel Castro's unfailing support through it all, which she reciprocated with her unswerving loyalty to the Comandante.

---

18. Martínez, afer becoming director of the Ballet de Veracruz, met Julian Schnabel who wanted to cast her in the scenes of the celebration in the chapel partially in ruins of San Francisco Xavier. This was where the mad yet extraordinary hot-air balloon was hidden ready to flee from Cuba, in the film *Before Night Falls* (2000). The film was based on the book *Antes que anochezca* by Cuban writer Reinaldo Arenas. Arenas was a dissident and homosexual, and this was why he was imprisoned. He managed to emigrate to the USA but later succumbed to AIDS.

3. FOUNDERS OF CUBAN BALLET: THE ALONSO DYNASTY

Alicia Alonso, Fernando Alonso, Alexandra Denisova in *Les Sylphides/Las Sílfides*, Ballet de la Escuela de la Sociedad Pro Arte Musical, Teatro Auditorium, Havana, 1942.

FERNANDO ALONSO

Fernando Alonso was born in 1914 in Havana and became one of ballet's greatest master teachers. He died in 2013 after dedicating his entire life to ballet.[19] Nothing during Fernando's days as a student could have suggested such a future. His family had sent him to Spring Hill College in Mobile, Alabama to distance him from the political

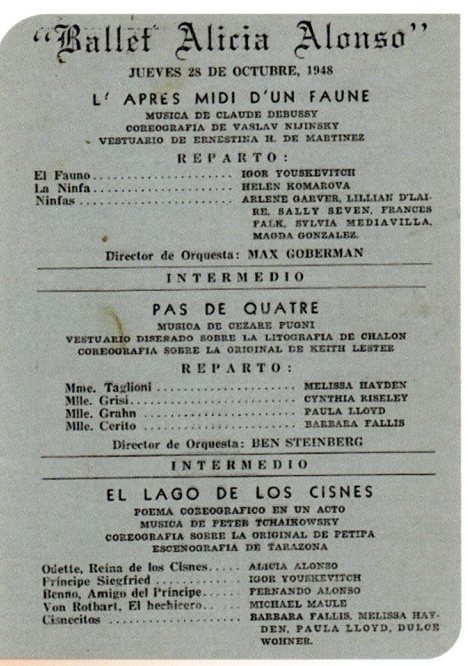

Program of the premiere of the Ballet Alicia Alonso.

---

19. Cf. Toba Singer, *Fernando Alonso, the Father of Cuban Ballet*, University of Florida, Gainesville 2013, with many testimonies of ballet artists from Cuba; Miguel Cabrera, *El Ballet en Cuba: nacimiento de una escuela en el siglo XX*, Balletin Dance Ediciones, Buenos Aires 2010, pp. 73-87.

3. FOUNDERS OF CUBAN BALLET: THE ALONSO DYNASTY

Alberto, Alicia, and Fernando Alonso, in the sixties.

disorders in Cuba at the time. He later attended a school in North Carolina and graduated in Commercial Sciences. He worked as a typist and stenographer in the sugar company Golodetz, and later in the Oficina Panamericana of a government ministry.

In 1935 Fernando left his office job and embarked on his path in the world of ballet. He began training at Pro Arte Musical under Nikolai Yavorsky. The master created *Claro de luna* on Beethoven's composition for the already budding couple Alicia and Fernando.

The couple married – Alicia was only sixteen – in New York in 1938. Their daughter Laura was born, and Fernando continued to train under Russian émigré ballet masters such as Mikhail Mordkin – one of the founders of today's American Ballet Theatre (ABT). Mordkin had Fernando make his debut in the company. Fernando also appeared with his wife Alicia in musical comedies.

Ballet Caravan was a company led by the wealthy ballet lover Lincoln Kirstein. Before it became the New York City Ballet, Fernando appeared with the company in ballets with American themes such as *Filling Station* (1938) and *Charade* (1939) by Lew Christensen (Brigham City, 1909 - San Mateo, 1984), and *Billy the Kid* (1938) by Eugene Loring (Eugene Le Roy Kerpestein; Milwaukee, 1911 - Kingston, 1982).

Fernando also maintained his ties with Pro Arte, whose ballet director was now George Milenoff (Bulgaria, 1901 - Florida, 1975). The latter, just as Fernando's friend Yavorsky, was already

Alicia Alonso and Fernando Alonso having fun during a speleological expedition.

a member of Ida Rubinstein's company.[20] With Pro Arte, the Alonso couple danced *Dioné* (1940). The ballet featured Cuban symphonic music by

---

20. Ida Rubinstein (1883-1960), was a very wealthy and fascinating figure of the arts. in 1928, she commissioned Ravel to create *Bolero* for her dance company. The company was the rival of of the Diaghilev's Ballets Russes.

3. FOUNDERS OF CUBAN BALLET: THE ALONSO DYNASTY

Fernando Alonso coaching Maria Elena Llorente and Alicia Alonso, in the late sixties.

Eduardo Sánchez de Fuentes (Havana, 1874-1944). The composer had also created the Havana hit *Tú* and the didactic *El folklore en la música cubana*.

When Fernando and Alicia returned to New York, they joined the Ballet Theatre, which was its name at the time. This put them in contact with figures of the stature of Mikhail Fokin, David Lichine (Rostov, 1910 - Los Angeles, 1972) and Jerome Robbins (New York, 1918-1988).

The year 1941 marked the couple's return to Cuba. While Alicia was regaining her strength following an eye operation, Fernando worked as executive secretary for Pro Arte. The following year, the Alonsos joined the dance and theatre troupe La Silva. Alicia's sister Anna Leontieva, from the Original Ballet Russe led by Colonel de Basil, also belonged to it, and there were foremost actors and literary figures such as Alejo Carpentier who were members. Fernando created *Pelleas y Melisande* on the music by Debussy and texts by the Chilean poet Pablo Neruda while with the troupe.

In 1943 the Ballet Theatre welcomed back Alicia and Fernando and in 1945, with some of the dancers from the New York company, they brought *Giselle* to Cuba.

The Alonsos continued to regularly come and go between Cuba and the United States and between the Big Apple and Havana. In the U.S. they danced together for Tudor and Robbins. In Cuba they staged *Petrushka* and *Les Sylphides* by Fokin. This was followed in 1947 by *Antes del alba*, the first work dedicated to purely Cuban themes. It was presented at the festival organized by Pro Arte with many guests from the United States.

From 1948, when the ABT ran into financial difficulty, until 1975, Fernando was director of a company that was destined to become the Ballet Nacional de Cuba after Fidel Castro came to power. The time was now behind them when the Alonsos, as "opposers" to the previous government of Fulgencio Batista, had suffered cutbacks that had sparked heated protest.[21]

From the historic year of 1959, the Alonso couple began to receive support from Castro's new regime. They had immediately come out in favor of it and Comandante Castro's backing was soon forthcoming for the esteemed "national ballerina". In the meantime, Fernando had been the ballet director of the Alicia Alonso Academy of Ballet since 1950. There he laid the foundations of the Cuban dance style of today. From 1962 to 1968 he directed the ENB, a fertile breeding ground for new generations of dancers nurtured on his expert training, with Alicia as Muse-model.

Fernando and Alicia divorced, and Fernando left Havana with his young second wife, Aida

---

21. Cf. Miguel Cabrera, El Ballet en Cuba, Apuntes Históricos, Cupulas. Havana 2011, Section Documentos, pp. 327-341.

3. FOUNDERS OF CUBAN BALLET: THE ALONSO DYNASTY

Villoch,[22] a promising prima ballerina talent and perfect for *La Fille mal gardée*. Fernando moved to Camagüey in 1975 where he directed the local ballet company. Aida was a Muse for Cuban dancer and choreographer Jorge Lefebre. Before he moved to Belgium, he was a member of the company founded by the pioneer of African American dance, Katherine Dunham. In 1976, he became director of the Ballet Royal de Wallonie, and directed the company until his death in 1990. Lefebre had led the company with the support of his wife Menia Martínez,[23] an exquisite blond ballerina and foremost figure at the BNC as well as Castro's *protégée*. Martinez had been a member of Maurice Béjart's Ballet du XXᵉ siècle and, in 2020, she returned to the Ballet de Cuba as a highly esteemed ballet teacher.

Fernando became director of the national ballet company of Mexico in 1992 and subsequently of the Monterrey Ballet. He remarried for a third time during that period and had two daughters by his third wife Yolanda. Fernando Alonso is buried at the monumental cemetery Colón dell'Avana. He had returned to Havana to a steady position at the ballet "headquarters" in 2001, after he had received the National Dance Award in 2000. Fernando was interested in psychology, kinesiology and anatomy, and had worked in radiology in the United States. A cultivated man who was never dogmatic, he is admired as the founding father of the teaching methodology of the Cuban ballet school ENB, which today bears his name. Fernando drew from the systems in Europe, America and Russia, to then infuse them with *cubanía*.

ALBERTO ALONSO

Alberto Alonso was born in Havana in 1917 and died in Florida in 2007. He had left Cuba in 1993 for the United States with his third wife, Sonia Calero (Havana, 1936), the sensuous, "brazen" ballerina who excelled above all in Cuban tradi-

Aida Villoch Ballet, in the seventies.

---

22. Cf. Octavio Roca, *Cuban Ballet*, Gibbs Smith, Layton (Utah) 2010, p. 93. See also https://www.facebook.com/Aida-Villoch-Ballet-472649129501097/.
23. **Link:** Interview with Menia Martínez. The Cuban ballerina was very young when she received a scholarship to study at the Vaganova School. She then became a member of the BNC and obtained authorization to join Béjart in Brussels directly – something very rare – from the Cuban Ministry of Culture. In 1960, as an interpreter, she accompanied the Cuban delegation to New York for the encounter Castro-Krushchev. Subsequently, in addition to becoming a teacher, notably at

La Scala of Milan, she also worked as *maître répétiteur* and remounted the works of her husband Jorge Lefebre for the Ballet Royal de Wallonie.

3. FOUNDERS OF CUBAN BALLET: THE ALONSO DYNASTY

Alexandra Denisova, 1938.

tional rhythms. Alberto was a professor all of his life. The last institution at which he taught was the Santa Fe Community College in Gainsville. After his passing, according to his wishes, his ashes were scattered at sea.

Alberto's biography was emblematic of Cuban existence in its trials and tribulations involving love, migration and dance. His first wife was Canadian ballerina Patricia Denise Meyers, known by her stage name — necessarily Russianized in those days — Alexandra Denisova. Alberto and Alexandra met while the ballerina was dancing in the Original Ballet Russe,[24] and they married in Melbourne in 1939. They separated in 1944 and Alberto married Elena del Cueto who was famous on the small screen for *Cabaret regalías* and *Casino de la alegría*. In 1962 Elena left Cuba for the United States with their two daughters. Alberto remarried a third time to Sonia Calero[25] and the couple had a son, Alberto Jr., born in 1964. Their son eventually left the island and did not work in the world of ballet.

Alberto Alonso had a sensitive affinity for the fine arts and music, and also a gift for physical culture. He was the second son of pianist Laura Rayneri de Alonso, who was known for her cultural activities. In 1933 Alberto became the first male pupil at the Escuela de Ballet de la Sociedad Pro Arte Musical de La Habana, led by Yavorsky.

In his younger years, Alberto perfected his ballet training with Lubov Tchernicheva (Saint Petersburg, 1890 - Richmond, 1976), who was the wife of Diaghilev's *regisseur*, Sergei Grigoriev. Alberto then continued his studies in Paris with Olga Preobrajenska and Stanislas Idzikovsky (Warsaw, 1894 - London, 1977), the latter was particularly active in Great Britain.

Alberto's teachers, all of whom came from Diaghilev's Ballets Russes, expressed their admiration for his gifts as an inspired character dancer.

During the thirties, Alberto joined the Ballet Russe de Monte Carlo. He performed *Petrushka*,[26] *Prince Igor*, *Spectre de la rose* and *The Prodi-*

---

24. The Original Ballet Russe of Colonel de Basil (formerly the Ballets Russes de Monte Carlo, created in 1931 to perpetuate the artistic legacy of the Ballets Russes of Diaghilev) took this name when the founders, René Blum and Wassily (or Vasily) de Basel, separated. Blum then founded his Ballet Russe de Monte Carlo. The Original Ballet Russe was dissolved in 1947.
25. **Link:** TV documentary on Sonia Calero and Alberto Alonso.
26. Images may be viewed of Alberto Alonso in Petrushka,

3. FOUNDERS OF CUBAN BALLET: THE ALONSO DYNASTY

gal Son with the company Colonel W. de Basil co-founded.

In 1941 Alberto became director of the Escuela de Ballet de Pro Arte. He worked as ballet master and choreographer from the staging of *Preludios* (1942) with music by Liszt, to *Concerto* with music by Vivaldi and Bach and Denisova in the leading role, and *Forma* (1943). Alberto also created *Sinfonía* based on music by Mozart, *Nocturnos* on Debussy, *El caballero de la rosa* on Strauss, *Nocturnal* on Chopin, *Sinfonía clásica* on Prokofiev, and *Espacio y movimiento* on Stravinsky, as he experimented in the fusion of neoclassicism and popular dance.

Sonia Calero, fourth from left, with artists from the television network CMQ as they read "El Imparcial" at the café Alaska, Havana, 1959.

Elena del Cueto in *Panoram* with music by Haydn and Brahms, 1950.

Alexandra Denisova in *Sinfonía*, Elena del Cueto and Sonia Calero in *Rapsodia negra* at: https://www.danzaballet.com/dance-of-my-heart-the-life-and-career-of-alberto-alonso/.

Among Alberto Alonso's creations was notably *Antes del alba* (1947) with music by Hilario González and stage design by Carlos Enríquez. Here for the first time in a ballet – and not without indignation from the White bourgeois audience – the social and ethnic issues of Cubans of African origin were treated. The libretto was by Spanish playwright Francisco Martínez Allende who had fled Francoism. Critics of *Antes del alba* accused the work of resorting to easy melodrama. Alicia Alonso was the protagonist Chela, a young consumptive widow overcome by disillusionment and shattered by feverish visions that finally drive her to suicide. The three Alonsos, Alicia, Alberto and Fernando, all appeared in the production, and Elena del Cueto played the exuberant Cachita. Certainly, Alberto Alonso's choreography benefited from the influx of innovative Ballets Russes choreographers such as Mikhail Fokin, George Balanchine (Alberto

3. FOUNDERS OF CUBAN BALLET: THE ALONSO DYNASTY

Alberto Alonso as the Dwarf in Léonide Massine's *Pavane*, Original Ballet Russe directed by Colonel W. de Basil, 1940.

danced in the latter's *Cotillon* in London), Léonide Massine (*Le donne di buon umore*), Anton Dolin, Bronislava Nijinska, and Serge Lifar. And there were the talents from the New World such as Antony Tudor and Jerome Robbins, the latter the multifaceted genius of theatre, cinema, and musical comedy.

Alberto joined New York's American Ballet[27] in 1943. In 1944, he danced the role of a sailor in *Fancy Free* by Robbins to music by Leonard Bernstein. This ballet-musical was presented in Havana at the 22nd Festival of the American Ballet Theatre (2010), a cultural ambassador and bridge between the United States and Cuba.

In 1945 Alberto appeared in the musical comedy *Yolanda and the Thief*. The film, set in a fictitious Latin American country, starred Fred Astaire and Lucille Bremer and was directed by Vincente Minnelli.

On 28 October 1948 Alberto began to lay the foundations with Alicia and his brother Fernando of what would become the Ballet Nacional de Cuba. Alberto's research into the concept of *cubanía*, "cuban-ness", that considered classical ballet from a modern point of view, led to the creation of his own ensemble in the early fifties. The ensemble not only appeared in groups such as Conjunto de Bailes of the Teatro Radiocentro and the ballet company of CMQ Televisión, but also in the shows of the capital's top nightclubs. These clubs, notably the Montmartre and the Sans Souci – French names colonial chic obliged – featured casts of more than a hundred dancers and fabulous shows such as *La calle*, *El pantano*, *El güije*, *Cha Cha Cha*, *Noche cubana*, *Sensemayá* and *El solar*.

Alberto Alonso's concept of "syncretic ballet" against a Caribbean backdrop gave birth to songs such as *Sombras*, *Maleficio*, *Quimbisá*, and *La rebambaramba*.

His ballet *Un retablo para Romeo y Julieta*[28] was created in 1969 for the Ballet de Cuba. With music by Hector Berlioz and Pierre Henry, it starred Alicia Alonso and Azari Plisetsky (Moscow, 1937). The ballet was filmed by Antonio Fernández Reboiro for the ICAIC (the national film board). Plisetsky was a very influential

---

27. The American Ballet was the first professional troupe directed by George Balanchine in the USA. It then became the American Ballet Caravan in 1936.

28. **Link:** Video of Alicia Alonso and Azari Plisetsky in *Un retablo para Romeo y Julieta* by Alberto Alonso.

3. FOUNDERS OF CUBAN BALLET: THE ALONSO DYNASTY

Maya Plisetskaya in *Carmen*, late sixties.

Alicia Alonso in *Carmen*, 1968.

Viengsay Valdés in *Carmen*, 2015.

presence in Cuba. He was aware of his impressive pedigree as the brother of Maya Plisetskaya and the nephew of Asaf and Sulamith Messerer, foremost figures of the Moscow Bolshoi. Reboiro also directed *Rumba* with Sonia Calero in 1972, with choreography by Alberto Alonso and music by Dámaso Pérez Prado. Eduardo Manet, however, directed the Cuban musical *Un día en el solar*, and Alberto did his best to choreograph the "entertainment dances".[29]

---

29. Cf. Yaima Redonet Sánchez *Un día en el Solar, Expresión de la Cubanidad de Alberto Alonso*, Argus-a Artes & Humanidades, Buenos Aires-Los Angeles 2018, for the pdf see http://www.argus-a.com.ar/archivos-ebooks/713-1.pdf. **Link:** Video of *Duo de la escoba* da *Un día en el solar* with Sonia Calero and Roberto Rodríguez, choreography by Alberto Alonso.

3. FOUNDERS OF CUBAN BALLET: THE ALONSO DYNASTY

Alberto Alonso was also the choreographer for Conjunto Experimental de Danza, the Teatro Musical de La Habana, and Conjunto Nacional de Espectáculos.

Among the many ballets created by Alberto Alonso – more than one hundred[30] – *Carmen* (1967)[31] remains his most internationally acclaimed. This ballet saw the light when Alberto was approached by Maya Plisetskaya,[32] star of the Moscow Bolshoi. It was in 1965 in Russia and Plisetskaya had just seen the performance of *El solar*. She was enthusiastic and wanted Alberto to choreograph a suite after a composition on Bizet which had been created by her husband Rodion Shchedrin. And it was precisely *Carmen* that became what was considered Alicia Alonso's signature role as "the Cuban gypsy". Fans in heated debate took sides defending one or the other ballerina's performance of the work.[33] Subsequently even the Cuban Classical Ballet of Miami proposed the Cuban *Carmen*. In 2006 in Moscow, the icy Bolshoi star Svetlana Zakharova danced the role under the guidance of Alberto himself who was by then in his eighties. This piece of technical virtuosity and fiery spirit also attracted Russian superstars Diana Vishneva, Uliana Lopatkina, and Natalia Osipova. At the BNC, these qualities were embodied in the vigor and character of Cuban star Viengsay Valdés. She had been assistant director of the company and later took over the running of the BNC. In January 2020 she was officially appointed to the function as successor to *Assoluta* Alicia. When the BNC included *Concerto DSCH* by Alexei Ratmansky in its repertory, this immediately signaled Viengsay Valdés' conscious desire to broaden the concept of visuals for the company.

Alberto Alonso's last important ballet was *Diario perdido*. A choral work on music by Alberto Bruni Tedeschi, it first premiered in 1986 in Havana and subsequently at the Rome Opera. The choreographer's first work abroad was *¡Si señor es mi son!* for the Ballet Hispano of New York in 1995. In 2006 Alberto Alonso was bestowed the Life Achievement Award "Una Vida por la Danza" by the Festival Internacional del Ballet of Miami.

LAURA AND IVÁN ALONSO

The Alonso dynasty, in addition to Alicia, Fernando and Alberto, also includes Laura Alonso, the daughter born to Alicia and Fernando in New York in 1938. She is today teacher and international *repetiteur*. Laura also directs AIDA (Asociación de la Danza para las Américas) and, in the aim of sharing Cuban know-how and methodology, courses at the Cuballet ballet school.

Laura Alonso was a soloist in the BNC for twenty-five years from 1959, and teacher at ENA and ISA (Instituto Superior de Arte). During the years from 1965 to 1967, she studied with Asaf and Sulamith Messerer, and danced in *Noche de amistad Cubano Soviética* in Russia, as an ambassador of culture and art.

---

30. Cf. Miguel Cabrera, *op. cit.*, 2011.
31. **Link:** Video of *Carmen* by Alberto Alonso, with Maya Plisetskaya, and dancers Nikolai Fadeyechev, Sergei Radchenko/don José, Alexander Lavrenyuk/Escamillo, Natalia Kasatkina/Fate.
32. Cf. *Dance of My Heart*, documentary by Ricardo Acosta, with Maya Plisetskaya, Sonia Calero, Alberto Alonso, Fernando Alonso, 2009, 79 min. The documentary can be viewed on Prime Video, whereas for the criticism that arose as a result of the bias of Cuban *émigré* Célida Villalón, who was part of the administrative staff of Pro Arte, see https://www.danzaballet.com/dance-of-my-heart-the-life-and-career-of-alberto-alonso/.
33. Cf. Eduardo Heras Léon, *Desde la platea*, Editorial José Martí, Havana 2010, pp. 23-25.

3. FOUNDERS OF CUBAN BALLET: THE ALONSO DYNASTY

Iván Alonso, 2017.

Laura Alonso, Centro Pro Danza, 2015.

Iván Alonso's *Yarini*, 2018.

3. FOUNDERS OF CUBAN BALLET: THE ALONSO DYNASTY

Laura has since directed the Centro de Promoción de la Danza de Cuba, known as Centro Pro Danza, and the Laura Alonso Ballet created in 1995. The repertory of the troupe Laura leads includes the great ballet classics of tradition but also *Los tres mosqueteros*, *Drácula/Dra-Cuba*, and *Le Chevalier de Saint-Georges*. In 2018, her dancers performed the musical *West Side Story* with choreography by Marta Bercy. The work was performed during celebrations for the 100th anniversary of the birth of Leonard Bernstein, an event directed by former BNC dancer Helson Hernández. The portfolio of Pro Danza notably includes *Yarini*, a ballet inspired by the figure who had been known as Havana's 'king of prostitution' and his women and rivals. The story is set during the Spanish War of Independence, with choreography by Iván Alonso, the son of Laura and Lorenzo Monreal. Iván trained at the ENA and was already a promising young dancer of the BNC "new guard". In 1966 he defected in Paris with nine other companions (the "*Gira de los diez*") to remain in Europe. *Yarini* was staged in 2018 at the Gran Teatro with a Cuban-American company, the Cleveland Habana Ballet.

An event to be remembered was when Laura – time and age do not seem to matter in Cuba – danced in the role of Giselle's mother with Alicia in the leading role.

Cleveland Havana Ballet, 2018.

4.

Cuban virtuosity consists in clean, prolonged balances, secure turns and jumps, sculpted *port de bras* and *épaulement*, with a quality of palpitating emotion. All of this is contained in a distinctive technique and style, imprinted with the stamp of Latin vibration and an aftertaste of respected classical tradition.

The Cuban school of dance has been built upon pride, courage, talent, and of being proud to be Cuban, of being the best, of being the most sought-after dancers in the world.

For decades Alicia Alonso, like a ruling sovereign, was the dominant figure in Cuban dance. The longevity of her stage career was unprecedented – indeed at ninety-two years of age Alicia even danced her cameo appearance in *Recuerdo*.[34] We can only express our admiration and render deserved homage to her tireless agitprop activity for ballet. It knew no limits, including her books.[35] And it is also important to pay tribute to all of those who, in Alicia Alonso's wake, have made the *caribeño* BNC one of the most highly esteemed dance companies in the world.

BALLET NACIONAL DE CUBA: STYLES AND GENERATIONS

MEN AND WOMEN OF THE BNC

In addition to the divine Alicia, the female dancers of the first generation at the artistic heights of the BNC were notably: exotic Loipa Araújo;[36] shining Aurora Bosch; superb Josefina Méndez, whose nickname was "Yuyi" and who passed away in

---

34. **Link:** Video of *Recuerdo* with Alicia Alonso.
35. Cf. Alicia Alonso, *Diálogos con la danza*, Editorial Letras Cubanas, Havana 1986; Editorial Galerna, Buenos Aires 1988; Editorial Complutense, Madrid 1993, for the "Alicia Alonso Chair" of the Universidad Complutense; Editora Politica, Havana 2000; Ediciones Oceano, Mexico 2004; Editorial Letras Cubanas, Havana 2010; *Dialogues with the Dance*, Editorial José Martí, Havana 2018, in English. The sequence of dates and places of publication, and the last release in English, are an indication of a far-reaching career over a broad span of time and show a constantly growing knowledge that was continuously cultivated as well as a global prestige on the stage and in the world of culture in general.
36. Loipa Araújo is a very sought after teacher in all the main companies, among which the ballet company of La Scala di Milano.

4. BALLET NACIONAL DE CUBA: STYLES AND GENERATIONS

Josefina Méndez, Mirtha Plá, Loipa Araújo and Aurora Bosch in Anton Dolin's *Grand pas de quatre*, 1948.

the *Grand pas de quatre*[38] was an extraordinary success and starred precisely these "four jewels". Originally, the term was used in reference to the historic performance in 1845 of the great divine rivals Carlotta Grisi, Maria Taglioni, Lucile Grahn, and Fanny Cerrito. Here, however, the four ballerinas performed Anton Dolin's delightful 1941 restaging. The work took its cue from the different styles of the original stars, and not without a touch of humor.

There are at least two other exceptional female 2007; and the suave Mirta Plá[37]. They were "*las cuatro joyas*" ("*the Four Jewels*"), as they came to be known. The English critic Arnold Haskell described them thus when he had been left spellbound by the 'Cuban miracle' and these 'gems' of dance, so adored by a Havana population of ballet lovers. Indeed the Cuban public was as analytical as it was fanatic. Their performance of

Alicia Alonso, Eva Evdokimova, Carla Fracci, Ghislaine Thesmar in A. Dolin's *Grand pas de quatre*, in the eighties.

---

37. Cf. Giselle Deyá, *Mirta Plá, una joya de la cultura cubana*, Ediciones Cumbres, Cuba-Spain 2013.

38. **Link:** Video of *Grand pas de quatre*.

Rosario Suárez, Amparo Bríto and Ofelia González, the "Three Graces" in George Balanchine's *Apollo*, in the seventies.

4. BALLET NACIONAL DE CUBA: STYLES AND GENERATIONS

figures of BNC's first generation to be cited. They were often known as "Soprano" and "Mezzo-soprano" and their careers marked the period that began in the sixties. These ballerinas were María Elena Llorente, today professor and *repetiteur*, and the late Marta García,[39] born in 1949, who was the dance partner and wife of Orlando Salgado. She passed away in 2017 in Madrid, where she had lived since 2005. There she had acted as 'ambassador' for Alicia Alonso who had been honored in 1992 with the Chair of the Department of Dance at the Universidad Complutense of Madrid.

Other admirable ballerinas of the BNC are no-

Viengsay Valdés and Carlos Acosta, principal dancer of the Royal Ballet in London, in *Le Corsaire*, 2007.

Yoel Carreño with Alicia Alonso, 2016.

tably the "*Tres gracias*": Rosario Suárez with her creative presence; Amparo Brito with her gift for flowing purity; and Ofelia González with her unique lyrical harmony. They are three figures who have shone as top performers, for example, as in Balanchine's *Apollo*.

Today at the BNC Viengsay Valdés[40] has emerged as a world-class star. She was born in 1976 in Havana to a family with an international background. She is a virtuoso performer gifted for a great variety of roles, as was Alonso, and is a very sought-after guest artist in companies ranging from the Washington Ballet to the Royal Ballet of London. "She could take a nap *en pointe*" boast her fans affectionately. In 2016 Viengsay Valdés was invited to represent her country on tour to Vietnam, Cambodia and Laos, where her father had served as ambassador.

---

39. Cf. Marta García, *Danzar mi vida*, Ediciones Cumbres, Madrid 2014. The editor for the Cumbres per la danza editions is Cuban Mayda Bustamante. The Preface is by the Cuban critic of "El País", Roger Salas. García was the director of the ballet company of the Teatro Colón in Buenos Aires and of the Gran Ballet of Cámara of the Alicia Alonso Institute of the Universidad Rey Juan Carlos of Madrid.

40. **Link:** Video of *Grand pas classique*, Viengsay Valdés with Elier Bourzac, now in Canada. Cf. also: Carlos Tablada, Viengsay Valdés, *De acero y nube*, Editorial Letras Cubanas, Havana 2017; Gabriel Dávalos, *Viengsay Valdés, Soy lo que ves*, Ocean Sur, 2017.

4. BALLET NACIONAL DE CUBA: STYLES AND GENERATIONS

José Manuel Carreño, *Le Corsaire,* 2006.

and Silicon Valley Ballet, and the Ballet de Monterrey in Mexico. José Manuel welcomes the idea of bringing new contemporary repertories to the BNC. His half-brother Yoelis is a principal dancer with the Norwegian National Ballet and performs ballets from the classical repertory – a Cuban specialty – and post-classical such as works by William Forsythe, Balanchine and Kylián.

In the Carreño family of dancers there is also Alihaydée Carreño, Álvaro's daughter, who joined the BNC in 1991. She subsequently emigrated to Spain and then to the Dominican Republic, though she returned to Cuba in 2013 to perform in *Cisne negro*.

Another important family are the Salgados. Orlando – whose wife, Marta García, is an extremely popular *bailarina/actriz* – and his brother Francisco, the father of Alina, Fidel Castro's granddaughter. Also of note is the Sarabia family including father Rolando and his son Rolando Jr., who can boast an impressive international

In Cuba the family – artistically too – is important. In fact, it is of central importance. And the BNC can boast quite a few families.

On the male dancers' front, the brilliant spearhead of the company is the Carreño dynasty. To begin with, there is Lázaro, the *"eterno primer bailarín"* and today a highly esteemed ballet master,[41] and then Álvaro, who is a soloist in the BNC. There are nephews José Manuel, star of the American Ballet Theatre and international guest artist, and director of California's San José Ballet

Paloma Herrera and José Manuel Carreño in *Don Quixote,* **1996.**

---

41. Lázaro Carreño was a *maître* in Spain for the ambitious Castilla y Léon/Barcelona Ballet, created in 2008 by the former Spanish star of the American Ballet Theatre, Angel Corella, a super-virtuoso dancer, who today directs the Pennsylvania Ballet. There are several Cuban dancers in the latter company including: Arián Molina, Dayesi Torriente, and Mayara Pineiro.

4. BALLET NACIONAL DE CUBA: STYLES AND GENERATIONS

Junor Souza (Benvolio), Yonah Acosta (Mercutio) and Carlos Acosta (Romeo) in *Romeo and Juliet*, English National Ballet, 2014.

career. The lineage also includes Victor Gilí, the son of the BNC 'jewel' Josefina Méndez. Gilí dances with the Ballet Concierto de Puerto Rico.

The prominent male dancers of the most recent generation include the Afro-Cubans Carlos Acosta, his nephew Yonah Acosta, and Osiel Gouneo. Also of striking presence among the first ranks is blond Dani Hernández, *danseur noble* of classical purity.

A further look at the great families of the BNC highlights, among the ballerinas of the last decades, the astounding Feijóo family. They are daughters and heirs of Lupe Calzadilla, who was also a ballerina with the BNC. Lorna Feijóo joined the Boston Ballet with her hus-

Osiel Gouneo at Kremlin Gala, 2018.

Rolando Sarabia, 2007.

4. BALLET NACIONAL DE CUBA: STYLES AND GENERATIONS

Lorna and Lorena Feijóo, 2012.

band Nelson Madrigal in 2003. The couple were both *maîtres* at the Houston Ballet, and in 2016 they opened their own Cuban school of dance in Dickinson, Texas. Lorna and her sister Lorena appeared on the American television program *Sesame Street* in an amusing educational show on pirouettes. Nureyev and Baryshnikov had also once appeared on the *Muppet Show*. The charismatic Lorna returned to the ENB to teach a masterclass in 2018. Lorna's sister Lorena was engaged by the San Francisco Ballet in 1999 and she retired in 2017. Lorena also made her debut as an actress in the film *The Lost City* by Cuban director Andy García (2005). The film was set in Havana at the time of the revolution.

"The San Francisco Ballet is a great company because it's full of Cubans" Alicia Alonzo proudly joked. Alicia was indeed the great mother of all her pupils, whether at home or émigré. Among some of "her" dancers who had joined the California ballet company: Joan Boada, until 2016; Taras Domitro, a principal dancer from 2008, and today an international guest dancer; Carlos Quenedit, principal dancer from 2014 and he too esteemed guest today.

What makes the Cuban dancers of the BNC so special? They are extroverted, musical, sensuous, and charismatic. The men are athletic and virile. They are capable of high, open lifts and multiple inimitable vertiginous turns. The women, as gentle as they are strong, manage to be as sensuous as their male partners, in adherence to academic codes, with flawless *aplomb* and rapid *tours* in crescendo, *ralenti*, and in the air. It goes without saying, virtuosity is essential for both men and women to quell the enthusiastic impassioned public fury.

"*El cubano es muy bailador*" declared Alonso, who felt that modernity was also an intrinsic trait of Cubans. So, just a matter of adding the classical. This was the magical recipe of the extraordinary Cuban school of dance. "They are the Russians of the twenty-first century" declared their countless aficionados and knowledgeable fans. Although the *escuela cubana* created a fusion of many elements of different origins, today the Cuban school of dance is immediately recognizable by characteristics that have created its own unique identity: *bailar hacia arriba*, *bailar encima*, *desprenderse del piso*, that is, dance that is elevated, rising from the floor, impeccable balance, cleanly executed batterie, mastery of the slow turn, expressive use of breathing, perfectly coordinated partnering, with both partners moving head and gaze together, appealing to every corner of the space, to achieve the triumph of dance.

Viengsay Valdés in the *pas de deux* of *Black Swan* with Romel Frómeta, 2010.

5.

CUBAN MALE BALLET DANCERS: A SPECIAL STORY

The *Escuela Nacionale Cubana de Ballet* means not only prestige but offers a complete training program and possibilities for a career. This has been achieved in a country where the population has suffered for decades from great hardships, also due to the embargo imposed by the United States. The School has obtained rare and precious results in the training of many top male dancers who are athletes and artists at once and much sought after everywhere.

Professional male dancers in Cuba were quite rare before – other than the Alonso brothers, Luis Trápaga, Enrique Martínez and Joaquín Banegas. Yet, along with Alicia Alonso's partners – from Igor Youskevitch and André Eglevsky[42] to Azari Plisetsky – they set an example for Cuban youths who could be chosen and offered the chance to study dance. At first the boys were selected from orphanages or from needy families – something that also occurred in Tsarist Russia – and they were offered the possibility to train as dancers with a scholarship accorded by a special commission. For some years the commission was headed by Joaquín Banegas, who had received a scholarship himself when he was a boy. Fencing, boxing, dance, cinema, reading and concerts were the cultural daily bread of these youngsters, in addition to their food and lodging. The career that might result from this regimen, if students were successful, would well be worth the sacrifices in terms of the status and esteem that awaited.

This educational program began to bear its fruit in one of its first most promising dancers, Jorge Esquivel. Born in 1950 into a poor family, he was a street kid who was destined to become Alicia Alonso's magnificent partner for more than fifteen years (1969-1986). They danced romantic ballets and also modern ballet works by Cuban choreographers Jorge Lefebre (*Edipo Rey*), Iván Tenorio (*La corona sangrienta*), Alberto Méndez (*El poema del fuego* on Prometheus,

---

42. In 1943, André Eglevsky appears barechested in an elegant artistic photo, taken in a New York studio by the famous photographer George Platt-Lynes. The photo appeared on the cover of the book by Peter Stonely, *A Queer History of the Ballet*, Routledge, London-New York 2007.

5. CUBAN MALE BALLET DANCERS...

Alicia Alonso with Argentinian Hugo Guffanti in Jorge Lefebre's *Oedipe Roi*, 1970.

that they had performed like "*cuatro Esquiveles*". Esquivel is an admired guest dancer not only in Cuba but in the world. Since 1993 he has been a ballet master in San Francisco and has also performed character roles in the city's ballet company.

There are many renowned dancers who graduated in the seventies and eighties, who had been trained according to the Cuban methodology. In addition to Lázaro Carreño and Orlando Salgado mentioned previously, they include Francisco Salgado, Pablo Moré, Fernando Jhones, Andrés Williams, José Zamorano, Jorge Vega, Rolando Candía, and Rafael Padilla.

Paso a tres in a comic vein, and *La diva*[43] on Maria Callas). Esquivel's elegance and virtuosity made him a *danseur noble* and model of Cuban virility. Indeed when the highly successful male ballet for quartet choreographed by Azari Plisetsky, *Canto vital* on music by Mahler, was danced by Raúl Barroso, Lázaro Carreño, Orlando Salgado and Andrés Williams,[44] general admiration was expressed

Miguelángel Blanco (in red), Romel Frómeta (in yellow), Taras Domitro (in blue), Javier Torres (in green), in the quartet *Canto vital* by Alberto Méndez, Havana, 2006.

43. **Link:** Video of *La diva* by Alberto Méndez for Alicia Alonso, early 1900s.
44. **Link:** Video of *Canto vital*, BNC, with Raúl Barroso, Orlando Salgado, Lázaro Carreño, Andrés Williams, 1979.

5. CUBAN MALE BALLET DANCERS: A SPECIAL STORY

Carla Fracci and Maurizio Vanadia in Alberto Méndez's *Cristoforo Colombo*, at the Teatro alla Scala, Milan, 1992.

Year after year a new wave of superb dancers complete their degrees. Some become ballet masters too.

Lienz Chang is also *maître de ballet* in Italy, at La Scala di Milano and the San Carlo di Napoli, and since 2019 he has taught at the Scuola di Ballo René de Cárdenas. Chang, a Cuban dancer formerly with the BNC and choreographer of the show *Sonlar*,[45] is a concentrate of *cubanía*, proud that there are other dancers in his

---

45. See https://www.renedecardenas.net/italiano/sonlar-italiano/.

5. CUBAN MALE BALLET DANCERS: A SPECIAL STORY

Lienz Chang is applauded for his *Don Quixote* at the Teatro Massimo di Palermo, with Olesja Novikova and Leonid Sarafanov, 2018.

family too (for example Yat-Sen Chang with the English National Ballet). Other impressive names from the Cuban National Ballet School are José Manuel Carreño (1992); Carlos Acosta (1994); Osmay Molina and Vladimir Álvarez (1997); Victor Gilí (1999); Rolando Sarabia, Yoel Carreño and Nelson Madrigal (2001); Octavio Martín (2003); Rómel Frómeta (2005); Taras Domitro (2007); Javier Torres, Elier Bourzac, Ernesto Álvarez and José Losada (2009); Dani Hernández, Osiel Gouneo (or Gounod)[46] and Alejandro Vire-

Viengsay Valdés with Patricio Revé in *The Nutcracker*, 2016.

Viengsay Valdés with Elier Bourzac in *Le Papillon*, 2010.

lles (2011). The latter was cast by Roberto Bolle for his gala *Bolle and Friends* (in the *Don Quixote* pas de deux with Polina Semionova, Teatro Regio di Torino, in 2018).

---
46. **Link:** Variation of *Atteone* with Osiel Gouneo.

5. CUBAN MALE BALLET DANCERS: A SPECIAL STORY

The style of dancers trained at the ENB, who move on stage with such ease, prowess and distinctive warmth *"a lo cubano"* make them quite understandably greatly admired and sought after.

Viengsay Valdés with Arián Molina in the *pas de deux* of *Black Swan*, 2011.

When considering the careers of male dancers trained in Cuba, a word should be said of the important contribution of Cuban prima ballerina assoluta Viengsay Valdés. She has personally trained some of the dance partners she has chosen such as Elier Bourzac, Romel Frómeta, Arián Molina, Víctor Estévez, and most recently, the young Patricio Revé, who joined the BNC in 2015 and very quickly became first soloist.

Some of the artists in this overview chose to continue their careers in other countries. Tentatively some updates: during a tour in Canada, Elier Bourzac remained in Toronto with his wife Patricia González, and companions Jorge Villazón, Hugo Rodríguez and Yadil Suárez. And Romel Frómeta, whose parents were also professional dancers, joined the Cincinnati Ballet in 2012 and, in 2016, the BalletMet in Columbus, Ohio. Miguel Anaya, also formerly with the BNC, dances for the BalletMet. Arián Molina is with the Pennsylvania Ballet since the 2015/2016 season, and Víctor Estévez joined the Queensland Ballet in 2016.

Marizé (or Marisel/Marizel) Fumero and Arionel Vargas in the *pas de deux* of *Swan Lake*, Cubanía en el Ballet, Ravello Festival, 2016.

CUBAN BALLET DANCERS IN THE WORLD

The ballet dancers trained in Cuba who left their country in waves made headlines. They left for various reasons, authorized or not. They were motivated by different reasons: economic (a higher standard of living and more comfortable lifestyle elsewhere); artistic (to be able to experiment in more innovative environments); sociopolitical (a desire for more personal freedom of movement). Nevertheless, the possibility to come and go from Cuba freely was the strongest desire shared by nearly all of those who left.

MIAMI

The Miami Hispanic Cultural Arts Center, known as the "White House of Ballet", is located in a nineteenth-century colonial neoclassical building with an archives annex. For decades it was directed with impassioned commitment by Pedro Pablo Peña (Havana 1944 - Miami 2018), an artist formerly with the BNC. Here the Cuban Classical Ballet of Miami founded by Peña became the chosen place for his fellow Cubans. When they made the crossing to Florida, they could rely on the support of Peña's Cuban Classical Ballet of Miami that gave them a first start. Peña was working as a choreographer with the Teatro Musical de La Habana when he left Cuba himself. This was during the great exodus that resulted when Fidel Castro's regime exceptionally granted general permission to leave the country. There were ships for this purpose that departed from the port of Mariel – familiarly called the *"marielitos"* – in

Pedro Pablo Peña in front of his building in Miami.

6. CUBAN BALLET DANCERS IN THE WORLD

Lourdes Lopez with two ballerinas from the Miami City Ballet.

1980. When Peña founded his dance company in Miami, his ambition was to compete with the BNC in Havana across the sea. The purely classical style and the repertory were in fact the same.

Among the Cuban artists whom Peña welcomed to his "*casa del ballet*" were notably Osmay Molina, who today lives in Puerto Rico, and Rayssel Cruz and Carlos Guerra, the latter then principal dancer with the Miami City Ballet. Marizé Fumero also joined Peña's company before joining the English National Ballet, and then the Milwaukee Ballet Company and the Georgia Ballet. There was Arionel Vargas, he too with the Milwaukee Ballet, who danced with the Royal Winnipeg Ballet in dazzling performances of the Balanchine repertory, to then join the English National Ballet. Vargas was invited to appear in the gala *Carlos Acosta and Friends* in Valencia and at the London Coliseum. Marizé and Arionel returned to Cuba together in 2018 to dance in the 26th Festival Internacional de Ballet de La Habana. This was the first festival without the presence of Alicia Alonso. Though she was ailing, many of her "children" had finally "come home".

Yolanda Correa was Yoel Carreño's favorite dance partner and just as Yoel, she was also for a renewal of the repertory of the mother school. After training at the Escuela Vocacional in Yolanda's hometown of Holguín, she joined the BNC. She subsequently went to Oslo to dance with the Nasjonalballetten and also with

François Llorrente and Michaela De Prince (Sierra Leone - USA) of the HNB in *Flames of Paris*, 2016.

the Staatsballett (Berlin) in 2018. This was also the year she performed for the first time in Miami, in the gala in memory of Pedro Pablo Peña, who had died a few months previously. Peña's last choreography had been *Habaneras*.

The Miami City Ballet, as noted previously, is

6. CUBAN BALLET DANCERS IN THE WORLD

also active in Florida. Lourdes Lopez has directed the company since 2012. Born in Havana in 1958, she grew up in Miami after her family left Cuba during the revolution. Lopez had previously been a principal dancer with the New York City Ballet. She became director of the MCB, succeeding Italian-American Edward Villella who was a Balanchine star dancer. Indeed, George Balanchine had carefully followed Villela since 1975. And finally, last but certainly not least, there were Cuban dancers Reyneris Reyes and Damian Zamorano with the MCB.

Lázaro Carreño, the maestro..

EXEMPLARY CAREERS: CARREÑO AND ACOSTA

Among the Cuban dancers who left the island nation with authorization from the BNC, there are José Manuel Carreño and Carlos Acosta.

José Manuel (1968) is the nephew of Álvaro and Lázaro Carreño. He joined the English National Ballet in 1990, already laden with prizes from competitions in New York and Jackson. Three years later, he was with the Royal Ballet in London, and in 1994, the American Ballet Theatre. He remained for fifteen years with the company, admired for the beauty, technique and nobility of his stage presence and his top performances in works by Balanchine, Robbins, Twyla Tharp, Mark Morris, and Alexei Ratmansky. He pursued a second career as artistic director: in San José (Silicon Valley Ballet), then with his own festival in Sarasota, Florida, and finally, with the Ballet de Monterrey in Mexico in 2016. Yet he never severed his ties with Cuba nor with the mother ballet company in Havana.

Carlos Acosta in his *Tocororo Suite*, 2015.

6. CUBAN BALLET DANCERS IN THE WORLD

Argentinian Marianela Nuñez of the Royal Ballet, with Carlos Acosta in his *Carmen*, 2015

the English National Ballet in 1991, at eighteen years of age. Just the year before, he had received the prestigious Grand Prix de Lausanne. In 1998 he was asked to join the Royal Ballet in London as principal dancer. This gave him the base from which he also developed a career as a choreographer (*Tocororo*[47] and *Carmen*[48]).

Carlos Acosta's nephew, Yonah Acosta was a principal dancer with the English National Ballet before joining the company of the Munich Opera. He was cast in *Tocororo* (the title refers to the white, red and blue national bird of Cuba) in the role of the protagonist, that is, of the author Carlos himself as a youth.

Carlos Acosta was born in 1973 to an Afro-Cuban family descended from former slaves. As a youth he was known as an unbeatable break dancer and as "*al moro de Los Pinos*", which referred to the extremely poor quarter of Havana where he spent his childhood. He was a very undisciplined student at the Escuela Provincial de Ballet Alejo Carpentier, until he was persuaded to put aside his preference for football – his idol was Pele. When he revealed such an explosive natural gift for dance, he was inevitably channeled into classical ballet. Yet it was necessary to keep Carlos away from the distractions of the capital and his environment. He was sent to study in Pinar del Rio and in Italy, at the Teatro Nuovo di Torino, under the attentive care of the artistic director of the ENB, Ramona De Sáa and her staff. This paved the way for him to join

TO DANCE *A LO CUBANO* IN A GLOBAL WORLD

Since 1966 and the "*diez de París*" incident, when ten Cuban dancers defected while performing in Europe, the Cuban exodus has never ceased.

One example is François Llorente, a brilliant promising twenty-year-old dancer with the BNC and gold medal holder at the 2017 Orlando competition. In 2016 he left for Sarasota, where Cuban dancer Ariel Serrano was also living. The

---

47. **Link:** Video of *Tocororo* by Carlos Acosta.
48. **Link:** Introductory documentary on Carlos Acosta's *Carmen*.

6. CUBAN BALLET DANCERS IN THE WORLD

latter had decided to remain in Miami in 1990, hoping for a better future in the United States than in Mexico where he and his wife were principal dancers with the Ballet de Monterrey. Today Serrano directs the Cuban Ballet School in Sarasota, after having been a principal dancer with the Sarasota Ballet company.

The dynasties of Cuban ballet dancers who have moved about, making their careers in various countries, include notably the fugitive Daniel Sarabia (1984). He left Cuba in 2004, first for Miami, and from there, to join the Boston Ballet. His brother Rolando Sarabia (1982)[49] joined Daniel a year later, after he himself fled Cuba. Daniel became a dancer in the Béjart Ballet in Lausanne, a company in which Cuban Julio Arozarena had been a dancer and choreographer, and subsequently *maître*. Daniel then danced with the Arts Ballet Theatre of Florida which was directed by Moscow-trained Vladimir Issaev. The two Sarabia brothers were welcomed back to the island in 2018, for the 26th Festival Internacional, and were moved to tears upon their homecoming. There were many dancers who returned to Cuba for the occasion. In fact, seventeen artists who had left the country decided to send a 'love letter' to the Govenor expressing their feelings for Cuba and the BNC. Among the artists who signed the letter were: Lissi Baez from Monterrey, Jorge Barani from Cincinnati, Dayesi

Daniel Sarabia in *Le Corsaire*, 2007.

---

49. **Link:** Video of *Aguas primaverales* by Asaf Messerer and *Tchaikovsky pas de deux* by George Balanchine with Lorna Feijóo and Rolando Sarabia, Sadaise Arencibia and Octavio Martín.

6. CUBAN BALLET DANCERS IN THE WORLD

Aliaydée Carreño and Osmay Molina in *Giselle*, 2007.

Torriente and Arián Molina from the Pennsylvania Ballet, Yanela Piñera and Camilo Ramos from Australia's Queensland Ballet.

Alihaydée Carreño[50] is the daughter of BNC dancers Álvaro and Haydée – Lázaro Carreño is her uncle – and she is now with the Ballet Nacional Dominicano. She had briefly danced with the Miami company and was asked by Pedro Pablo Peña in 2007 to perform *Giselle*. In 2013 she returned to Cuba to perform with Yanier Gómez.

Xiomara Reyes, from the "new guard" at the BNC, had studied with Laura Alonso, and was welcomed back to Havana some time ago. After seven years with the Royal Ballet of Flanders, from 2003 to 2015, she was the only Cuban principal dancer with the ABT, after the "creole diva" Alicia. Reyes returned to the stage of Cuba's capital during the 2010 Festival Internacional at the Teatro Karl Marx, as a member of the North American delegation.

---

50. **Link:** Video of *Il cigno nero* with Alihaydée Carreño and José Manuel Carreño.

In Italy there are four very well-known Cuban male dancers. Amilcar Moret (1977) is the son of Ofelia González and Pablo Moret (or More/Moré) who were both master teachers at the Scuola di ballo dell'Opera di Roma. His mother was one of the historic dancers of the Havana hit *Tarde en la siesta*. Amilcar danced in the ballet companies

Xiomara Reyes in *Seven Sonatas* by Alexei Ratmansky, ABT, 2011.

of Monte Carlo, Zurich, Munich and Hamburg – where he performed John Neumeier's *Othello* – and is popular for his appearances on Maria De Filippi's television show *Amici*.

José Pérez (1976) is also known for his appearances on *Amici*. As an international dancer since 1997, he has pursued his career principally in Brazil, Germany (Dresden), and Italy. Pérez

6. CUBAN BALLET DANCERS IN THE WORLD

Cubanía en el Ballet, a gathering of the artists in Michelangelo Pistoletto's *Terzo Paradiso*, Ravello Festival, 2016.

has danced in leading roles that include the role of protagonist in *Otello* by Fabrizio Monteverde at the Teatro San Carlo di Napoli, and as Don José in Luciano Cannito's *Carmen*.

Also of note is Maykel Fonts (1976), the brilliant Cuban maestro-partner in the show presented by Milly Carlucci on Rai, *Ballando con le stelle*. Fonts was formed at the school of the legendary cabaret Tropicana, in Havana.

Ricardo Núñez (1945-2014) was an international ballet master while he was at the BNC. In Italy, he worked with the Teatro Massimo di Palermo. He staged *Swan Lake* at the San Carlo di Napoli, as well as the dances for Verdi's *Un ballo in Maschera*. In 1998, Núñez also choreographed *B come Bach* and *Giselle*.

Arianne Lafita Gonzálvez, who studied with Laura Alonso and danced with the BNC in the early years of 2000, is a ballerina with an impressive career. Born in Matanzas, she is the most active Cuban ballerina in Italy today. Gonzálvez had come to Europe with Victor Ullate's company after having decided to form a couple, in life and on the stage, with Vittorio Galloro. The latter, a Neapolitan dancer, had studied at the San Carlo and then went on to specialize at the ENB in Cuba. They are presently working as freelance dancers.

The 2016 Ravello Festival,[51] with *Cubanía en el Ballet*, was instrumental in reuniting quite an impressive group of the vast family of Cuban artists, whether from the BNC, the company Acosta Danza, or from various European companies and beyond. Many of these names are top performers on American stages. They are dancers who have excelled after making the crossing to the opposite shore, to Miami, only miles from their beloved homeland, with the nostalgia of having gone back and forth so many times during the pre-Castro age.

---

51. **Link:** Video of *Cubanía en el Ballet*.

The Beauty of the Alhambra, a 1989 film with choreography by Gustavo Herrera.

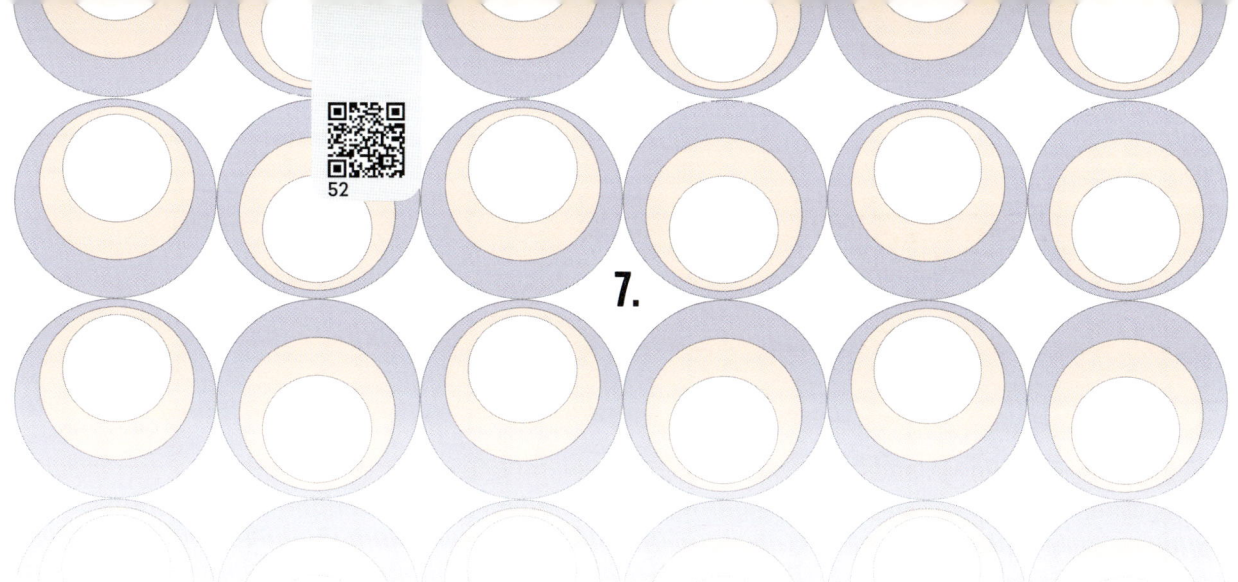

7. BNC: CHOREOGRAPHERS

During the seventies and eighties, there was an all-male 'triad' in Cuban choreography that consisted of Alberto Méndez, the most famous abroad, Iván Tenorio and Gustavo Herrera.

ALBERTO MÉNDEZ

Alberto Méndez was born in Pinar del Río in 1939 and was a student of architecture before becoming involved in athletics and dance. He was introduced to dance through the founding father of modern dance in Cuba, Ramiro Guerra (*Mambí*, *Mulato*). This led Méndez to study ballet, and he became a dancer with the BNC in 1960. He remained with the Company until 1999.

As choreographer, Alberto Méndez created the work *Tarde en la siesta* with music by Ernesto Lecuona (1973). The dance is set in the early 1900s, during the colonial period, and is the story of four sisters – Consuelo ("Comfort"), Dulce ("Gentleness"), Esperanza ("Hope"), and Soledad ("Solitude") – with their different qualities expressed in their names. Other famous choreographies by Méndez are: *Muñecos* (1978), in which a couple become animated dolls; *Ad Limitum*, a work created especially for Alicia Alonso and Antonio Gades (1978); the admirable *La Diva* (1982), a tribute to Maria Callas, to the music from her operas and created for Alicia Alonso; and *La viuda alegre* (1986), again for Alicia, surrounded by wonderfully handsome dancers for this version of *The Merry Widow*.

His staging of *Péri* to nineteenth-century music was filmed by the ICAIC.

The *Talismán pas de deux*,[52] a composition by Petipa rarely performed in Western Europe, is included in the BNC repertory. Its "conservative" vein takes pride in highlighting ties with ancient European roots.

An unforgettable work is *Poema del amor y del mar* created for Alicia Alonso and Rudolf Nureyev.

---

52. **Link:** Video of *Talismán* with Rosario Suarez and Lienz Chang.

7. BNC: CHOREOGRAPHERS

Antonio Gades and Alicia Alonso during the filming of *Ad Libitum* directed by Alberto Méndez, 1978.

Staged in Palma de Maiorca in 1990, the cast also featured soprano Victoria de los Ángeles. The event was filmed, and the video also included footage of rehearsals held at Nureyev's home on Li Galli island, formerly owned by Léonide Massine.

Alberto Méndez has often been invited to stage his works in Italy, and starring world-famous dancers and ballerinas to whom he is pleased to offer well deserved prominence. In addition to those above, works by Méndez that have featured great names have been: *La signora delle camelie* with Carla Fracci at the Teatro San Carlo di Napoli

Tarde en la siesta **with Mirta Plá, Marta García, Ofelia González, Maria Elena Llorente, 1974.**

(1982); *Cristoforo Colombo* with music by Donizetti at La Scala di Milano (1992), during the year of celebrations for the Genoese explorer's discovery of the New World. The work was based on an idea by Beppe Menegatti for his wife Carla Fracci in the role of queen Isabella, opposite Maurizio Vanadia, who later directed the Scuola di Ballo della Scala (2017-2020); and *Sogno di una notte d'estate* for the Balletto dell'Arena di Verona (1995).

IVÁN TENORIO

Iván Tenorio (Matanzas, 1941 - Havana, 2014) began his training in New York with the dance school founded by Martha Graham in the late fifties. He returned to Cuba to continue his studies in modern dance and ballet though he was above all known as an actor at the time.

Tenorio joined the BNC and Fernando Alonso's troupe, the Ballet Coreográfico. He created *Rítmicas* (1973) for the company, a work to the pulsating rhythms of *rumba*.

His interest in narrative theatre marked the works of *La Casa de Bernarda Alba* (1975) and *La corona sangrienta* (1980). The latter was Tenorio's first ballet created for Alicia Alonso.

Works from 1986 include notably: *El pensamiento revolucionario cubano*, to music by Rafael Gómez and Chucho Valdés; *El programa de Moncada*, in reference to the barracks where in 1953, young opposers to Fulgenico Batista attempted an attack led by Fidel Castro to overthrow him, though this was unsuccessful; *El triunfo de los humildes*, a succession of three dances with a clear sociopolitical intent and conceived for an open air venue and popular audience; and *Virgiliando* (2012), dedicated to the great Cuban writer Virgilio Piñera, "the Cuban Proust", who had been banned and subsequently rehabilitated by the cultural establishment.

Poster of Iván Tenorio's *La casa de Bernarda Alba*.

GUSTAVO HERRERA

Gustavo Herrera (Remedios, Villa Clara, 1946 - Mexico City, 2016), admired as the 'choreographer of Cuban sensuality', began his career with the Grupo Experimental de Danza de La Habana directed by Alberto Alonso. He then joined the Ballet del Instituto Cubano de Radio y Televisión, and the Ballet de Camagüey (1969-1975), directed by Vicentina de la Torre and later by Torre's successor Joaquín Banegas.

7. BNC: CHOREOGRAPHERS

Dioanea by Gustavo Herrera, restaged in 2016.

During this period Herrera created works such as: *Presencia de Camilo* (Cienfuegos, one of the leaders of the revolution) and *Elegías Antillanas* (1970), based on poems by Nicolás Guillén, the creator of "afrocubanità"; *De cara al sol* (1972), dedicated to the national hero José Martí; *Cantada a Céspedes* (1974), in tribute to the "Father of the Fatherland" Carlos Manuel de Céspedes; *Sikanékue* (1973), inspired by the theme of a secret religious sect; *Al Mayor* (1977), in homage to the heroism of Ignacio Agramonte during the War of Independence of Cuba from Spain.

Beginning in 1975 and during the years that followed, Herrera created 46 works for the BNC including: *Tula* (1975), to the music of Ravel and inspired by the life of writer Gertrudis Gómez de Avellaneda; *Cecilia*

Flora by Gustavo Herrera, restaged in 2013.

7. BNC: CHOREOGRAPHERS

53

Valdés (1975), again drawn from literature, a work based on the progressive novel by Cirilo Villaverde; *Dan-son y Flora* (1978), in tribute to painter and sculptor René Portocarrero, a friend of Chinese Cuban artist Wilfredo Lam, one of the leading exponents of modernity; *Dionaea* (1984), from the name of the carnivorous plant; *Electra Garrigó* (1986), based on the writings of Virgilio Piñera; and *Alfonsina* (1987). In addition, Herrara also created: *Los pinos nuevos, Concierto en mi menor, Badanesa, Déjame amar al pájaro del amor, Amor 1800,* and *La Giraldilla*.

His artistic choices in sets, costumes, and music consistently demonstrated his high-profile collaboration with the sister arts in the name of *cubanía* and the values of national culture.

In addition to working with numerous Cuban and Latin American dance companies, Gustavo Herrera also participated in the production of the charming, piquant musical comedy *La bella del Alhambra* (1989), a film directed by Enrique Pineda Barnet.[53]

EDUARDO BLANCO: *ENFANT PRODIGE*

A choreographer emerged during the following generation who seemed to possess the natural

Cuba dentro de un piano by Eduardo Blanco, 2011.

53. **Link:** Video of *La bella del Alhambra* by Enrique Pineda Barnet.

7. BNC: CHOREOGRAPHERS

gift to make "dance caress music" — that is, *cubanía*. Eduardo Blanco (Santiago de Cuba, 1982) revealed his vocation at an early age. Indeed Eduardito *"El niño coreógrafo"* created his first ballet *Baila y juega* at the age of twelve. By 2002 he had become a resident choreographer of the BNC, for which he created such works as *Souvenir* and *Final obligado* (2002); *Verano* and *Tiempo de danzón* (2003); *Inocencia* and *Homenaje a Saint-Saëns* (2004); *Homenaje*, *Integración* and *Pieza en forma de Habanera* (2006); *Acentos* (2008),[54] which was a spectacular barrage of feats by male dancers; and *Por una voz* (2009).

Blanco created a series of works for the students of the University Chair of Dance of the Ballet Nacional de Cuba: *Aladino* (2001), *El camarón encantado* (2002), *Hansel y Gretel* (2003), *El sol-

Anette Delgado and Dani Hernández in *Vilma*, a ballet by Eduardo Blanco in honor of Vilma Espín, revolutionary and activist, 2015.

dadito de plomo (2004); *Sueño de abuelos* (2005) and *La eternidad de los cuentos* (2007). In 2009, he was invited to Brazil, Argentina and Para-

Vilma Espín on the second front of the Castro advance, in the east of the island, 1958.

guay for the project *La leyenda del agua grande*, organized by the Brazilian government. This project was intended to draw attention to the native tribes of Iguazú in an appeal for the preservation of their culture.

In 2010, the choreographer conceived the graceful *Idillio pas de deux* for the 22nd Festival Internacional de Ballet, and directed the first flash mob in Cuba, *Valses para un fin de año*, in collaboration with UNICEF, and also featuring singer Raúl Paz and the Camerata Romeu.

Among Eduardo Blanco's many choreographies in recent years, there is notably *Vilma* (2015), a work dedicated to the life of Vilma Espín, a famous revolutionary and activist who tragically disappeared in 2007.

---

54. **Link:** Video of *Acentos* by Eduardo Blanco with Yonah Acosta, Serafín Castro, Janier Gómez, Camilo Ramos, Alejandro Silva on the theme *Havana Calipso*.

8.

BNC: REPERTORY

The BNC repertory includes the works of countless world-renowned choreographers. It has placed these works alongside its "made in Cuba" ballets that express the unfolding of the country's political and artistic history over the decades. The works from the fundamental grand repertory of international academic tradition, on the other hand, include not only *Giselle*, *Swan Lake* and *Don Quixote*, but also *The Sleeping Beauty*, *The Nutcracker*, *Coppélia*, *La Fille mal gardée*, and *Paquita*.

Also to be cited are the creations of Cuban choreographers, among whom Ramiro Guerra (*Toque* and *Habana 1830* in 1952, *Ensueño* in 1955, *Chacona* in 1980); Enrique Martínez, who passed away in 1998 at seventy-two years of age (*Coppélia*, 1968);[55] Jorge Lefebre (*Oedipus Rex*, 1970 and *Salomé*, 1975); Jorge Esquivel and Carlos Acosta (*Enlaces coreográficos*, London 2007); and choreographers of Russian origin working in Cuba such as Azari Plisetsky and Anna Leontieva.

The BNC included the work by George Céspedes (1979), from the Danza Contemporánea de Cuba, *Por favor, no me limites* in 2002, a programmatic title.

Among the ballets in the repertory conceived ad hoc by Cuban artists, there is *Venceremos* (1982) – the Castro revolutionary slogan – by Chilean dancer Patricio Bunster (1924-2006). Bunster, a member of the Ballet Jooss, was an

Alicia Alonso in *La avanzada* created by Azari Plisetsky, Guantánamo, 1964.

---

55. This *Coppélia* was also mounted at: La Scala in 1986, with Oriella Dorella and Marco Pierin; at the Colón of Buenos Aires; and in Uruguay upon invitation by Julio Bocca, Argentinian director of the Ballet Nacional Sodre, former star of the ABT.

8. BNC: REPERTORY

Alicia Alonso and Azari Plisetsky in *Don Quixote*, 1968.

Alicia Alonso in *Coppelia*, 1931.

actor and political activist who had been living in exile in Germany after the 1973 coup in his home country. He taught in Dresden until 1985, at the historic school founded by Gret Palucca, and ultimately returned to Chile.

BNC FEMALE CHOREOGRAPHERS

There are an impressive number of choreographies created by women in the BNC repertory. Some of these artists have several works in the repertory: Cuca Martínez, Alicia Alonso's sister (*Versos y bailes* and *Sóngoro cosongo* based on texts by Nicolás Guillén, 1953); Elena del Cueto (*Remembranzas cubanas*); Sonia Calero (*La guagua*, that is, "the bus" in popular jargon); Menia Martínez, Josefina Méndez, Aurora Bosch, Ramona De Sáa, Gloria Contreras from Mexico (*Huapango*); Gladys González (notably her *Leningrado*, 1977). Choreographers with several titles in the repertory also include Hilda Riveros, Gloria Marín, Lupe Calzadilla, Marta García, Tania Vergara; also of note are Laura Domingo Agüero (*Ígneos* 2011), María Rovira from Spain (*Loss, Escape and Earth and Moon*), and the modern Marianela Boán (*Degas* 1990).

Alicia Alonso herself choreographed *Pedro y el lobo* (*Peter and the*

Alicia Alonso poses in perfect balance as the Black Swan for Maurice Seymour, 1953.

8. BNC: REPERTORY

Amaya Rodríguez in *Tula* by Alicia Alonso, 2014.

Wolf) from the original by Adolph Bolm (1979), *Le Ballet Comique de la Reine* (2002) a homage to the first staging of ballet as court entertainment (Paris, 1581); *Tula* (1998), based on the life and writings of Gertrudis Gómez de Avellaneda, and remounted in 2014 for the bicentennial celebration of the author's birth; and *Shakespeare y sus mascaras*, which was an original version of *Romeo and Juliet* (2003).

For as long as Alicia Alonso, BNC's artistic director and star was center stage, the BNC proposed works by/for her. And this was motivated by the declared objective to celebrate the greatest moments in the history of ballet. Among the ad hoc works in the BNC repertory, *Dido abandonada* is of particular interest. The ballet premiered at the Gran Teatro in 1988 and Alicia Alonso herself was both choreographer and protagonist.

The work was performed again during the 25th Festival Internacional of Havana. In four acts, *Dido abandonada (Dido Abandoned)* was based upon the ballet pantomime of 1766, that evoked the verses by Virgil and Metastasio with libretto and music by Gasparo Angiolini. Transcribed by Italian specialist Lorenzo Tozzi, Alicia Alonso explained that it was recreated without turning its back on present-day academic ballet technique. The indisputable protagonist despite her years was Alicia Alonso, borne to triumph by her glorious BNC male dancers, dressed by Salvador Fernández in classical tunics designed to highlight their beauty and vigor.

La flauta mágica also belonged to this same line of pride and nobility in the assertion of a high-profile historical and cultural background. The work was also choreographed by Alicia Alonso, based upon the work by Lev Ivanov (Saint Petersburg, 1893) and to music by Riccardo Drigo.

ballet in Cuba in 1917 with Anna Pavlova. The musical score, which was first given to Pavlova and later entrusted to maestro Richard Bonynge, was offered to Alonso by the conductor himself. He had wanted to personally conduct the orchestra on that occasion. Dancer Luca Giaccio, who had pursued specialized training precisely in Cuba, gave an exceptional performance.

CULT BALLET AND *CUBANÍA*

Skakespeare y sus máscaras by Alicia Alonso, 2003.

This ballet of thwarted love in a rural world premiered at the 19th Festival Internacional in 2004. It was in remembrance of the performance of the

Luca Giaccio in *The Magic Flute*, 2004.

Another distinctive feature of the BNC repertory are the works that exalt its roots, in this case, Spanish. This is reflected in various creations by resident choreographers who were motivated by this aim. An example is *Majísimo*,[56] by BNC dancer Jorge García (1965). This bubbling divertissement with music from Jules Massenet's opera *El Cid*, was an immediate and prolonged success. It is a succession of five dances: Catalana, Aragonesa, Andaluza, Aubade, and Navarra. The title refers to the so-called Goyaesque in vogue movement of "*majismo*", characterized by a chastened elegance among the privileged classes, but also a robust impudence among the common people. The iconography used for reference was vividly expressed by toreador-inspired brocade jackets and swirling skirts with lace frills.

The works of the BNC repertory range from the rare pearls of the 1800s, to the works of the grand tradition conquered title by title, partially

---

56. **Link:** Video of *Majísimo* by Jorge García, with Ofelia González, Dagmar Moradillos, Gloria Hernández, Galina Álvarez, Jorge Vega, Alberto Terrero, Rafael Padilla. Francisco Salgado, Malaga 1990.

8. BNC: REPERTORY

Majísimo (2011) by Jorge García: (from left) Paloma Herrera, Argentinian, and José Manuel Carreño, Cuban, both from the ABT; Xiomara Reyes, Cuban also of the ABT, and Reyneris Reyes, Cuban from the Miami City Ballet; Lorena Feijóo, Cuban of the San Francisco Ballet, and Nelson Madrigal, Cuban from the Boston Ballet; Lorna Feijóo of the Boston Ballet, and Joan Boada of the San Francisco Ballet, both Cuban.

and then totally. The repertory also embraces the era of the Cuban Revolution and presents works rooted in the culture's artistic and political history. There are also original works by twentieth-century artists that became international hits, as well as new projects by Cuban and foreign choreographers. All through the decades of its existence, the BNC repertory has thus reflected an extraordinarily varied profile.[57]

ALICIA ALONSO GRAN TEATRO DE LA HABANA

The Gran Teatro de La Habana (GTH), since 2016 named after Alicia Alonso, celebrated its 100th anniversary in the spring of 2017. The event took place in the Sala García Lorca with the performance of recent new works.

Ely Regina Hernández – a ballerina who began at the BNC, then joined Acosta Danza, and returned to the BNC – presented *Invierno*,[58] a duet on the music by Tchaikovsky. This is a delightful journey to the Kingdom of Sweets from *The Nutcracker* that, as the choreographer explained, "acts as a support for a work built on a classical base and along a modern line."

Hernández had previously created several works for the BNC within the Taller creative workshop program such as *El Relato*, *Dueto* and *Yo, Tu, El, Ella* on music by Alexia Moore (Pink).

---

57. Cf. Miguel Cabrera, *op. cit*, 2011.

58. **Link:** Video of *Invierno* by Ely Regina Hernández.

Anette Delgado, Adrián Sánchez and Darío Hernández in *Anyali* by Ely Regina Hernández-Ezio Bosso, 2017.

8. BNC: REPERTORY

Oscurio by Anabel López Ochoa with Viengsay Valdés and Ariel Martínez, 2013.

Airel Martínez in *The Corsair*, 5th South African Ballet Competition, 2017.

She is also the creator of *Anyali*, for which she also designed sets and costumes. The music was by the Italian composer Ezio Bosso, whose works include dance compositions for Christopher Wheeldon, Edward Liang, and Bonachela. *Anyali* is performed by a trio, two men and a woman – the latter role was either danced by the young Bárbara Fabelo or étoile ballerina Anette Delgado. The piece aims to subvert the academic canon with its stark contrast of light and darkness, and the delineation of faceless characters. The title is a proper noun yet at the same time a polysemic word that alludes to dream images.

Also, in 2016, Colombian Belgian Annabelle López Ochoa choreographed *Oscurio* for the BNC. The music was by the duo Raime and Michael Gordon, with costumes by Aviad Arik Herman and lighting design by Michael Mazzola.

Many new dancers are constantly arriving on the scene in Cuba, and through their experimentation, they guarantee renewal at home. Yet young Cuban dancers are also very much in demand abroad too and are called in impressive numbers to countries around the world. The School churns out dancers, the Company trains them, and the world welcomes them with open arms. Cuba is truly a special case.

Among the most prominent young dancers: Ginett Moncho, Daniela Gómez, Ana Lucía Prado, Glenda García, Maureen Gil, Ariel Martínez, Daniel Barba, and Patricio Revé.

Among the latest recruits, of note is Rafael

8. BNC: REPERTORY

Sadaise Arenciba and Raúl Abreu in *Swan Lake*, 2017.

The young dancers Diana Menéndez and Narciso Medina (son of Narciso Sr. who is one of the most influential personalities in Cuban modern dance), appeared as guest artists in the cast of *The Nutcracker* with the Ballet Nacional Dominicano.

Grettel Morejón,[60] prima ballerina of the BNC, was the star of the world premiere of Jimmy Gamonet's *Romeo and Juliet*. Gamonet is choreographer and director of the Ballet Nacional de Perú in Lima. In 2014 he asked Cuban Pepe Hevia to mount *Preludio* for his company. This was a neoclassical piece on music by Rachmaninoff, Chopin and Bach. This is an example of how Cuban methodology and dance know how have had repercussions throughout Latin America.

Quenedit – well-known for having participated, along with his brother Carlos, in the Italian television show *Amici*[59] – and Chanell Cabrera. They performed *The Nutcracker* in Texas, with the Quenedit Dance Theatre directed by Ernesto Quenedit – a Cuban dancer formerly with the BNC and who is Rafael's uncle. Rafael Quenedit and Cabrera also appeared with the Joffrey Ballet, thus confirming that dance and ballet open doors of communication that on other fronts might well seem to be closed.

In November 2017 a favorite classical work, *La Fille mal gardée,* was performed again. Yankiel Vázquez, a dancer trained at the national school and a soloist since 2015, made his stage debut in the role of Colin. Daniel Rittoles, award winner at the 4th Beijing Competition in Peking in 2017, and the previously cited Narciso Medina Sr., award winner at the Youth America Grand Prix 2016, performed the role of Alain.

In 2018, seventy-five years after Alicia Alonso's stage debut as Giselle, this signature ballet of the BNC repertory, along with the Cuban *Don Quixote*, were both restaged in the United States. There were performances in Chicago (Cu-

---

59. In 2020, the Cuban dancer Javier Royas also participated in *Amici*. Royas was a member of the Royal Swedish Ballet and appeared in the film *Yuli* on the life of Carlos Acosta. Quenedit and Royas played competing pupils in the fillm, but in real life they were working professionals.

60. **Link:** Video of *Vals* by Alberto Méndez with Lorna Feijó and Rolando Sarabia.

8. BNC: REPERTORY

Narciso Medina Jr. and Katherine Ochoa, ENB, in *Don Quixote*, 2017.

bans Miguelángel Blanco and Alberto Velázquez danced with the local company, the Chicago Joffrey Ballet), then Washington (the Cuban dancers who appeared with the Washington Ballet were Javier Morera, Oscar Sánchez, Giancarlo Pérez, Rolando Sarabia – already with the Houston Ballet and the Miami City Ballet – and Venus Villa, of Italian Cuban origin), and finally in Tampa and Saratoga. The press reviews, other

8. BNC: REPERTORY

Grettel Morejón and Rafael Quenedit in the "Waltz of the Snowflakes", *The Nutcracker*, 2017.

Yolanda Correa and Yoel Carreño in the *Esmeralda pas de deux*, 2015.

than some reticence concerning the taste of the mise-en-scène, were excellent, with praise and applause for the dancers and their performances.

GREAT CHOREOGRAPHERS: RARITY AND SPECIFIC IDENTITY

Historically the BNC has introduced many 'patents of nobility' into its programs: *Napoli* Act 3, the *Festival de las flores en Genzano pas de deux*, the divertissement from *Willliam Tell*, and *La Sylphide*,[61] all of these ballets by Bournonville; *Esmeralda* by Marius Petipa; *La vivandière*, *Nathalie o la lechera suiza* by Pierre Lacotte, who was the French specialist on reconstruction of historic ballets; *La muñeca encantada (The Fairy Doll)* by Nikolai and Sergei Legat on music by Riccardo Drigo; *The Corsair pas de deux*, *Diana y Acteón pas de deux*, *Paquita grand pas*, *El talismán* by Petipa; *La Cachucha*, in the 1992 version by Eduardo Veitía; and Fokin's *Carnaval,* reconstructed by Italian dancer and choreographer Toni Candeloro.

Cuban maestro Pedro Consuegra (1929), who resided in France, was commissioned the "antiquated and kitsch" reconstruction (*investigaciónes-reconstrucciónes*) of *Los milliones de Arlequín* (1998), with décors by Ricardo Reymena. Consuegra also reconstructed the 2004 complete version of *El despertar de Flora* ("*The Awakening of Flora*"), and *Le roman d'un bouton de rose* (2006), all choreographed by Marius Petipa. Consuegra

---

61. **Link:** Video of *La Sylphide* with Anette Delgado and Yoel Carreño, BNC.

8. BNC: REPERTORY

Arián Molina, José Losada, Camilo Ramos, Serafín Castro in *Canto vital* by Azari Plisetsky, 2014.

had previously mounted *Cenicienta* for the BNC. This was his merry *Cinderella* to the music by Johan Strauss Jr. The work premiered in 1988 in Marseilles,[62] where it was above all identified with the works of Roland Petit. A revised version followed in 1996 performed by Alicia Alonso and Consuegra's *Cenicienta* was restaged at the 26th Festival Internacional de La Habana in 2018.

The BNC repertory also includes Soviet creations: *Aguas primaverales* by Asaf Messerer (on Rachmaninoff, 1953); *Las llamandas de París* ("Flames of Paris"), choreographed by Vasili Vainonen, and based upon the French Revolution; *Arlequinada* and *Canto vital* to Mahler (1973), and the *Spartacus pas de deux*, by Azari Plisetsky.

The works of "Cubanized" Argentinian Rodolfo Rodríguez are also noteworthy. During the early sixties he mounted works by Léonide Massine such as *El sombrero de tres picos* (*The Three-Cornered Hat*, 1919) and *Gaîté Parisienne* (1938).

---

62. **Link:** Video of *Hommage Pedro Consuegra*, 2014.

CHOREOGRAPHERS OF THE 1900s

The BNC has gathered many works over the years by famous choreographers. These works, mainly from the twentieth century, include: *L'Après-midi d'un faune* by Nijinsky;[63] Fokin's *Petrushka*, *La muerte del cisne*, and *Espectro de la rosa*; Balanchine's *Apollo*, *Sylvia pas de deux*, *Ballo della regina*, *Agon pas de deux*; *El bello Danubio* by Massine; *Grand pas classique* by Gsovsky; *Bhakti* by Béjart; *Estudios y preludios* (1974) and *Sonata* (1976) by Roland Petit.

In 1978, there were works added to the BNC repertory such as: *Bodas de sangre* by Antonio Gades, *In the Night* by Jerome Robbins, followed by *Quando la hojas caen* (*The Leaves are Fading*) by Antony Tudor; *Steptext* by William Forsythe (1988);[64] fragments of works by John Cranko, *pas de deux* from *La fierecilla domada* (*The Taming of the Shrew*), and *Onegin*. The company also gave extraordinary performances of *Le papillon* (1981), *Lilith* (1990) and *Fuera del silencio* (1990) by Ann Marie DeAngelo. This latter work so impressed Cuban audiences with its innovative classical and contemporary mixed style that it was performed at the Festival, in Havana, seven times from 1976.

Also of interest are the creations by José Parés (Puerto Rico, 1926 - San Juan, 2006). Parés was a maestro with Maurice Béjart's Mudra School.

---

63. In the fantasy novel by Abilio Estévez, *Los palacios distantes* (2002), Nijinsky lives clandestinely under the Teatro dell'Avana, just as Maria Callas does.
64. **Link:** Video of *Steptext* by William Forsythe, with Gladys Acosta, Alberto Terrero, Javier Sánchez, Vladimir Álvarez of the BNC.

José Parés, in the center of the troupe Tele Ballet, New York, 1948.

In 1952, he created *Un concierto en blanco y negro* for Alicia Alonso. The work, tinged with Balanchine and with music by Haydn, is included in the BNC repertory today. Parés joined the BNC in 1959 as a dancer and teacher, and then began

Hor che'l ciel (1997) and *Orfeo* (1993) by Massimo Moricone; *Concerto Conciso* by Karole Armitage (2000); *Les patineurs pas de deux* by Ashton, *El combate (The Duel)* from Tasso's *Jerusalem Delivered*, conceived in 1949 for the company of Roland Petit; *The Duel* by William Dollar; *Una rosa, una rosa,* and also *Habanera Suite* by the Spanish contemporary choreographer Ramón Oller; *Tres virgenes y un diablo* from Boccaccio and *Una rosa para Miss Emily* from William Faulkner, both by Agnes De Mille; *Samsara* by Victor Ullate; *Non, je ne regrette rien* by Ben Van Cauwen; and *Siéntate* (2011) by Cina Espejord, from Oslo.

The Italian choreographer Vittorio Biagi, formerly principal dancer in Béjart's company, created *La muerte de Cleopatra* in 1979 for Alicia Alonso; and Jiri Nemecek, from Prague, staged Euripides' *Medea* for Alicia in 1982.

Marta García in *Bodas de Sangre* by Antonio Gades, since 1978 a work in the BNC repertory.

***Un concierto en blanco y negro* by José Parés, 2016.**

choreographing for the company as well.

Works also of note are *Cantares* by Argentinian Oscar Araiz; *Percusión para seis hombres* and *Nuestros Valses* by Venezuelan Vicente Nebrada;[65]

All decisions concerning courses of action, programming, and staging were always the sole responsibility of the divine Alicia: the "Assoluta" for her fans, or the "Cobra negra" for her detractors, by virtue of the supremely indisputable, unconquered position that she held right up to her death.

---

65. Cf. Carlos Paolillo, Vincente Nebrada, *La ruta del coreógrafo*, Editorial Balletin Dance, Buenos Aires 2018.

A poster of the Conjunto Nacional de Danza Moderna.

9. CUBAN MODERN DANCE: FROM RAMIRO GUERRA TO TODAY

Fidel Castro implemented a general reform of the country's educational system when he came to power. Dance was also concerned by the reform, with the creation of the Departamento de Danza Moderna del Teatro Nacional de Cuba. This later was called the Conjunto Nacional de Danza Moderna, before finally becoming Danza Contemporánea de Cuba (DCC).

Ramiro Guerra (Havana, 1922-2019), after graduating in law to please his parents, became a renowned dancer, choreographer, essayist, and critic.[66] He proudly claimed his *mestiza* descent, which was a mixture of European, African and Chinese origins. Guerra's work had a profound impact on contemporary dance in Cuba. In fact, he was the founding father of all that came after him, whether on a practical or theoretical level, or in terms of teaching and popularizing the art form.[67] Yet he was also controversial. He enjoyed a period of recognition for his work but fell into disfavor when his ideas and projects were not considered in line with the regime's plans.

In 1971, the premiere of Guerra's *El decálogo del Apocalipsis* ("Decalogue of the Apocalypse") was banned. As a result, Ramiro Guerra, in determined defense of his aesthetic and social causes, was obliged to leave the DCC as director. He turned to the study of dance and research instead, as he considered the art of movement in terms of content, and its emotional and psychological aspects. This encompassed everything about the art, wherever, whenever, from yesterday or today, without preclusions or prejudices.[68]

---

66. Cf. Carolina Riera Sanz, *Ramiro Guerra. Bailarín, coreográfo y maestro*, Santiago de Chile: Universidad de Chile, Facultad de Artes, Departamento de Danza, p. 63. 2012. On the practice of Cuban modern dance cf. María del Carmen Mena Rodríguez, *El cuerpo creativo, taller cubano para la enseñanza de la composición coreográfica*, Buenos Aires (Argentina), Colección Súlkary Cuba, Balletin Dance, p. 27, 2009.

67. Cf. Elfride Mahler, Ramiro Guerra, José Limón, *Fundamentos de la danza*, Editorial Orbe, Havana 1978.
68. Cf. Ramiro Guerra, *Siempre la danza, su paso breve...*, Ediciones Alarcos, Havana 2010; Iliana Polo, *Panorama de*

9. CUBAN MODERN DANCE: FROM RAMIRO GUERRA TO TODAY

Ramiro Guerra.

Guerra translated texts by American founders of dance companies. He published articles in *Dance Magazine* in the U.S. and *Por la Danza* in Spain. He contributed essays to books of compilations.[69] In 1994, Guerra founded the Centro de Desarrollo de la Danza, and the newspaper *Toda la danza-La danza toda*, in which his studies appeared along with those of other Cuban scholars.

Having attained this indisputable mastery – concrete, enduring and penetrating – documented by his own writings,[70] Guerra's far-reaching contribution to Cuban artistic and cultural life was finally recognized. In 2000 he was awarded the Premio Nacional de Danza.

In 2017, at the age of ninety-five, Guerra received a tribute to his artistic contribution in the form of the documentary-conversation *Mi vida, la Danza*. The film was produced by Yadira Herrera/Almargen and directed by Alina Morante Lima. The images and documentation had been gathered by Lissette Hernández García. She was a consultant for the project and had directed a film on Ramiro Guerra twenty-five years previously. The film *Mi vida, la Danza* also included several interviews of the maestro's famous pupils such as Santiago Alfonso and Roberto Pérez León.[71]

Ramiro Guerra had a profound impact on dance in many different areas. He influenced many of the dance companies with which he worked. In 1978, when he could return to choreography, Guerra worked with the Ballet de Camagüey (*El canto del ruiseñor* on music by Stravinsky) and the Conjunto Folklórico Nacional de Cuba (CFNC), for which he created *Tríptico oriental*.

Guerra also conceived *Trinitarias* for the CFNC, with sets by primitive artist Benito Ortiz. In this work, Guerra takes a fresco depicting Trinidad folklore and transforms it into dance. He included typical *pregones*, *trova* and *fiesta Sanjuanera*, based upon research by the scholar Samuel Feijoó. For the same troupe, Guerra then produced

---

la danza moderna y contemporánea en Cuba, Editorial Adagio, Havana 2010; Graciela Chao Carbonero, *De la contradanza cubana al casino*, Editorial Adagio, Havana 2006.

69. Cf. Ramiro Guerra, *My Experience and Experiments in Caribbean Dance*, in Susanna Sloat, *Making Caribbean Dance*, University Press of Florida, Gainesville 2010, online 2012.

70. Cf. Ramiro Guerra, *Fundamentos de la danza*, Pueblo y Educación, Havana 1982; *Teatralización del Folklore*, Editorial Letras Cubanas, Havana 1989; *Una metodología para la enseñanza de la danza* (1989). *Coordenadas danzarias*, Ediciones Unión, Havana 1999; *Eros baila*, Editorial Letras Cubanas, Havana 2000; *Apreciación de la danza*, Editorial Letras Cubanas, Havana 2003; *De la narradividad al abstraccionismo en la danza*, Centro de Investigación y Desarrollo de la Cultura Cubana Juan Marinello, Havana 2003; *El síndrome del placer*, Editorial Capiro, Santa Clara de Cuba 2003; *Calibán danzante*, Editorial Letras Cubanas, Havana 2008. All of the previous online at http://artesescenicas.uclm.es/index.php?sec=artis.

71. Cf. Roberto Pérez Léon, *Por los orígenes de la danza moderna en Cuba*, Departamento de Actividades Culturales, Universidad de La Habana, Havana 1986.

9. CUBAN MODERN DANCE: FROM RAMIRO GUERRA TO TODAY

The company Danza Voluminosa, founded by Juan Miguel Mas, 2016.

De la memoria fragmentada, DCC, 1989.

Refranes, dicharachos y trabalenguas. This was an evocation of sayings, tongue-twisters and incessant repetitions.

Projects of more recent date were produced with the Teatro Nacional de la Pantomima (*El reino de este mundo*, based on a novella of the same title by Alejo Carpentier); with Danza Libre de Guantánamo, and finally, with Danza Voluminosa. This latter troupe consisted of dancers who were not – or who no longer were – "normal weight". It was founded in 1966 by Juan Miguel Mas (Guerra's pupil). For these extra-large dancers, Guerra created *¿Fedra?* in 2001. He accepted the challenge "to organize new bodies and new harmonies in a non-conventional aesthetic approach".

In 1989, on the thirtieth anniversary of the DCC, Guerra conceived *De la memoria fragmentada*. This was a collage of all his works created for the Company. Symbolically, the dancers are condemned to move about in wheelchairs onstage as images are projected on a screen and on televisions that gradually switch off. The images show the dress rehearsal of *El decálogo del Apocalipsis*, Guerra's boldest work, that was never allowed to premiere as planned in 1971. The title *De la memoria fragmentada* was also the name adopted in 2017 for a convention that analyzed every aspect of twenty-first-century dance, from dialogues, physiques to sets. Organized by the Departamento di Danzología de la Facultad de Arte Danzario de la Universidad de las Artes, the convention hosted scholars from various countries in the world (including France, Mexico, and Colombia). A second convention was held under the same name on contemporary works in 2019. It celebrated the five hundred years of Havana and the sixty years of existence of the DCC.

9. CUBAN MODERN DANCE: FROM RAMIRO GUERRA TO TODAY

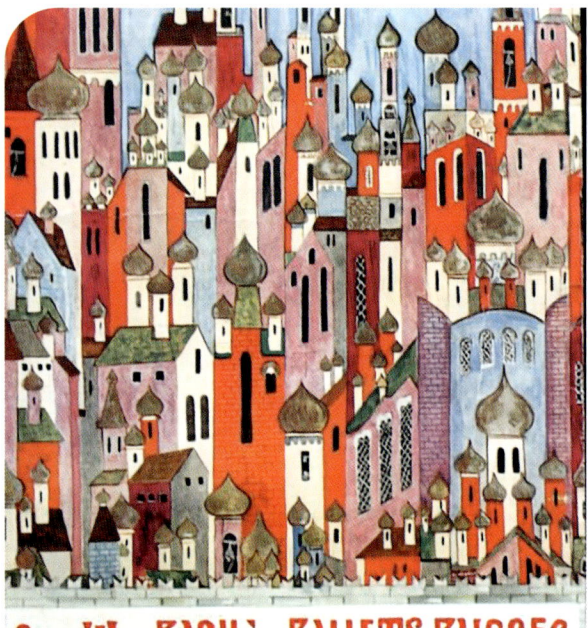

An American poster of Colonel de Basil's Ballets Russes.

Artists from Colonel de Basil's company travelling on the ship *Maloja*, 1938.

TRAINING ABROAD

Guerra's first approach to dance was through the Pro Arte Musical[72] with maestro Nikolai Yavorsky, under the direction of Alberto Alonso. Nina Verchinina, who in the words of Guerra himself was "a kind of dissident of the academic style"[73] also contributed to his training. He followed her example and joined the dance company that owed its aesthetic heritage to Colonel de Basil's Ballets Russes. Guerra chose the stage name Pedro Suárez and began to dance in modern ballets such as *Petrushka* and *Polovetsian Dances* from *Prince Igor*, choreographed by Mikhail Fokin. He also went on tour in Brazil and the U.S. When Guerra moved to New York in 1946, he met founding figures of modern dance such as Doris Humphrey and José Limón. Most important of all, he was able to

Nina Verchinina, in the forties.

---

72. Foremost modern artists such as Anna and Irma Duncan (season 1930/1931) were invited to Cuba. Anna Duncan is seen on the cover of the Pro Arte Musical magazine: http://madios.com/listm/m0287r.jpg-; Ted Shawn (1937), Harold Kreutzberg (1938), Kurt Jooss (1940), and Martha Graham (1941).
73. Cf. Fidel Pajares, *Ramiro Guerra y la Danza en Cuba*, Casa de la Cultura Ecuatoriana, Quito 1993; see also http://www.casa.co.cu/publicaciones/revistaconjunto/126/fidel126.htm.

9. CUBAN MODERN DANCE: FROM RAMIRO GUERRA TO TODAY

study with Martha Graham who let him follow her classes for free. When Guerra returned to Cuba in 1948, he was ready to show everything he had learned during his stay in the United States.

RETURN HOME

Guerra taught modern dance in 1950 at the Alicia Alonso Academy of Ballet. He was also a teacher at the affiliated Escuela de Arte Dramático directed by Violeta Casal (actress and voice for Radio Rebelde), and Fernando Alonso's troupe Danza

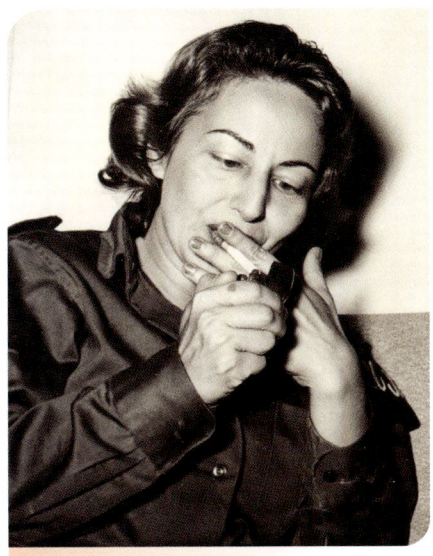

Violeta Casal, Havana, 1959.

Experimental. Guerra staged his first work two years later, one that he had created for the Alicia Alonso Ballet: *Toque*, to music by ethnologist and musicologist Argeliers León. The work sparked controversy right from the start, both because of its references to the world of the Afro-Cuban *Orishas*, and for its suggestive erotic scenes. Only the authoritative words of Fernando Ortiz,[74] who termed the work "art with the soul of Cuba"[75] (that is, with the true soul of the island), could serve as a shield against the violent criticism. Guerra also created the subsequent works *Habana 1830* and *Crónica nupcial* (1962), for what was by now called the Ballet Nacional de Cuba.

In the meantime, Guerra continued to travel and teach in all Latin America. He also spent a time in Spain, where he toured with his *Drama-Danza* and, in Granada, he presented *Llanto por Ignacio Sánchez Mejías* (based upon *A las cinco de la tarde* by García Lorca). The latter theme had already been treated by Limón in 1946 with actor Osvaldo Pradere. Guerra returned to Cuba in 1954 and staged his works at various institutions: *Dos danzas cubanas* by Ignacio Cervantes, *Dionisiaca Mulata,* and *Sensemayá,* with texts by Nicolás Guillén, the Cuban national poet who was of African descent. A series of Guerra's works were also restaged: *Zarabanda* on music by Bach, and the previously mentioned *Llanto*; *Tres Tiempos* again to music by Bach, *Dos Soliloquios: De mí de ti* to music by Satie; *Muerte de Antoñito el Camborio* based upon the work by García Lorca, and *Presagios* by Eduardo Manet.[76] Then followed the works: *Gesta de América* on music by Heitor Villa-Lobos, and *Son para turistas* on music by Juan Blanco.

In 1956, Guerra founded the "Taller Experimental de la Danza" at the Alicia Alonso Ballet Academy. It was during this period that Guerra was experimenting in an uninhibited and uncompromising approach to multicultural

---

74. Cf. Fernando Ortiz, *Africanía de la música folklórica de Cuba*, Editorial Universitaria, Havana 1965.
75. Cf. Letter from Fernando Ortiz to Alberto Alonso in Ramiro Guerra, *Siempre la danza, su paso breve…*, Ediciones Alarcos, Havana 2010, pp. 360-363.
76. Writer born in Santiago in 1930 but who lived in Paris, he was director of the Teatro Nazionale a Cuba from 1960 to 1968.

9. CUBAN MODERN DANCE: FROM RAMIRO GUERRA TO TODAY

Día de Reyes **by Pierre Toussaint Frédéric Mialhe, from *Album Pintoresco de la Isla de Cuba*, 1851.**

hybridization. He created such works as *Orientalita*, *Rítmicas* to a score by Amedeo Roldán (Paris, 1900 - Havana, 1939), *Cantata a la paz* to music by Heitor Villa-Lobos, and *Suite para niños*.

In his writings, Guerra once remembered how Roldán's composition, *La rebambaramba* (1928), had inspired Sergei Diaghilev shortly before he died. Diaghilev had planned to use the music in a new work for his cosmopolitan, exotic Ballets Russes.[77] Ruth Saint Denis and Ted Shawn had also been inspired by the music for a dance, but nothing ever came of the idea. The libretto of *La rebambaramba* (1928)[78] was the work of the highly esteemed writer and musicologist Alejo Carpentier.[79] His mother was Russian and his father French (Lausanne, 1904 - Paris, 1980) and Alejo was a typical European-Cuban bridge between cultures. The musical score was by Amadeo Roldán (Paris, 1900 - Havana, 1939) whose father was Spanish and mother of mixed race. The pianist was Albertina Gardes. Roldán graduated from the Madrid Conservatory and was a fervent

---

77. Cf. Ramiro Guerra, *op. cit.*, 2010, p. 80.

78. On writing for musical purposes and not only literary - looking for a rhythmic prose already in itself musical, as a musical composition in its own right – see statements by Alejo Carpentier at: https://cvc.cervantes.es/literatura/aih/pdf/16/aih_16_2_269.pdf.

79. On Alejo Carpentier, see *La música en Cuba*, Fondo de Cultura Econónima, Mexico 1946; Editorial Letras Cubanas, Havana 1979, Havana 2004.

exponent of the Afro-Cuban movement.[80] In addition to his compositions, he also set texts to the music of Nicolas Guillén. During the twenties, he was conductor of the Havana Symphonic Orchestra and of the capital's string quartet. *La rebambaramba* (or "the big uproar") by Carpentier and Roldán, was a "musicorama" of multicolored rhythms. It was performed in Paris in orchestral form in 1931. To create a folkloric version of the work for the Cuban stage, Carpentier himself had declared that the island had magnificent popular dancers with all the qualities to bring to life the work's vivid scenes in movement. In 1957 a dance to the score was also prepared for television by Alberto Alonso, with no fewer than eighty performers. One of them was Sonia Calero, *rumbera* and BNC prima ballerina of folkloric character roles. She later became *répétiteur* of the company's *Carmen* that went to Miami and around the world.

The libretto by Carpentier and Alberto Alonso was even more complex. It was packed with characters from the colonial period and characterized by the nuanced tones of romantic nineteenth-century landscapes. These had been inspired by the scenic settings by Pierre Toussaint Frédéric Mialhe (1810 - 1868). He had come to Cuba in 1838 by invitation of the Real Sociedad Patriótica, and remained until 1854.

This version of *La rebambaramba* seemed strongly folkloric in its high color both visually and musically and was striking to Guerra as well. In 1961, he staged his own interpretation in a choreography for the Conjunto Nacional de Danza Moderna and took the ballet to Paris. The sets and costumes (so painstakingly recreated in every detail that they seemed like oleographs) were designed by Cuban painter and illustrator José Hurtado de Mendoza. A contemporary of Carpentier and Roldán, Mendoza was associated with the Grupo Minorista just as they were. This was a movement whose focus was the non-European, vernacular and mixed-race cultures. Guerra was also inspired by the primitivism and Africanism expressed in European artistic avant-garde circles and attempted to avoid slipping into false representations.

A NATIONAL MODERN DANCE

The year 1959 and the rise to power of Fidel Castro were a turning point for the country. Many artists who had left Cuba returned to their homeland. They were witness to the creation of new institutions such as the Departamento de

Ramiro Guerra's *Mulato*, 1960.

---

80. Cfr. Robin D. Moore, *Music and Revolution, Cultural Change in Socialist Cuba*, University of California Press/Center for Black Music Research, Chicago 2006.

Danza Moderna del Teatro Nacional, headed by Isabel Monal (1931). An important intellectual

9. CUBAN MODERN DANCE: FROM RAMIRO GUERRA TO TODAY

A poster of *Tierra* by Elena Noriega.

figure of the revolutionary period, Monal had studied in the United States and been an activist in the underground militancy. Upon her return to Cuba, she offered Guerra the chance to create the Conjunto Nacional de Danza Moderna with 30 dancers: "10 White, 10 Black, 10 Mixed Race". Among them were future protagonists of Cuban dance such as Eduardo Rivero, Gerardo Lastra, Luz María Collazo, and Eddy Veitía.

In February 1960, the newborn dance troupe performed two key works by Ramiro Guerra that premiered at the Teatro Nacional. They were *Mulato* and *Mambí*, alongside *Estudio de las Aguas* (*Water Study*, 1928) and *La vida de las abejas* (*Life of the Bee*, 1929). These latter works were by Doris Humphrey and remounted by Lorna Burdsall,[81] an American dancer who had come to Cuba in 1955. Burdsall worked with dedication to make the technique and works of her American teacher Humphrey known in Cuba.

Her aim was to give deserved importance to the patrimony of Cuban dances of African origin

Suite Yoruba by Ramiro Guerra, 1960.

– Katherine Dunham's[82] commitment in the U.S. for the recognition of the value of Black culture also comes to mind. In Cuba, the crucial role of modern dance in achieving this was played by Elena Noriega, the author of *Huapango* (Matanzas, 1965), *Tres Preludios*, and *Folklore Mexicano II*.

And thus, with the support of the government, the "movimiento danzario nacional" was born. Guerra went forging ahead immediately, not only in practice, but also in theory. He con-

---

81. See the documentary by Estela Bravo, *Americans in Cuba, Those Who Came, 1988-1989*, Tamiment Library and Robert F. Wagner Labor Archives, New York.

82. **Link:** Video of *Ballet Creole*, performed by Katherine Dunham.

9. CUBAN MODERN DANCE: FROM RAMIRO GUERRA TO TODAY

tributed to the publication *Lunes de Revolución*,[83] under the leadership of Carlos Franqui and Guillermo Cabrera Infante. The latter was the writer destined to boldly represent the transgressive side of Cuba with his famous *Tres tristes tigres*.[84] He was the author of two incisive articles on dance, one that negatively critiqued *Mambí*,[85] and the other that applauded *Mulato*. He clearly declared his position as the enemy of tutus and pointes on the island.[86]

Guerra was made responsible for organizing the Departamento de Danza at the Teatro Nacional (from 1962 it was called the Conjunto Nacional de Danza Moderna, and from 1974, the Danza Nacional de Cuba). He began by putting together a group of keen young people and purposely composed a multi-racial troupe. He chose young men and women from different artistic fields – dance, cabaret, television, or some with no experience at all, yet who were active in sports. To carry out this new undertaking, he could count on the help of several figures: Nieves Fresneda (1900-1981), a top ballerina with the Conjunto Folklórico Nacional and expert folklore informant; Oreste Suárez (Papo) to conduct the orchestra; Trinidad Torregosa, musician and *batá* drum maker; Jesús Pérez, singer and conductor of the percussions section of the Conjunto de Danza Moderna; and the contribution of Lorna Burdsall.

Guerra's open, progressive horizon included the *Yoruba* pantheon, the rites of the Abakuá, and the elements of the Cuban cross culture "*blanquinegra*". Popular music and dances such as *mambo* and *cha-cha-cha* also gained his respect

Isidro Rolando in Ramiro Guerra's *Orfeo Antilliano*, 1964.

and took their place, despite the American and European commercialization of these dances. With Paris leading the way, they had pillaged this heritage during the forties, to make it sell they had eroticized these dances (*rumba-fox*, *canción slow*, *capricho afro*) and adulterated their image.

---

83. Cf. Leandro Estupiñán, *Lunes: un Día de la Revolución Cubana*, Editorial Dunken, Buenos Aires 2015; Amelia Duarte de la Rosa, *Cuba danza los lunes*, Guantanamera, Sevilla 2017, contains all of the articles on dance that appeared from 1959 to 1961 in *Lunes de Revolución*, cultural and literary supplement of the periodical *Revolución*.
84. Cf. Guillermo Cabrera Infante, *Tre tristi tigri*, Il Saggiatore, Milan 1993.
85. Eutimio Mambí, a Spanish officer of color who deserted and became a fighter in the War of Independence of Cuba from Spain at the end of the nineteenth century. Thus "Mambises" was how Mambi's followers were called.
86. Cf. Guillermo Cabrera Infante, *Un milagro postergado*, *Lunes de Revolución*, n. 60, p. 15.

9. CUBAN MODERN DANCE: FROM RAMIRO GUERRA TO TODAY

Medea y los negreros by Ramiro Guerra, with Cira Linares as vindicative Medea, 1968.

Medea y los negreros was gesturally and rhythmically archaic and was accompanied by separate male and female choruses. Jason was a European adventurer who sails to Cuba with Medea — a voodoo priestess and woman of noble birth taken into slavery. In Cuba Jason meets Creusa, the daughter of a slave driver.

Guerra would also enthusiastically cite as his favorite works *Tríptico oriental* and *Trinitarias* which were for with the Conjunto Folklórico Nacional. Guerra also invented his own technical-spiritual-creative training method for dancers. This

Guerra personally planned the stages of production and decided on the main works to be performed. The first was *Suite Yoruba* (1960), based on the reading of *Los bailes y el teatro de los negros en el folklore de Cuba* by Fernando Ortiz. The story developed around four divinities: Yemayá, Changó, Ochún and Oggún. The film version of *Suite Yoruba* by José Massip in *Historia de un ballet* (1962), influenced later versions of the ballet for the stage with richer effects. Other cardinal works were *Orfeo antillano* (1964) and *Medea y los negreros* (1968), with the brilliant contribution of painter, graphic artist, and designer Raúl Martínez (1927-1995). All these works were dramatic pieces.

In *Orfeo antillano*, Orpheus is a *tamborero* and the gods are the divinities of the Afro-Cuban pantheon. The atmosphere is set by the Carnival and *conga* music with a trumpet solo composed by Leo Brouwer (1939), Ernesto Lecuona's great nephew. Brouwer was a guitarist and orchestra conductor who was also open to contemporary music. The divination that gives rise to the story of Orpheus and Eurydice comes from the religion Ifá.

Lorna Burdsall, Elena Noriega, Ramiro Guerra, in the sixties.

Elfriede Mahler, in the forties.

methodology in fact later became a theatrical work entitled *Ceremonial de la danza*, in response to encouragement from Maurice Béjart (1927-2007) who had been impressed by the dance class led by maestro Guerra.

Guerra's aim was to reaffirm the freedom of choreography in terms of music, and he also used silence to this end. This seemed to reflect his knowledge – in the realm of theatre – of the innovations of Konstantin Stanislavski and also Andrés Castro. The latter had studied at the school led by Erwin Piscator in New York, and was director of the Cuban Las Máscaras theatre company. Guerra also embraced the ideas of Bertolt Brecht, the epic theatre and cathartic Marxist playwright.

lication 1937) and music by Roldán. This was a dance set in a sugar cane plantation and structured along the lines of the *buffo* theater genre.

Guerra's portfolio also includes certain works based upon a formal aesthetics style. They draw upon the history of European dance and its structures. An example of these works is *Chacona* created in 1966. It consists of five dances to a theme and variations danced by three couples. The style mixes elements of the low dance of the European-Spanish court and the spirals of Afro-Cuban movements with erotic overtones. The music by Bach, however, leaves space for the dancers themselves to perform the percussions with their hands.

Chacona **by Ramiro Guerra, 1966. (right) Study by Eduardo Arrocha for the show.**

Brecht was a theoretician on the distancing and alienation of actors. Finally, Guerra shows his familiarity with the ideas of Polish director Jerzy Grotowski, who advocated the stage as life experience in a search for essentiality.

In 1960, Guerra completed *El milagro de Anaquillé* with libretto by Carpentier (1927, pub-

In 1970, Guerra created *Impromptu galante*, an almost entirely improvised work. Here Guerra did not limit himself to using the stage only, but also the boxes and aisles of the theatre. He used the dancers' voices as well, and projected images on a maxi screen. The attraction between two people was the theme, with moments of seduction – in reference to Ochún, Yemayá and Oyá – and conflict. The audience was given a chance to participate as contenders. The plot could change every evening. Music and sound, both recorded and live, included noises and cries. In the seven scenes presented at the Teatro Nacional – a modern building inaugurated in 1960 – and in the outside gardens, there were also humorous moments. The work sought dimensions outside the serious commitment of many of Guerra's creations.

Impromptu galante was followed by *Ordalía* in the same ironical-critical vein. *Ordalía* was characterized by its unusual performance spaces (including Guerra's apartment) and ludic, subversive "*carnavalización*" elements. Another work was *Tiempo de quimera*, built upon recurring sayings and proverbs.

THE DECALOGUE OF THE APOCALYPSE

El decálogo del Apocalipsis of 1971, was the fruit of a year's work. The project was even more demanding than the previous creations, with its performance taking place not only on stage, but also outdoors and against the façade of the Teatro Nacional. Three Sibyls served as links between the parts and sequences of the work. They were meant to guide the audience through the twelve scenes of the work. The Ten Commandments

Study by Eduardo Arrocha for *The Decalogue of the Apocalypse*, 1971.

were turned upside down in their meaning and intention, and a Prologue and an Epilogue gave further substance to the story.

– Thou shalt worship the gods: the golden calf against the masses of the poor.

– Thou shalt kill: the crucifixion staged as the lynching of a Black man by the Ku Klux Klan.

– Thou shalt dishonor thy mother and father: the prodigal son, half-man and half-woman, with three umbilical children.

– Thou shalt blaspheme the tower of Babel: swearing in various idioms rise from the tower of Babel.

– Nothing will be sanctified: the fallen angels staged as students in revolt.

– Thou shalt steal: the good thief represented by cartoon superheroes.

– Thou shalt desire the wives of others: foolish-looking virgins participate in a bizarre fashion show with suffocating metal armors.

– Thou shalt fornicate: the *Song of Songs* for a

biblical couple *blanquinegra* among phallic elements.

– Thou shalt give false testimony: false prophets like marionettes are to be thrown into a cesspool.

– Thou shalt desire what others have: *The Seventh Seal* in futurist tones, with an astronaut, amidst fireworks, gestures suggesting oriental sculpture and violent acts.

So many elements suggesting rupture and rebellion pompted the censors to react. They banned the performance of this problematic decalogue "for technical reasons" and interrupted the career of Ramiro Guerra as director and choreographer of the troupe.

The Conjunto del Departamento de Danza Moderna, as it was called at the time, no longer performed Guerra's choreographies. During the seventies, he thus turned to writing and critical reflection, and contributed articles to the magazine *Prometeo*. In the eighties, Guerra returned to work with the Conjunto Folklórico Nacional and his loyal friend Eduardo Arrocha, who had designed the costumes for *Chacona*, *Orfeo antillano*, *Tríptico oriental* and *Medea y los negreros*. His aim was also to demonstrate the merits of an innovative use of backlights, as had been the case in *Décalogo del Apocalipsis* itself.

Guerra is unanimously recognized as having been the driving force behind the creation of a national dance style. This style was influenced by the unique characteristics of Cuban folkloric dances: pelvic movement, muscular fluidity, sinuosity of gestures, and undulating mobility of torso and hips.

The basics of methodology and modern Cuban didactics also establish the correct progression of body work on several fronts, from the development of strength and extensibility to the use of weight and expressivity.

In the text *Hacia un movimiento de danza nacional*,[87] of 1959, Guerra argues why all of the arts of the New World, as expression of the multiethnic "American race", must be bearers of national values and existential truths: "The rhythmic agility, the physical expressivity, the Dionysian impulse, and the quality of improvisation are imperative in the making of a national dance".

MODERN DANCE IN THE USA AND CUBA

Lorna Burdsall (Preston, 1928 - Havana, 2010)[88] studied at the College of New London. From 1948 and for thirty consecutive years this was

Lorna Burdsall with Fidel Castro, 1983.

---

87. Cf. Ramiro Guerra, *Siempre la danza, su paso breve…*, Ediciones Alarcos, Havana 2010, pp 68-72.
88. See http://journal.juilliard.edu/journal/lorna-burdsall-dancing-connecticut-cuba.

9. CUBAN MODERN DANCE: FROM RAMIRO GUERRA TO TODAY

the headquarters of the American Dance Festival, the crucible of the most significant figures in dance in the United States. Later Burdshall trained at The Juilliard School in New York, and attended workshops led by key figures such as Martha Graham, Doris Humphrey, Antony Tudor and José Limón. Burdshall was destined to play a central role in establishing American-style modern dance in Cuba.[89] She arrived in 1955 after her marriage to a Cuban student from Matanzas. The son of rum and beer traders,

Gabriela Piñeiro Burdsall.

Manuel Piñeiro was studying business administration at Columbia University when he decided to join Fidel Castro and the guerillas of the Sierra Maestra. *Barba Roja* or "Red Beard", as Piñeiro came to be nicknamed, later became head of intelligence services for the entire country.

In Cuba under Castro, Lorna danced with the Conjunto Nacional de Danza Moderna and performed in works by Ramiro Guerra. She staged the creations of Doris Humphrey and created her own choreographies in a revolutionary spirit. She joined the ENA as a member of its faculty. As a teacher, Burdshall implemented the technique of floor work that was now an integral part of the patrimony of Cuban methodology. Gabriela Piñeiro (1989), the daughter of Lorna's son, Kahlil, also joined the DCC. She and her father paid a visit to the Palmer Auditorium of Connecticut College in 2017. Here was where her grandmother Lorna had made her professional debut before embarking on her adventurous life in Cuba.

In 1981, Lorna Bursdall founded her company "Así somos" with a focus on dance and theatre, both image and performative, as well as research. Bursdall's creations featured dialogue between spectators and performers, interaction with performers from different origins, and artists of the plastic and visual arts. Recycled materials were used, based on themes from every day life seen as instruments of play, irony and improvisation. Under the difficult conditions of the *periodo especial*, even non-theatre spaces were used by the troupe to reach the public, and the Casa de la Cultura de Plaza hosted therapy workshops of dance and music.

Elfriede Mahler (Pennsylvania, 1928 - Cuba, 1998) studied ballet with Gertrude Prokosch in her native Bryn Mawr and then modern dance with Martha Graham. She worked with Alwin Nikolais (1910-1993),[90] maestro and pioneer of

---

89. Cf. Lorna Bursdall, *More Than Just a Footnote: Dancing from Connecticut to Revolutionary Cuba*, self published in 2001.

90. See https://www.nikolaislouis.org/index.

9. CUBAN MODERN DANCE: FROM RAMIRO GUERRA TO TODAY

A performance by Lorna Burdsall's company Así Somos in the eighties.

"total theatre", that combined the use of movement, light, color, form, sound and technology. Mahler subsequently became a university professor and director of the company YMHA in

Alma Guillermoprieto.

Philadelphia. She moved to Cuba in 1960, and in 1966 she became head of the school of dance of the ENA. Mahler mounted a choreography dedicated to *Playa girón* (the Bay of Pigs), where the failed attempt by the U.S. to invade Cuba and topple Fidel Castro was launched. She founded the troupe Danza Libre in Guantanamo where she worked until her death, and where choreographers such as Alfredo Velázquez and Isaías Rojas had also created.

Another young American, Alma Guillermoprieto, was invited to Cuba in 1970 under the protective wing of Lorna Burdsall. Just twenty years of age, of Mexican ancestry, Alma was asked to share with the students her experiences studying with Merce Cunningham, the father of American postmodernism. She also evoked her training with Twyla Tharp, a foremost figure of a new dance style that transversally drew from modern, postmodern, ballet, and the musical. At the ENA, Guillermoprieto found herself faced with students with little preparation – as she wrote in her book about this phase of her career in Cuba.[91] Yet she found them combative and skilled in Afro-Cuban dance, despite the unequipped rooms – without mirrors to avoid narcissism – and lack of goods and services, or personal freedom.

Morris Donaldson, a dancer and choreographer with the Juilliard School, choreographed *Los discípulos del Diablo* and *Malcolm X* for Anna Sokolow (1910-2000), and the works premiered in 1969 at the Teatro Garcia Lorca, the name of

---

91. Cf. Alma Guillermoprieto, *Dancing with Cuba*, Vintage Books/Random House, New York 2005.

9. CUBAN MODERN DANCE: FROM RAMIRO GUERRA TO TODAY

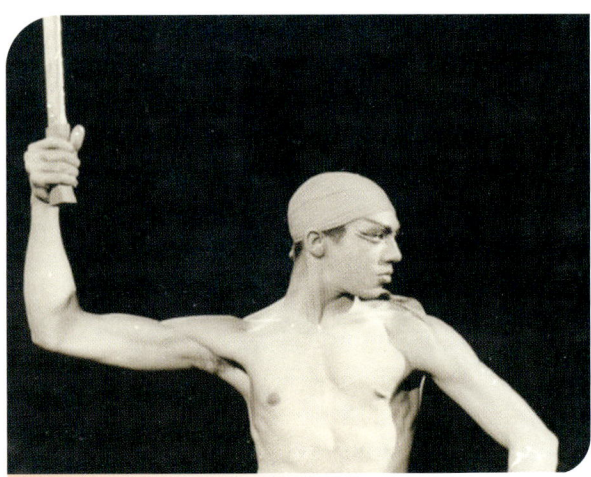

Eduardo Rivero as Oggún in *Súlkary*, 1971.

the theatre at the time, in Havana. Morris Donaldson was an African American artist who intensely felt the spirit of the Black Panther movement. He later founded his own troupe in the U.S. His work *Los discípulos del diablo*, with decors by Donaldson himself and music by Edgar Varèse, referred to the racial discrimination in the U.S., with themes such as conflict, oppression, struggle and justice. Donaldson's words were unequivocal as he referred to the 'humiliated' Black person. The plot included 'the Blacks', among whom Eduardo Rivero (who later authored Súlkary), and 'the Whites', the police, the Ku Klux Klan, and the people. *Malcolm X,* to music by Miles Davis, and a vigorous male trio, was presented in the program thus: "A poem, an abstract dance that attempts to reflect on the qualities of this great man, the majesty of his character, his illuminated research".

Dr. Suki John[92] is a dancer, choreographer and writer from progressive New York, who is a recognized scholar on the history of Cuban modern dance. She has written frankly of the practical shortcomings and problems of free expression the country has faced. Yet she has also expressed her deep feelings for the human and artistic qualities of Cuban dancers. Indeed, she created *Amor y cólera* (now *Cartas de amor*, "love letters") for the company DCC (1993), and *Pandora* (Festival de Ballet, 1994) for the BNC. Suki worked above all with the Compañia de la Danza Narciso Medina, in Havana, until 1992. With the support of the Cuban Artists Fund and the Guggenheim Museum, she promoted the invitation for the DCC to perform at Guggenheim's Works and Process series in 2002. Among her works for the company: *Festina lente*, *Ariel*, *Shake it up*, *Dyad*, *Microwave Suite*, and *Barriga Bestia*. The latter premiered in 1996 at the first Cuban modern dance festival, "Los días de la danza".

Narciso Medina and Marlene Carbonell in rehearsal for *Caverna Magica*, 1998.

---

92. See http://www.sukijohn.com/.

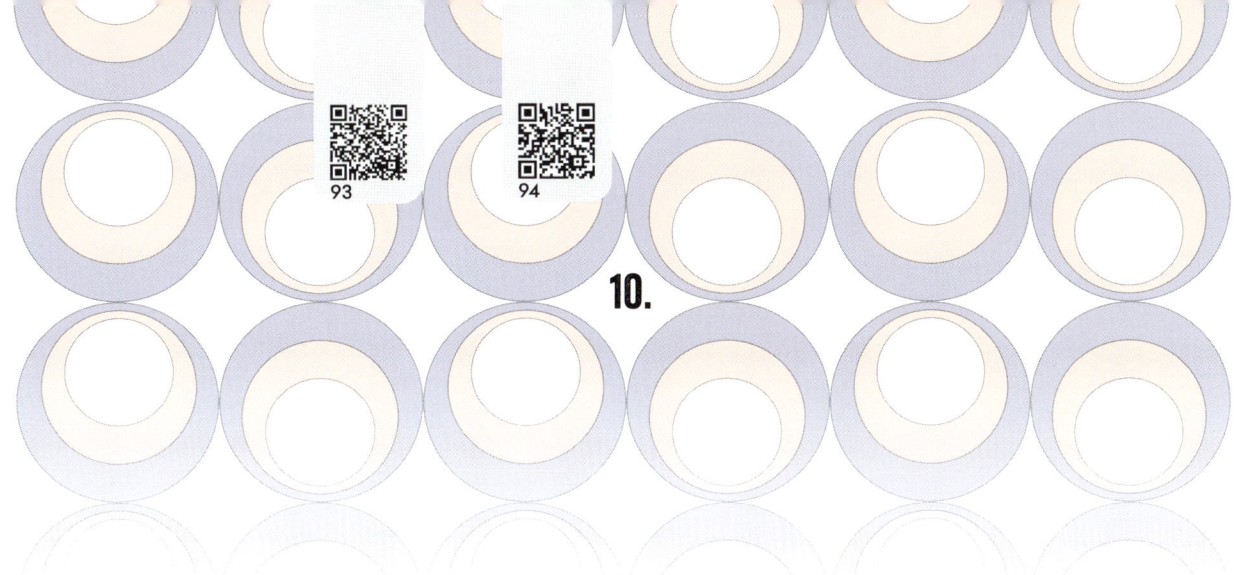

10.

DANZA CONTEMPORÁNEA DE CUBA

Danza Contemporánea de Cuba (DCC) is the dance company that is officially responsible for cultivating and promoting modern dance on the island. With its many versatile performers, the DCC has consecutively produced no fewer than 250 creations[93] over the years. The DCC's active repertory keeps sixty of these works in performance with a broad range of types of works. DCC's historic titles clearly indicate the inheritance accumulated over the different periods of the troupe's existence: *Suite Yoruba* by Ramiro Guerra, *Súlkary* by Eduardo Rivero, *Grifos* and *Dédalo* by Rosario Cárdenas, *Cara o cruz* by Jorge Abril to music by Leo Brouwer and Guido López Gavilán, and *Michelangelo* by Víctor Cuellar.

The permanent director of the DCC company[94] since 1984 has been Miguel Iglesias. After obtaining a degree in Physical Education, he began dancing with the Cuban Television Ballet in 1967. He then joined the Ballet de Camagüey. Iglesias entered Conjunto Nacional de Danza after being completely won over by Ramiro Guerra's *Medea y los negreros*. The DCC also includes original works by foreign choreographers as a part of its repertory, and has often been invited to perform these works by the choreographers' respective countries with the support of

DCC on Plaza de la Revolución, in Havana.

---

93. **Link:** Video on the DCC, profile over the years with excerpts of various choreographies. Mats Ek is glimpsed while working with dancers in the studio.
94. **Link:** Video on the DCC.

Tangos Cubanos by Billy Cowie, DCC, 2015.

10. DANZA CONTEMPORÁNEA DE CUBA

Reversible by Anabel López Ochoa, DCC, 2015.

Otros Caprichos by Àngel Margarit, DCC, 2015.

Demo-n/Crazy by Rafael Bonachela, DCC, 2008.

cultural institutions. Indeed the unique suppleness of the technical and expressive qualities of Cuban dancers is invariably irresistible. Some of these works by foreign choreographers are *Reversible* by Colombian-Belgian Annabelle López Ochoa, and *Tangos cubanos* by choreographer and technological visuals artist Billy Cowie, who also created music and texts.[95] Cowie had pre-

---

95. **Link:** Video of *Tangos cubanos* by Billy Cowie (DCC).

Folía by Jan Linkens, DCC, 2011.

Compás by Jan Linkens, DCC, 2003.

Sombrisa by Itzik Galili, DCC, 2012.

viously drawn inspiration from tango for *Tango de Soledad* in 3D, and *Tango Brasilero* as a video dance work. Also to be considered are works such as: *Sombrisa* by Israelian Itzik Galili in tribute to Cuban Olympic boxing champion Teófilo Stevenson; *Misa en el piso* by Italian Luca Bruni (2003); *Carmen?!* by Swedish Kenneth Kvamström; *Compás* and *Folia* by Dutch Jan Linkens; *Demo-n/Crazy* by Catalan Rafael Bonachela; *Otros Caprichos* by Catalan Àngels Margarit (remounted

10. DANZA CONTEMPORÁNEA DE CUBA

Drama, by Ibsen by Luvyen Mederos, 2014.

er, actor, and singer who has had an impact on many dancers who are impressed by his original approach to the narrative body. Cruz achieved renown for his performance in Sasha Waltz's Havana hit *Zweiland* – an example of expressive theatre-dance that keeps constant tension between vulnerability and irony. Cruz himself admitted that he did not truly know how to use the extraordinary bravura of Cuban dancers. Also invited to work with the DCC have been Algerian artist Samir Akika, who was trained in Essen and is active in Germany, and Italian Giovanni Di Cicco.

The intersecting of cultures and different

in 2015 with her own troupe Mudances) and *Equilux* by Scottish Fleur Darkin.

Swedish dancer and choreographer Mats Ek anthologically reworked parts of *Casi casa*. DCC dancers very effectively combined the rigorously Nordic dynamics with the vigorous, exuberant spontaneity of Cuban dance.

Juan Cruz is a multifaceted danc-

The Listening Room by Theo Clinkard, 2016.

Identitad-1 by George Céspedes, DCC, 2013.

itineraries gave birth to *Drama, by Ibsen*, choreographed by Luvyen Mederos, who had also worked with the cabaret Tropicana. His work was created in 2014 in collaboration with Norwegian singer and guitarist Thea Hjelmeland. Critics referred to the work as minimalistic, "work in progress", and even sometimes as "non-dance", and a "journey through human interactions".

Prior to the DCC repertory, however, there had already been works by foreign choreographers: American Abigail Levine with her *Desatar* that premiered at the 2003 festival Los días de la Danza; Spanish Joaquín Sábate (who lives in Holland) with *El riesgo del placer*; and British artist Cathy Marston with *Araña*. Marston had also directed the Ballet of Berne and was associated with the Royal Opera House.

The DCC mounted *Listening Room* (2016) by British dance maker Theo Clinkard with the project *Islas creativas* ("Creative Islands") funded by the British Council. This choreographic structure had no specific theme but was based upon a few creative instructions and an innovative concept. In fact, the music the audience heard was not the same as what the dancers were listening

Mambo 3 XXI by George Céspedes, DCC, 2009.

Carmina Burana, choreography by George Céspedes and Miguel Iglesias, 2017.

Rasta Thomas in *Requiem*, 2018.

to in their headphones. While the dancers heard Missy Elliott, Bach, Vivaldi, Calle 13, or Capital Cities, the audience was listening to *Variations for Vibes, Piano and Strings* by Steve Reich. The dancers, instead of executing a fixed written choreography, had the enriching experience of facing the complete unknown. The audience, on the other hand, had to deal with a process that it had never been confronted with before.

Dancers and choreographers of the company had to measure up to creations. There was Jorge Abril's *CC Canillitas*, based on Charlie Chaplin's *The Kid*. George Céspedes, who had won the Alicia Alonso Certamen Iberoamericano de Coreografía (CIC) award with *Identidad-1*, created the tremendously successful *La ecuación*[96] and *Mambo 3XXI*, the latter to the rhythms of Caribbean music of the fifties. In 2017 Céspedes was commissioned to create a dance to the formida-

---

96. **Link:** Video of *La Ecuación* by George Céspedes, DCC, *Cubanía* program organized by Carlos Acosta, Royal Opera House, London 2014.

10. DANZA CONTEMPORÁNEA DE CUBA

Cénit by Laura Domingo Agüero, DCC, 2016.

La Consagración by Christophe Béranger and Jonathan Pranlas-Descours for DCC, 2018.

Miguel Altunaga in a jump.

presented his *Más allá del polvo*. Altunaga was already a member of the DCC, and in 2017 he also joined the London company Rambert,[97] as dancer and choreographer. He focused on themes of distance, separation and

---

97. The first British modern dance company, founded in 1926 by Mary Rambert, formerly with the Ballets Russes, to then evolve through various creative phases. See http://www.rambert.org.uk/about-us/our-history/.

ble *Carmina Burana*. He contributed to a Mozart inspired event, *Réquiem, espectáculo monumental*, directed by Pepe Olivares. The dance was then taken to Mexico with Rasta Thomas as star dancer.

In 2016, the young Cuban writer and choreographer Laura Domingo Agüero created the dynamic trio *Cénit*. And in 2018, Miguel Altunaga

everyday struggles, and had already been attracting attention for his solo choreography *Memoria* performed by Carlos Acosta at the 2012 Festival Internacional de Ballet de La Habana.

The year 2018 also marked the premiere of a grand production for the DCC, *La Consagración*,

10. DANZA CONTEMPORÁNEA DE CUBA

El Cristal by Julio César Iglesias, DCC, 2015.

La Sagra della primavera to the music of Igor Stravinsky. The work was by Christophe Béranger, former member of the Ballet de Lorraine, and Jonathan Pranlas-Descours, active in the plastic arts and theatre, and with training at the Brussels school, P.A.R.T.S. Both of these artists also direct the company Sine Qua Non Art in La Rochelle, France.

THE DCC AND OFFSPRING

In 2013, George Céspedes founded his dance company Los Hijos del Director (LHD), that is, 'The Children of the Director'. "A rock band's name" he explained. And the following year he presented *La tribulación de Anaximandro*, a work centered on man's relationship with the world and the notion of chance. In 2016, at the Gran Teatro LHD he proposed *Innermost*, with a focus on conflict and disagreement, dispersing and reuniting.

Julio César Iglesias, who is in fact the son of DCC director Miguel Iglesias, became known for his theatre works such as *Mercurio*; *El Cristal*, in episodes after an opening sung *en travesti*; *The Family*, *Coil*, and *El regalo*, for which he was awarded first prize in the European Community competition "Unità nella Diversità"; *Quisiera ser tu perro* and *Restaurante El Paso*, on alienation and everyday existence. His works for the screen have been popular, with effective fusion between different art forms, such as in the music video *Amargo pero dulce* for Diana Fuentes. Iglesias has also conceived works for other troupes, such as the Spanish company Macana (*Invisible Wires*, presented in Cuba in 2017).

Osnel Delgado has also followed in the wake of the DCC. His mother, Idania Wambrug, is a professor at the ENA. His father, Esteban Delgado, a dancer and co-director of the troupe Ebony, was a dancer with the DCC (2003-2011) and choreographer for the group Rakatán. In 2012, the independent company Malpaso,[98] "false step" or "reckless", saw the light. The company was co-founded by Osnel Delgado with Daileidys Carrazana — a graduate of the ENB and ballerina with the DCC — and his friend Fernando Sáez — a graduate of the ENA/ISA, actor and founder of the Estudio Teatral Santa Clara in Pinar del Rio, and administrator of the *Fundación Ludwig de Cuba* for the arts. Though everyone thought that leaving the DCC would be a big mistake, it was in fact with Malpaso, and its rich repertory, that

---

98. **Link:** official video link of Malpaso 2018.

10. DANZA CONTEMPORÁNEA DE CUBA

Malpaso.

Malpaso and the Afro Latin Jazz Ensemble, 2016.

international fame awaited.[99] The company was based at the Havana Centro Hebreo Sefaradi in Vedado, and each year resided at the Joyce Theater in New York, the city's hub of modern and contemporary dance.

For the U.S. market, the company was discovered by African American choreographer Ronald K. Brown (1967). He was spellbound by the Malpaso performers with their "liquid joints" and realized they would be perfect to perform his energetic work *Why You Follow* at full throttle. And there was also Trey McIntyre, associate choreographer for the Houston Ballet and with the David Parsons Dance Company. In 2015, he conceived *Under Fire* for Malpaso with music by Grandma Kelsey. The work was co-commissioned by the historic festival Jacob's Pillow in Massachusetts. The dance centered upon memories, and the need to cast into a fire of purification anything that weighs down the past to get to the essential. McIntyre also remounted his *Bad Winter* for the Delgado troupe.

It was also during 2012 that Osnel Delgado gained recognition with his *Anoxia* at the competition Alicia Alonso Certamen Iberoamericano de Coreografía. In 2013, he created the duo *Ocaso*[100] to the non-Cuban sound of Autechre (an English electronic band), and the multifaceted Kronos Quartet of San Francisco, as well as Max Richter (with a post-minimalist Anglo-German sound).

Malpaso received general acclaim in the U.S. with *Homenaje al Benny* (*Homage to Benny*), in tribute to the Cuban musician Benny Moré, and also with *24 horas y un perro* (*24 Hours in a Dog's Life*). This latter work was pure dance, structured on music by Arturo O'Farrill, the son of Cuban musician Chico O'Farrill (Havana, 1921 - New York, 2001). Chico was the master of "Cubop" (the Bebop of the island) and was a pianist and composer himself. Arturo O'Farrill's music here flirts with the tangoes of Astor Piazzolla. It was performed live at the Joyce Theater by his Afro Latin Jazz Ensemble (2014).

---

99. For the Malpaso repertory, see https://www.malpasodance.com/repertoire.

100. **Link:** Video of *Ocaso* by Osnel Delgado.

For *Despedida* (*Farewell*), Osnel Delgado again worked in collaboration with O'Farrill and his band, with inspiration from a poem by Jorge Luis

Why You Follow by Ronald K. Brown, 2014.

Under Fire by Trey McIntyre, 2015.

Borges. Delgado and his favorite musicians were again united for *Dreaming of Lions* (2016), an allusion to waves at sea and battles as in Hemingway's *The Old Man and the Sea*. This was another coproduction with the Joyce Theater as well as American foundations.

The Malpaso New York program in 2017 explained that the company had "left Cubanismo at home in Cuba" for a more international style of staging, lights and costumes. The program included two guest choreographers. The first was American Sonya Tayeh with *Face the Torrent*. She had choreographed for Martha Graham's company and for Bill T. Jones, and gained popularity for her work with the TV contest show *So You Think You Can Dance*. Her music videoclips for stars such as Miley Cyrus and the Kylie Minogue shows were also very popular. The second guest choreographer was Canadian Aszure Barton — with *Indomitable Waltz*, to the music of the quartet of Alexander Balanescu and Michael Nyman. Mikhail Baryshnikov, the Russian-American ballet divo, during his second "contemporary"

Trey McIntyre.

10. DANZA CONTEMPORÁNEA DE CUBA

Liquidotopie by Cecilia Bengolea, 2018.

of Canada, Les Ballets Jazz de Montréal, and La Scala di Milano. *Liquidotopie* was also choreographed by Cecilia Bengolea,[101] an Argentinian residing in France. She was a bold choreographer and dancer, and interested in infinite hybridizations.

The 100th anniversary of the birth of Merce Cunningham, father of the postmodern dance movement in the United States, was celebrated in 2019. For the occasion, Malpaso presented *Fielding Sixes*. This was part of a mixed program in which *Tabula rasa* by Ohad Naharin, the foremost Israelian choreographer, also appeared. In 2020, Mats Ek worked for Malpaso on an augmented version of *Woman with Water*.

Despedida by Osnel Delgado: (from left) Tahimy Miranda Ruiz de Villa, Osnel Delgado and Joan Rodiguez, Malpaso, 2015.

Indomitable Waltz by Aszure Barton, 2016.

career, expressed admiration for Tayeh. Barton choreographed for companies such as the Nederlands Dans Theater, the National Ballet

---

101. Cf. Elisa Guzzo Vaccarino, *Eros e Danza*, Gremese, Rome, Paris 2017, in Italian and French.

Francesca Raballo and Andrea Carozzi during rehearsals of *Historia de un adiós* by Laura Domingo Agüero, Eko International Dance Project.

(above) Caridad Martínez (Cherité), "*Prima Mulata Assoluta*", and Lázaro Carreño, BNC, in *La Fille mal gardée*, Honorable Mention, 5th Varna International Ballet Competition. (below) Javier Royas, Royal Swedish Ballet.

(above) Rita Montaner in *El romance del palmar*, 1938.
(below) Orquesta Anacaona at the Broadway nightclub
La Havana Madrid, New York, 1937.

(above) Jorge Barani.
(below) A scene from the docu-film *Cuban Dancer*, choreography by Laura Domingo Agüero, screenplay co-written with director Roberto Salinas, 2020.

Amilcar Moret González.

(above) Viengsay Valdés in *Diana y Acteón*.
(below) A workshop on Mats Ek's *Giselle*, led by Pompea Santoro,
Escuela Nacional de Ballet, FAC, Havana, 2019.

11. IN THE WAKE OF GUERRA: FOR AN ETHNO-CUBAN DANCE

More than a generation of Cuban modern dance choreographers are indebted to the teachings of Ramiro Guerra. This has been evidenced by Guerra's official historian, Fidel Pajares Santiesteban (Camagüey, 1962). As a dancer, choreographer and scholar, he is the curator of the Ramiro Guerra archives.[102] Pajares was trained at the ENA in modern and folkloric dance (1965-1971). He was one of the performers in *Suite Yoruba*, and a featured soloist in the groups that ultimately became today's Danza Contemporánea de Cuba. He is also a professor in Cuba and Venezuela, and was founder and director of the company Ecodanza and Compañía Regional de Etnodanza in the region of Lara, Venezuela. He has been a consultant to Yolena Alonso, daughter of the musician Pachito, and the Cuban company Yoldance.

In addition, Pajares is an essayist and lecturer and is also active in television (*Amalá*, *Páginas del diario de campana*, *Simparalé*, *Panorama de la música y la danza*, *Elogio a la danza*, and *Patakín*[103]). He is a firm believer in the importance of a dual approach to work, one that is theoretical and operative. He is presently committed to obtaining a Dramaturgy section in the Unión de Escritores y Artistas de

---

102. See https://www.ecured.cu/Fidel_Pajares. For Fidel Pajares' career see: https://www.ecured.cu/Danza_Moderna_en_Cuba._La_cargada_una_forma_m%C3%A1s_de_movimiento_(Book). For some of his writings cf.: Fidel Pajares Santiesteban, *Ramiro Guerra y la danza en Cuba*, Editorial Casa de la Cultura, Quito 1993; *Danza moderna en Cuba. La cargada como una forma más del movimiento*, FEDUPEL, Caracas 1998; *La danza moderna cubana y su estética*, Editorial Unión, Havana 2005; *Danza contemporánea cubana* (Multimedia), Editorial Cubarte, Havana 2005; *Dramaturgia de la danza en Cuba*, Editorial Adagio, Havana 2010; *Escuela cubana de danza moderna*, Editorial Adagio, Havana 2011; *La danza moderna y la crítica de la danza en Cuba*, Editorial Tablas-Alarcos.

103. The term "*patakín*" refers to the myths of Cuba that have come from African culture and tradition. A 1985 film also was entitled *Patakín* and was directed by Manuel Octavio Gómez. It featured "Latinized" choreographies by Victor Cuéllar in the style of Jerome Robbins. The film was most probably the first Cuban musical in the style of the famous American movies of the fifties. **Link:** Video of the film *Patakín*, choreography by Victor Cuellar, with *rumba*, tango and jazz.

11. In the wake of Guerra: for an ethno-Cuban dance

Cuba (UNEAC).[104] In his text *La danza moderna cubana y su estética*, Pajares presents the profiles of three generations of important creators who have been inspired by Ramiro Guerra's training and concepts.

The first generation includes Eduardo Rivero, Santiago Alfonso, Victor Cuéllar, Clara Luz Rodríguez, Isidro Rolando, Luz María Collazo, Nereida Doncel, Hedí Veitía, Isabel Blanco, Manuel Vázquez, Dulce María Vale, Armando Martén, and Miguel Iglesias. The second generation notably consists of: Susana Pous, Marianela Boán, Rosario Cárdenas, and Narciso Medina. The main exponents of the third generation are Jorge Luis Abril and Lídice Núñez.

The following are the works of some of the most well-known of these artists residing in Cuba and abroad.

FIRST GENERATION

Eduardo Rivero

Eduardo Rivero Walker (Havana, 1936 - Santiago, 2012) first studied at the Havana Conservatory of Music before he decided to train in dance. He was cast in Ramiro Guerra's *Suite Yoruba* in the role of a *Mulatto* man in love with a White woman. Rivero's career then evolved towards works visually inspired by the paintings of the Spanish

Súlkary by Eduardo Rivero, 1979.

artist Víctor Patricio de Landaluze (an exponent of what was known as *costumbrismo*). He staged the everyday universe of peasant farmers, landowners, and slaves in a typically Cuban context.

Rivero was the creator of *Okantomí* (1970), a dance modelled after the bronze and ivory sculptures of Benin and Ifé – an ancient Nigerian city of *Yoruba* culture. He choreographed, above all, one of the masterpieces of Cuban modern dance repertory, *Súlkary* (1971). This title refers to an ancient dance from Upper Volta (today Burkina Faso). It is accompanied by *Yoruba* chants and percussions, but also visually draws inspiration from the engravings on rock in the Sahara.[105] The interweaving of cultures recurs in his *Duo a Lam*, in reference to Wifredo Lam (Sagua La Grande, 1902 - París, 1982). The painter and plastic artist Lam was of African, Chinese and Cuban descent and was

---

104. F. Pajares Santiesteban publishes his writings under the aegis of the Dirección Municipal de Cultura Santa Clara – Cátedra Antropología de la Danza "Ramiro Guerra".

105. **Link:** Video of *Súlkary* by Eduardo Rivero.

11. IN THE WAKE OF GUERRA: FOR AN ETHNO-CUBAN DANCE

Building of the Ballet Español de Cuba.

the ethno-contemporary dance that pulsates from the heart of the Caribbean.

Alvin Ailey[106] was an inspiration. This genius of American modern dance, magnificently innervated by the Black touch, had pointed out an ideal, accessible way of promoting the diverse dance heritage of all the people of Cuba. It was a means of overcoming a vernacular image, and to transform this patrimony into the national cultural identity. It would have its own profile and own methodology. Rivero analyzed each of the characteristics of this legacy and highlighted its features: *off center* position of the hips; undulations of the spine; strong contact with the ground; energetic circular movements of the head, shoulders and chest yet the strong, elongated lines of academic ballet in the rest of the body. In modern Cuban technique, these elements create a specific type of aesthetic and form. For brevity's sake, this is usually referred to simply as *técnica*. It is a mixture of the floorwork of Martha Graham, the 'falls' and recoveries of Doris Humphrey, and the plasticity of José Limón.

a leading figure of the international avant-garde movement. Yet Rivero's greatest masterpiece is still considered *Súlkary*. This creatiion is a fusion of elements of Afro-Cuban *Yoruba* and *Arará* dance, with rhythmic, almost ceremonial steps performed to beating drums, a solo voice, and responding chorus. There are moments of statuary freezes and an evocation of totem-like sacredness in the finale danced by three women and three men. *Súlkary* has been performed by numerous companies, among which the Ballet Español de Cuba, organized by Alicia Alonso and directed by Eddy (Eduardo) Veitía (Havana, 1964; a graduate of the ENA/ISA, and BNC dancer) with a cast of Cuban and Brazilian dancers.

The National Dance Theatre Company of Jamaica, founded in 1962, also staged the work for its fiftieth anniversary. *Súlkary* has an erotic, ancestral charge. With its male and female couples offering representations of seductive and belligerent rites, it has become a classic of

SANTIAGO ALFONSO

The multi-faceted Santiago Alfonso (Havana, 1939) was a student of Ramiro Guerra and

---

106. See http://www.alvinailey.org/; http://www.theaileyschool.edu/. Cf. also: Alvin Ailey, A. Peter Baily, *Revelations: The Autobiography of Alvin Ailey*, Citadel Press, New York 1995, Jennifer Dunning, *Alvin Ailey: A Life in Dance*, Da Capo Press, Boston 1998; Thomas F. DeFrantz, *Dancing Revelations, Alvin Ailey's Embodiment of African American Culture*, Oxford University Press, Oxford 2006.

11. IN THE WAKE OF GUERRA: FOR AN ETHNO-CUBAN DANCE

Class with maestro Santiago Alfonso.

also trained with Tomás Morales (Matanzas, 1936 - Havana, 2019). The latter was a singer, choreographer, and dancer who began his career under the direction of Alberto Alonso at the famous Cabaret Sans Souci. He was also one of the co-founders of the Conjunto Experimental de Danza. Santiago is noted for his performance dances such as *El Rey Cristóbal*, *¿Quien le teme a Virginia Woolf?*, *María Antonieta*, *Ochosi y el venado* ("The god and the deer"). Yet he is equally famous for his floor shows at the Tropicana, his choreographies for television, and as a jury member for the popular dance championship *Bailando en Cuba* for the selection of the island's best dancers.

By 2007, Santiago Alfonso[107] had his own company, the GEDE (previously known as the Diáspora de la Danza or Grupo de Experimentación de la Danza y el Espectáculo). With classy flair, he stamped its style with the typically Cuban mark of undulating and sensuous corporeality. He created a synthesis between cabaret, performance and entertainment dance, thanks to his artists trained in both classical and modern dance. They had what it took to make popular rhythms and dances into an elegant showcase of bravura, without preconceived ideas of "high" or "low" culture.

Victor Cuéllar

Victor Cuéllar (Havana, 1945) is unquestionably a narrative choreographer. Since *Juegos poliformes* in 1971, he has always worked across all the dance sectors, from performance dance, to television, to entertainment. And in all of these forms, he has put folkloric elements in the spotlight.

His many works include notably: *Panorama de la Música y la Danza Cubanas*, *Michelangelo*, *Diálogo y Escena para bailarines*, and *Fausto*.

---

107. **Link:** Video of a dance class led by maestro Santiago Alfonso.

SECOND GENERATION

Marianela Boán and DanzAbierta

Marianela Boán (Havana, 1954), a DCC dancer and choreographer, founded DanzAbierta in 1988. Her work sparked discussion in Cuba on such concepts as the new dramaturgy of dance, contamination, stepping beyond technique, and organic corporeality. These are common concepts in the discourse of European dance today, but they were highly innovative in Cuba at the time of her first choreographies.

Among Boán's works that soon brought her recognition: *Mariana* (1980), on the history of Cuba and its heroes and patriots; *Adán y Eva* (1980); *Guernica* (1983); *Teoría de Conjunto* (1985); *Lunetario* (1986), on marginalization; *Un elefante se balancea sobre la tela de una araña* ("An elephant swinging over a spider's web", 1988); and her immediately acclaimed *Godot* (1992). An intriguing work is *Cruce sobre el Niágara* (1987), based upon a highly successful play by Peruvian playwright Alonso Alegría (1969). Tightrope walker Charles Blondin, with his young friend Carlo on his shoulders, crosses Niagara Falls on a tightrope. Yet it is a search for authenticity in life, rather than commercial sensationalism. The work was again performed by the company Acosta Danza in 2017.

With her own group, Boán focused on overcoming the limits of pure movement. Yet she also pursued kinetic experimentation based upon *contact improvisation* and *release* (a breathing and muscular relaxation technique). As always, the aim was to achieve maximum naturalness and fluidity. The American methods of avant-garde multi-artistic minimalism were put into practice: Boán with DanzAbierta, Víctor Varela with the Teatro del Obstáculo, and José Ángel Hevia,

Mario Sergio Elías and Raúl Reinoso, Acosta Danza, in *Cruce sobre el Niagara* by Marianela Boán, 2017.

a dancer with the company from its beginnings, and author of *Dos para cero*.

What also played an important role for Boán was the influence of Germanic dance-theatre. And there was the impact of Roberto Blanco's work. In the eighties he had staged a work of strong innovative impact, *Yerma*. The cast featured Rolando Isidro (Havana, 1941), a singer, dancer and choreographer (first noted for his performance in *Ireme*), and who was also a dancer in Guerra's works; and Vicente Revuelta (1929-2012), actor, film director and avant-garde educator. Revuelta co-founded the Grupo Teatro Estudio with his sister Raquel, a famous actress – after whom the Theatre "Sala Raquel Revuelta" was named in Vedado (Havana).

11. IN THE WAKE OF GUERRA: FOR AN ETHNO-CUBAN DANCE

Defilló by Marianela Boán, 2017.

Even the Flying-Low Dance Technique became part of DanzAbierta's treasure of learning. It also drew from this approach as it pursued a vocation of training professionals, amateurs, and the disabled. The creator of the Flying Low concept was Venezuelan-New Yorker David Zambrano. He developed exercises based upon respiration and the release of energy through the body. This was achieved through floorwork, spiral energy, and breathing with a focus on the skeletal structure.

Boán proposed to treat themes strictly related to existential and social reality.[108] She did this while giving full range to the individuality of her performers: applying the "how to do" rather than the "what to…" She hoped to close the creative lag in the country by bringing to the Cuba of the eighties what had existed elsewhere twenty years before. The crystallization of modern dance on the island following Guerra's decision to give up his experimentation led to this gap.

In 1996, Boán created a very successful surreal piece performed by her company entitled *El pez de la torre nada en el asfalto*[109] ("The fish from the tower swims in asphalt"). Its theme dealt with Cubans in a time of crisis, and it was a mixture of cabaret, popular dance and contemporary ballet. The work evoked the Malecón Habanero, known as "the longest bench in the world", a seafront that symbolizes *cubanía*, but also *rumba*, and the

---

108. For a list of the most important works by Marianela Boán from 1999 to 2017 see https://boandanza.wixsite.com/marianela-boan/sinopsis.

109. **Link:** video of *El pez de la torre nada en el asfalto* by Marianela Boán.

124

11. IN THE WAKE OF GUERRA: FOR AN ETHNO-CUBAN DANCE

Hablemos de cosas bonitas by Marianela Boán, 2015.

willing escorts for tourists known as *jineteras*.[110]

Boán demonstrated a new way to use academic dance freely when in 1990 for the BNC she presented *Degas* to a music score by José María Vitier. Boán's approach was also apparent in 1999, with her dance based upon *A Streetcar Named Desire* by Tennessee Williams for the DCC. The work was performed live to original music by pianist Roberto Carcacés. As an artist, he had been an important figure in the protest movement.

Boán created her umpteenth work on the theme of the individual and the individual's relationship to society called *Chorus perpetuus* to music by Pergolesi, Mozart, and Gershwin, as well as Cuban traditional songs. After this creation, in 2001, Marianela left DanzAbierta to pursue her own international direction. She was invited to perform as soloist (*Blanche Dubois*, *Fast Food*, *Seagull*, and *Lifting*) and to dance, create, and teach in various universities in the U.S. Boán continued to choreograph for herself and for other companies and institutions such as the American Dance Festival. In 2005, she founded her own troupe, Boan Danz Action, in Philadelphia. That same year, she created *Map*, *Fluid*, *Quiereme mucho*, and *Eighth Commandment* for the company. In 2006, she staged the multimedia duo *False Testimony*. While heading today's Compañía Nacional de Danza Contemporánea de República (CNDC), founded in 2010 as ProDanCo, Boán choreographed *Defilló*. Her work was also presented in 2017 in Cuba at the 17th Festival de Teatro de La Habana. This dance, to the music of Wim Mertens and Chucho Valdés,

---

110. Cf. Alejandro Ruiz Torreguitart, *Vita da jinetera*, Associazione Culturale Il Foglio, Piombino 2011.

11. IN THE WAKE OF GUERRA: FOR AN ETHNO-CUBAN DANCE

was inspired by the paintings of the Dominican artist Fernando Peña Defilló with his subjects and settings from Creole culture. Boán had also returned to Cuba in 2011 to participate in the workshop Danza en Construcción under the auspices of the Consejo Nacional de las Artes Escénicas, with the support of the French Embassy and the Paris Brownstone Foundation. In 2013, she had presented *Caribe Deluxe* with the CNDC at the theatre Sala Raquel Revuelta in Havana.

SUSANA POUS AND DANZABIERTA

With Boán no longer at the head of DanzAbierta, it was Guido Gali (Santa Clara, 1974), organizer and playwright (*El arte de la fuga*), to give the company a new identity. He sought out various creators and finally in 2008, the Spanish dancer and choreographer Susana Pous (Barcelona, 1971) took over the direction of the company. Pous had been trained in Europe and America. She had studied at the Martha Graham Center for Contemporary Dance and the José Limón Institute. She was a dancer in Boán's company, she had been an assistant to the Spanish choreographer María Rovira, and interpreter in Spain for Selene Lux Dance and Tránsit Danza.

Her interest in Cuba and its dance was sparked by the inspiring discovery of the poetic style of Pepe Hevia (José Ángel; Havana, 1971)[111]. Hevia was a dancer with DanzAbierta and choreographer for his own company, Pepe Hevia Danza, and for other troupes such as the national modern dance company of Costa Rica and the national company of Ecuador (*Carmen*). His works reflected an original classical and modern hybridization, with even video dance works. The latter were produced with/for his sister *trovadora* Liuba María Hevia, a famed tango singer.

Pous' first work for DanzAbierta was *Qué se*

Belleza efímera by Pepe Hevia, 2010.

Welcome by Susana Pous, 2016.

---

111. See http://www.danza.es/multimedia/biografias/pepe-hevia. **Link:** Video of and on Pepe Hevia.

11. IN THE WAKE OF GUERRA: FOR AN ETHNO-CUBAN DANCE

puede esperar cuando se está esperando inspired by her coming motherhood – her daughter Luna's father was the composer X Alfonso, a musician of Afro-rock fusion and Havana hiphop. The work was such a big change for the troupe that it completely threw them. But with Pous' *MalSon*[112] (2009) a new horizon had indisputably opened up for the group. The more than one hundred performances of *MalSon* were undeniable proof of the success of the "Spanish-born Cuban" artist. This success was further confirmed with Pous' *ShowRoom*, a work inspired by observing dancers behind the scenes.

In 2018, the troupe directed by Susana Pous changed its name to Micompañia. The previous year it had also moved its headquarters to Villa Lola, which was Pous' home in Miramar, with its spacious, luminous dance studio.

"Danza combinatoria" at work.

Rosario Cárdenas

A graduate in Art History with her thesis *Para un concepto de Combinatoria en Danza*, Rosario Cárdenas (Havana, 1953) was first a dancer with the DCC from 1971 to 1990. While with the company, she created the works *Dédalo*, *Imago*,

---

112. **Link:** Video of *MalSon* by Susana Pous.

11. IN THE WAKE OF GUERRA: FOR AN ETHNO-CUBAN DANCE

Afrodita, ¡Oh, espejo! by Rosario Cárdenas, 2017.

concept of choreographic composition for variations and permutations. Danza Combinatoria tended to favor formal and mathematical compositional values rather than emotional or narrative ones. Nevertheless, literary inspiration was not lacking, and Cárdenas' work drew upon the writings of innovative, committed writers who could be provocative. This was the case of José Lezama Lima (1910-1976) for *Dador* (2000), on the eros of adolescence. The piece was imbued with symbolism as it staged a hermit, knights, and boys masked in gold. In *El ascenso* (2004), again based on a work by Lezama Lima, a trio becomes the protagonist that attempts to climb the path to spirituality. *María Viván* (1997), on the other hand, refers to the work by the same name by Virgilio Piñera (1912-1979) on the sensual figure of the "photogenic consumptive" and other texts by the author.

In Rosario Cárdenas' dances, movements range from the most everyday to the most refined. She has introduced the Afro-Cuban influence, evident in *Combinatoria en Guaguancó* created in 2002 to music by Guido López Gavilán. She combines theater, performance dance, body art and video such as in *Zona-Cuerpo* (2010). In this work she brought a hint of parody to sensuality in its treatment of anatomy and human feelings. Also of note is *Tributo a El Monte* (2013), a homage to the fundamental writings of the anthropologist and woman of letters Lydia Cabrera. This becomes a Bible of sorts of the Afro-Cuban religion. From drums to rap.

Grifo, *El angel interior*, and *Canción de cuna* ("Lullaby"). Her master teachers were Eugenio Barba and Yuriko Kikuchi, the latter being Martha Graham's preferred dancer. While studying, Cárdenas also embraced the Alexander technique to release repetitive strain and tension. She also trained in the technique of David Zambrano.

In 1990, Cárdenas founded her own troupe, Danza Combinatoria, and worked to develop her

In 2017, Rosario Cárdenas presented *Afrodita, ¡Oh, espejo!*. In this work, the Greek goddess of Beauty is brought into the resonance of Ochún, the *Yoruba* divnity of eros. The original music score was by Frank Fernández, one of the greatest classical and popular Cuban pianists of all times.

11. IN THE WAKE OF GUERRA: FOR AN ETHNO-CUBAN DANCE

NARCISO MEDINA

Narciso Medina (Guantánamo, 1961), principal dancer and choreographer with the DCC, is the director of his own working troupe, formerly the Compañía Gestos Transitorios, and later the Compañía de Danza Moderna Narciso Medina. The company was founded in 1993 at the Teatro Favorito, formerly the cinema Calle Belascoaín at the corner of Peñalver, where it has its training academy and studio.

Medina has often been invited to Finland and has taught for many years in Japan, where he created his multi-disciplinary company, the Danza Estudio Ventana. Medina is also the founder of the Cuba Japan Festival in Tokyo. In 2015 he proposed the show *Japon baila en Cuba* to the Teatro Nacional dell'Avana. This was a fusion between the two cultures based upon an imaginary trip to Santiago de Cuba made by Japanese tourists in search of the musical roots of the Isla Grande.

Medina is above all famous as the creator of *Metamorfosis* (1986).[113] Despite his young age at the time, the work immediately set him apart: plastic protean figures, three male bodies, emerge like monstrous creatures from the mouth of a barrel to become human beings. It was a piece imbued with Kafka's disturbing novel, *The Metamorphosis*, and set to the music of Jean-Michel Jarre.

As a standard bearer of *cubanía*, Medina developed his own teaching method called *movimiento transitorio*. It begins from the cycle of breathing, to then expand this vital energy into the sur-

**Narciso Medina.
(left) Teatro Favorito, the
company's location in Havana.**

rounding space. This is through the impulse of a movement, fall, suspension, concentration, and projection. It uses the gestural expressiveness of theatre dance. Indeed improvisation is one of the key creative principles in Medina's work: *Caverna Mágica*; *Espacio, hombre, solo*; *Génesis para un carnaval*; *Cantoral*; *Últimos sucesos de fin de siglo*; *Dialogo con el vacío* and *Habitantes del hormiguero* ("Inhabitants of an anthill"). The latter, particularly exemplary, was mounted for the 20th Anniversary of the company.

Medina's creations are very strongly

---

113. **Link:** Video of *Metamorphosis* by Narciso Medina.

11. IN THE WAKE OF GUERRA...

influenced by Carpentier's renowned concept that was coined "magic realism". Carpentier was a supporter of "the marvellous real", as opposed to surrealism, and this walked the tightrope between primitivism and post-modernism. It considered the practical aspects, body contact, minimalism and other currents of "universal" contemporary dance. Medina was the creator of *La Vida en rosa* (*La Vie en Rose*). This was made with a complex multimedia dramaturgy and was accompanied by a video clip that he also directed. The work was based upon the songs of Edith Piaf and Cuban popular music. Medina also presented non-Cuban choreography pieces such as *Fujin-Raijin* ("God of air-god of light") based upon the Kabuki theatre of Yoko Saito and Idalmys Arias, and *O uva de Lune* by Martinican Jean-Claude Zadith. In this work, disciples of Mephistopheles appear among the characters, and the soundtrack includes Stravinsky's *Sacre du Printemps*.

THIRD GENERATION

JORGE LUIS ABRIL

A graduate of the ENA, a dancer with the DCC since 1981 and in Lorna Burdsall's troupe "Así somos", Jorge Luis Abril (Havana, 1962) is the founder of the Santiago company Teatro de la Danza del Caribe. He staged *Balada de los dos abuelos* with this company, a work inspired by Nicolás Guillen. Abril is also the creator of *Canillitas*[114] for the DCC. This was a dance-pantomime inspired by Charlie Chaplin who is a universal cult figure in Cuba. Abril is also a professor at the Lizt Alfonso dance school,[115] and choreographer for video dances (*Crisálidas*, 2007) in collaboration with director Isabelle Million.

LIDICE NÚÑEZ LOPEZ

Lidice Núñez Lopez (Havana, 1969) graduated from the ENA and became a dancer with the DCC. She gained renown for her choreographies *Flavio*, *La tempestad*, *Terriblemente innocente*, *Trastornados*, and *Cuida de no caer* for the DCC. Her work *El violín descalzo*[116] to a music score by Philip Glass and Ravi Shankar also brought her acclaim.

IN HAVANA AND BEYOND: OTHER COMPANIES

Lizt Herrera Alfonso (Havana, 1967) is also a foremost figure. A professor of Spanish and ethnic dances for Laura Alonso's Pro Danza, she also founded her own company in 1991. She represents different techniques and practices

Lizt Alfonso.

---

114. **Link:** Video of *Canillitas* by Jorge Abril with Julio César Iglesias and George Cespedes.

115. See http://liztalfonso.com/en/. **Link:** Video of *Suite Lecuona*, Lizt Alfonso's troupe.

116. See https://www.facebook.com/pg/nunezlidice/posts/.

The troupe Codanza.

11. IN THE WAKE OF GUERRA: FOR AN ETHNO-CUBAN DANCE

Carcinoma by Yoel González Rodríguez, Compañia Médula, 2015.

and has conceived several musicals for the stage such as *Vida*, which was a Canadian and German coproduction. In addition, she has also choreographed music videos among which notably *De mis recuerdos* by Juan Formel, for Van Van, the top of the charts band in Cuba and abroad. She also choreographed the music video *Bailando*, a hit by Enrique Iglesias with Descemer Bueno and Gente de Zona. Lizt has also devoted herself intensively to training dancers. She is the recipient of many awards, including the International Spotlight Award, bestowed upon her by Michelle Obama. For television, Lizt is a member of the jury for the program *Bailando en Cuba*, alongside Susana Pous and Santiago Alfonso.

There have been many companies founded by the third generation of dancers and choreographers who are indebted to the teachings of Ramiro Guerra. One of the first of these companies was founded in Matanzas in 1987. This was the troupe Espiral, under the direction of Lillian Padrón. From 1994, the company fostered the choreography competition for duets, Danzandos, at the Teatro Sauto of the city of Matanzas (1863). The theater was designed by the Italian architect Daniele Dall'Aglio after the model of La Scala di Milano.

In 1988, in Santiago de Cuba, Eduardo Rivero undertook the creation of the Teatro de la Danza del Caribe. This continued in the wake of Cuban modern dance trends such as the dramatization of folkloric elements.

Danza Libre was founded in 1990 in Guantánamo by Martha Graham's follower, Elfride Malher. It was imbued with a mixed folkloric and modern style and also developed elements rooted in Franco-Haitian tradition. The company was directed by Alfredo Velázquez Carcassés (who died brutally in 2013 at only forty-four years of age). He was a principal dancer, choreographer (*Wemilere*) and master teacher who developed his own system of training based upon the concatenation of movement.

Elio Orestes Reina Figueredo had trained with

Yoldance in *Besame mucho*, with a *transformista* dancer in the cast, 2018.

11. IN THE WAKE OF GUERRA: FOR AN ETHNO-CUBAN DANCE

Velázquez himself and was known as "the athlete of dance". As a performer, he was an award winner at the Concurso Internacional de Danza del Atláno Norte Gran Prix "Vladimir Malakhov" (1968). The event was named after the great Ukrainian dancer who had a great love of Cuba and who had led the event.

One of the dancers with Danza Libre was Joel González Rodríguez, a twenty-year-old experimental artist inspired by Malakhov. He created his own troupe in Guatánamo called Médula ("Marrow"), that is, go straight to the core of reality. He mounted his own versions of *Swan Lake*, *Giselle*, and *Carmen* with this company.

Danza Fragmentada was created in 1993 by Ladislao Navarro Tomasén. Based in Guantánamo, it mixes techniques and origins, modern and folklore.

The company Codanza was founded in Holguín in 1992 by Maricel Godoy with a group taken from the ENA. Its name alludes to *cohesión, conjunto, compacto, combinación*. It explores contemporary styles, from formal work to theatrical. One of Codanza's key creations was *Año cero* with the participation of plastic artist Cosme Proenza with his symbolist and surrealist vision. *Ritual* by Godoy was a veritable calling card for the group. Its repertory also included *Muerte prevista en el guión* ("Death foreseen in the script") by Argentinian choreographer and dancer Susana Tambutti. In her work, the history of dance is treated in a humorous vein. *Pasajera la lluvia* by Nelson Reyes treats the theme of homosexuality, a topic that had been considered taboo in Cuba for a long while. *Fuerza, vitalidad y destreza*, force, vigor and eros, are characteristics that Maricel Godoy feels belong to her Codanza.[117]

---

117. **Link:** Video of *Ritual* by Maricel Godoy, Codanza.

Danza del Alma was a predominantly male group that was created in Santa Clara in 1995 with Ernesto Alejo Sosa (*Danzar peces de luna* and *Pido permiso*). The titles in its repertory were already a declaration of a certain stance: *Machos, Baile para hombres con deseos inconfesos o Machos y hembras*, and *Juegos de guerra*. Among the dancers in the company, there were some who contributed original choreographies such as Yusniel

Another spectacular Yoldance moment.

González Broches with *Panes y peces*, and Jean Michel Díaz Montenegro with *Tanto para nada*.

In Cuba, therefore, the way was being paved for the expression of one's own gender identity.[118] Fidel Castro himself had commented positively on this development in the dialogue-documentary by Oliver Stone, *Comandante* (2003).

---

118. Cf. Abel Sierra Madero, *Del otro lado del espejo*, Casa de las Américas Award, Havana, 2006, in which there is a careful and explicit examination of themes such as sexuality, identity, and gender. There is a wealth of library documentation. See the blog also: https://siluetasdecuba.wordpress.com/2012/05/12/desterremos-la-homofobia-fotos/.

11. IN THE WAKE OF GUERRA...

Ballet Rakatán.

Yoldance saw the light in 1999 led by Yolena Alonso Zequeira (Havana, 1978). She resided in Cuba and in Germany and was the niece of the great *bolerista* Pacho Alonso. A pupil and dancer under Narciso Medina, Yolena worked above all in theater and musical comedy. A famous example was *Viva Cuba!* with an original music score that drew from all the island's musical richness. It ranged from *bolero* to *pilón*, the *conga* to the *cha-cha-cha*, with the orchestra of the "Star of Salsa" billed "Pachito Alonso and his Kini Kini". Among Yoldance's most famous pieces:[119] *La Habanera* (2001), *Mambo Club* (2003), *Sugar Island* (2004), *Viva Cuba!* (2005), *Havana Buena Vista Show* (2008), *Bésame mucho* (2011), and *La Guarapachanga* (2016).

In 2001, Nilda Guerra, class of '75, founded Ballet Rakatán. The name was actually an onomatopoeia that helped her count out the beat during rehearsals. This pulsating rhythm drives the company's work that combines classical, modern, folk, popular, Afro-Cuban, with veins of flamenco and Latin Jazz. The company's emblematic international hit *Viva Cuba!*[120] is set in an airport with its constant arrivals and departures. It is the embodiment of Cubans' desire to dance, make music and travel.

The Ballet Contemporáneo Camagüey Endedans emerged in 2002. Founder and choreographer Tania Vergara Pérez proposed to give a privileged place to contemporary dance that would embrace a broad spectrum. Themes included the condition of women (*La fuente de todos* to music by Händel) and male virtuosism, in the solo *La muerte del hombre* based upon Mikhail Fokin's *The Dying Swan* (1905). In addition to this revamped version of the sublime neo-romantic piece, the company presented a bold reference to transvestism in its 2013 *Carmen* to the music by Bizet. Endedans has also presented numerous works abroad. Notable examples are multiple award-winner *A los confines de la tierra*, *A Él*, *Abrazo perdurable*, *Retrato de tus ojos*, and *Media Noche*. Since December 2014, the co-director of Endedans is Cuban American Pedro Ruíz. His professional background is impressive, as professor and principal dancer in Alvin Ailey's talent forge, and with the Ballet Hispánico of New York.

---

119. **Link:** Video of Yoldance.

120. **Link:** Video of *Vamos Cuba!* at the Birmingham New Street Station, 2016.

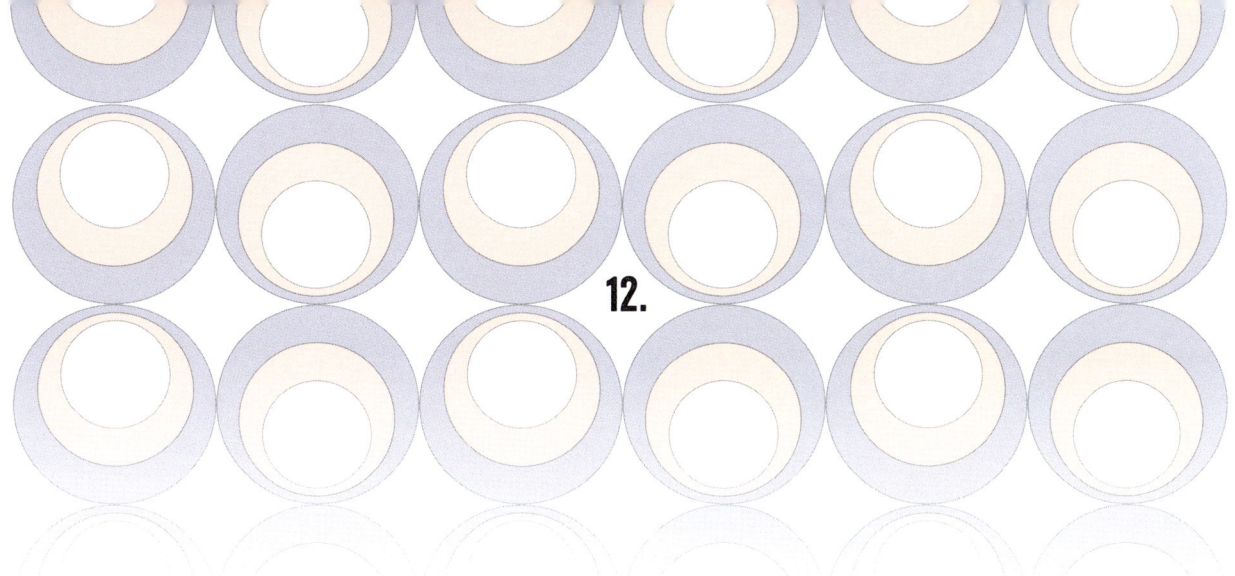

12.

CUBAN CONTEMPORARY DANCE: THE NEW MILLENNIUM

Modern and contemporary dance, or "non classical" – in the familiar Cuban sense – is today blossoming into a new period of development and expansion.

Sandra Ramy Aparicio (Havana, 1976) is a dancer and choreographer with a decidedly innovative vocation. She is considered one of the most interesting creators of the last wave. She was a dancer with DanzAbierta and Danza-Teatro Retazos in Cuba, and with Constanza Macras and Norbert Servos in Germany. In 1997, she began working as an actress with the Teatro Estudio under the direction of Vicente Revuelta. She also worked with the Teatro El Público, directed by Carlos Díaz. She is a professor of Stage Arts at the Universidad de las Artes di Cuba and has taught summer courses in Theatre at the New York University of Havana, with the support of the Fundación Ludwig.

In 2010, Ramy launched the project Se Estudio, a creative arts center that is open to children and non-professional adults. Since 2014, she leads the dance program of the Fábrica de Arte Cubano (FAC). This is a space for experimental projects located in a vast multi-disciplinary space in Vedado, in a former electricity plant. The activities organized at the FAC are coordinated by a commission that is responsible for their promotion. The programs are for the most part funded by the revenues from the many Cuban and foreign visitors keen to explore this popular spot. Sandra Ramy regularly selects opportunities for training at the FAC. These include open classes from tango to Afro-beat, and high-profile master classes for professionals. Among the latter, there were notably master classes led by teachers from Martha Graham's company in the U.S. The company was invited to the 2016 Festival de Ballet, returning for the first time to Cuba since its last visit in distant 1943.

In 2019, the principal dancer of the Cullberg Ballet, Pompea Santoro, gave a master class on the repertory of modern remakes of classical

12. CUBAN CONTEMPORARY DANCE: THE NEW MILLENNIUM

Mi trabajo es Usted by and with Sandra Ramy, 2012.

ballets by the Swedish creator Mats Ek. The works included *Giselle*, with the students of the ENB, *Swan Lake* and *Carmen*.

In 2013, Ramy created a multi-disciplinary collectivity called Persona consisting of actors, musicians and dancers. This was under the auspices of the Consejo Nacional de Artes Escénicas de Cuba and the Cuban Ministry of Culture. Among its most notable works: *Busca la cabeza con el pie* (2002), *Detrás de Nadie* (2005 National Critics Award), *Algunos ritos inútiles* (2007), *Ave María Didáctica* (2009), *Uno en uno* (2010), *Peso* (2010), *Cabaret de Reparaciones imprevistas* and *Mi trabajo es usted* (2012), based upon the story *The Egg and the Chicken* by Clarice Lispector. Other works followed such as: *¿De qué está hecha tu casa?* (2014) or *Yilliam de Bala coming soon*,[121] whose theme was an imaginary fashion show. The opening of the work featured an ironic sign saying *Hasta la Victoria Beckham* – paraphrasing Castro's epic words *Hasta la victoria siempre* with an additional reference to David Beckham's popular fashion creator wife – though neither the designer nor the victory ever materialized.

The year 2018 marked a particularly challenging undertaking by Sandra Ramy as choreographer of the work *Consagración de la primavera*. The focus was on the individual and society, with the figure of male soloist, Abel Rojo, multiplied to infinity by a play of mirrors. In Italy, for the project Cubita,[122] during 2016 Ramy mounted *Cubanología*, in residence in Naples with Campania dancers from the company Körper led by Gennaro Cimmino. Ramy's *Cubanología* was also presented in the program *Abballamm!* for the Ravello Festival[123] directed by Laura Valente. It was also performed in Turin (at the "Lavanderia a Vapore" of the Piemonte dal Vivo foundation), with the young troupe Eko Dance International Project directed by Pompea Santoro. *Cubanología*, to Cuban traditional music – just as *Siboney* by Ernesto Lecuona, and *Guantanamera* by Joseíto Fernández – evokes the poetic words of *Lo que prolifera*,[124] a text by writer and musician Omar Pérez. The theme is that of "a return to the eternal question of identity". It considers the musical archetypes, movements, rhythms,

---

121. **Link:** Video by *Yilliam de Bala Coming Soon*.
122. *Cubita* (a term that combines Cuba and Italy and recalls a famous brand of Cuban coffee), a project organized by the author of this book. Born out of the harmony and collaborative experiences with people sensitive to the possibilities for opening and exchange in the field of the contemporary dance of the new generation.
123. See the section "Media" with photos and videos of: http://fondazioneravello.com/website/.
124. Omar Pérez wrote *Crítica de la razón puta*.

12. CUBAN CONTEMPORARY DANCE: THE NEW MILLENNIUM

Ylliam de Bala by Sandra Ramy, 2014.

with works (see *De invocaciones y otros límites*) that have been translated into several languages. She is a contributor to magazines such as "La Jiribilla"[125] and "DanzaBallet".[126] She is a choreographer active in Cuba and in many countries of Latin America, and a director of dance videos. She was awarded the Coreografo Elettronico 2017 prize for *Circunloquio*, shot in an abandoned hospital with dancers from the DCC.[127] Laura Domingo Agüero also co-wrote the docu-film *Cuban Dancer* with director Roberto Salinas (an Indyca

gestures, and the most authentic characteristics behind the stereotype of *cubanía*. In Ravello and Piemonte, *Cubanología* was presented in diptych with *Historia de un adiós* by Laura Domingo Agüero. The work was inspired by the memory of a love, the recollection of a time of romance that vibrates in the pure emotion of dance. The music score is driven by evocative songs — such as *Veinte años* sung by Omara Portuondo, *Un día de noviembre* by Leo Brouwer, *Adiós a Cuba* by Ignacio Cervantes with Javier Ruiz on piano — and a poetic text by the author herself.

Laura Domingo Agüero (Havana, 1985) is noted as one of the most eclectic of the new Cuban talents. As a writer, she is a member of UNEAC,

***Consagración de la Primavera* by Sandra Ramy, 2018.**

---

125. Digital cultural magazine activated in 2001 with a paper version of 2003.
126. See https://www.danzaballet.com.
127. **Link:** Video of *Circunloquio* by Laura Domingo Agüero.

Historia de un adiós by Laura Domingo Agüero, troupe Körper, Ravello Festival 2016.

12. CUBAN CONTEMPORARY DANCE...

128

129

production). The film retraces the development of dance in Cuba and the U.S., in theatres, dance halls and the street, and also tackles the topic of emigration. Laura teaches at the ENB, where her mother Raquel is a professor. She created the trio *Cénit* for the DCC to *La catedral* by classical guitarist Augustín Barrios Mangaré. Laura's portfolio of works also includes: *Igneos, Dulce es la sombra,* in the ambit of the BNC, the modern solo *El desequilibrio* (2014)[128] for super-classical star Viengsay Valdés. In 2020, on the occasion of the 61st anniversary of the DCC, she created the literary *Pedro Páramo* based upon the work by Juan Rulfo. In November 2018, the FAC hosted *Dove sei?*[129] for Cubita 3. The piece was conceived by Laura Domingo Agüero for the Balletto Teatro di Torino, founded forty years previously by Loredana Furno, and directed by her daughter Viola Scaglione. It drew inspiration from the writings of the philosopher Maurizio Ferraris. A rich platform of Cuban contemporary dance was featured with the troupes Persona, Retazos/Memory Wax, Los Hijos del Director, and Malpaso.

The FAC had previously presented Cubita 2 and Daniele Ninarello's choreographies *R-Evolution*, with the company Persona, and Simona Soledad Rinaldo, *The Dancing Truck.*[130] These were presented during

Rehearsal for *Cubanología* by Sandra Ramy, Eko Dance International Project, Turin, 2016.

***Cubanología* by Sandra Ramy, Ravello Festival 2016.**

---

128. **Link:** Video of *El desequilibrio* di Laura Domingo Agüero for Viengsay Valdés.
129. **Link:** Video of *Dove sei?* in Havana.

130. See http://lasa-cuba.blogspot.it/2017/11/the-dancing-truck-simona-soledad.html.

"Lavanderia a Vapore", Piedmont "House of Dance", Collegno-Turin.

FAC, Fábrica de Arte Cubano.

the 2017 Italian Culture Week, under the auspices of the Italian Embassy. Ninarello's creation was based upon electronic rhythmic cells developed in a minimal mood by multimedia artist Matteo Vinti. A Cuban touch was brought by Guido Gali, the eclectic cultural figure and artistic director for DanzAbierta, for Susana Pous and Sandra Ramy. The work reflects upon the evolution of dancing bodies as interconnecting signs and communicating rhythms. *The Dancing Truck* was created through an international appeal for mobility/residency "On the Move" at the Laboratorio Artístico de San Agustín (LASA), which was created in 2008.[131] It is the motor of the WASA (Wifi Alternativa de San Agustín, a local social and cultural intranet network). The workshop LASA is based upon concepts of "projects of contextual art", "open works", to be a framework for participative activities inspired by the "theory of needs" developed by the American psychologist Abraham Harold Maslow (1908-1970). LASA was launched by the artist Candelario with French curator Aurélie Sampeur to organize a wide range of activities (including restoration, which supports the work

R-Evolution by Danielle Ninarello, Compañia Persona, FAC, Havana, 2017.

---

131. Cf. AA.VV, *Si estuvieras en una isla, Diez Años de LASA*, Havana 2019.

12. CUBAN CONTEMPORARY DANCE: THE NEW MILLENNIUM

Where are you? by Laura Domingo Agüero, BTT, at the FAC, 2018.

The Dancing Truck by Simona Soledad Rinaldo – Lasa, 2017.

Simona Soledad Rinaldo.

of the center) in a neighborhood on the city's outskirts. Simona's *The Dancing Truck* traces the encounters that occur in public places between the people of this neighborhood. It evokes their memories and daily lives to suggest the idea of an 'Itinerant Dance School' where passengers in a bus exchange "dance phrases". In 2019, Simona

142

12. CUBAN CONTEMPORARY DANCE: THE NEW MILLENNIUM

Hardly Ever by Francesco Scavetta/Wee, Havana, 2016.

Dime quanto es quella vale by Simona Soledad Rinaldo, Milan, 2019.

Soledad Rinaldo mounted *Dime quanto es que ella vale* with three dancers from the company Persona. It was a reflection on the role of women in Latin pop music and mainstream erotic fantasy. After the work premiered at the FAC in Havana, it was staged in Milan at the Fondazione Arnaldo Pomodoro, at the theater Noh'ma.[132]

Another Italian, Francesco Scavetta, who is based in Norway with his company Wee, has impressed the Cuban dance theatre scene most interested in innovative projects. His *Hardly Ever*, performed at the Centro Cultural Bertold Brecht de La Habana in 2016, explores the concept of "*intercorporalidad*". Scavetta questions the meaning of stage performance, its aesthetic and political sense, and of being on stage suspended between surprise and chance, in a playful spirit. This has been an alternative approach to the tenets of narration in theatrical dance.

CENTRO DE LA DANZA DE LA HABANA

The official entity, Centro de la Danza, is located in Havana's very central area of Paseo del Prado, and figures among the spaces and organisms dedicated to the promotion of contemporary dance. It was opened in July 2006 and is directed by María del Carmen Borroto Alfonso. Dance companies that use the Centro, which is equipped with work rooms, are: Rosario Cárdenas, DanzAbierta-Micompañia, Narciso Medina, Danzas Tradicionales JJ, Folclórica Raíces Profundas, Flamenca Ecos, GEDE di Santiago Alfonso, Ban-Rarrá, Yoldance, Ballet Rakatán, Havana Queens, Así somos, Los Hijos del Director, and the non-subsidized Malpaso. The company "*de técnica mixta*" Acosta Danza also uses their facilities, as previously the companies Compañía Danzares and Compañía Pinos Nuevos.

---

132. See https://www.nohma.org/teatro_nohma.html.

12. CUBAN CONTEMPORARY DANCE: THE NEW MILLENNIUM

Façade of the Centro de la Danza on Paseo del Prado.

Compañia Ban-Rarrá, Paseo del Prado, 2009.

NEW FACES

In Cuba, training is canonical and state-run, and workplaces and performance venues are not privately owned, unless performances are in one's own home. Therefore, every creative wave of newcomers must learn to be yielding and live with the idea that institutional opportunities are few and far between.

Every year on 29th April, "Los días de la danza" (International Dance Day) is celebrated with a highly varied program. Interesting solos were seen in the project *Todos x Uno* (2013), such as Gabriela Burdsall at the DCC, where *Medea Reloaded*[133] was staged. Lorna's granddaughter works with playwright Maikel Rodríguez, as well as Adolfo Izquierdo of Así somos. She also creates for videodance. The list of new talents who have achieved the most acclaim includes Luvien Mederos, who has pursued his career principally abroad, and Norge Cedeño Raffo, creator of *Transire* for the DCC, *Happy Ending*, and *Trailer* for Codanza.[134] Cedeño, formerly with the DCC, today heads his own troupe Otro Lado, with DCC colleagues such as Thais Suárez and Niosbel González.

NEW DANCE AND NEW CRITICS

The vision shared by the generations most directly influenced by Ramiro Guerra's position — to modernize dance by including different cultures — is subject to objection. This is often voiced by those who refer to studies in the United States on the issue of race. Indeed, they see the institutional recognition of "negritude" as an obligation to remain as such and act as such. They argue that this only goes to nourish the stereo-

---

133. **Link:** Video of *Medea Reloaded* by Gabriela Bursdall with Luis Enrique Carricaburu at the Fábrica de Arte Cubano.

134. See https://www.facebook.com/CodanzaHolguinCuba/videos/1222205807911039/.

type of the 'White-dancer' of controlled verticality, adapted to the European academic language, and the 'Black-dancer' of unlimited flexibility, adapted to folklore and modern dance, in addition to having that exotic and erotic aspect so popular with the entertainment market.

Recently there have been observer-activists such as Lourdes Ulacia and Noel Bonilla Chongo who have openly taken a position on this, adopting an innovative postmodern approach.

Lourdes Ulacia, a dancer with the DCC, was trained by master teachers such as Carlos Horta, on the style of José Limón, and Yuriko, on Graham. She attended the workshops of Sasha Waltz and David Zambrano held in Havana at DanzAbierta. Ulacia taught modern dance at the ENA and from 1990 to 2015 at the ISA. She has been Professor of Methodology in Enseñanza de la Técnica. Her aim is to concentrate on combining elements specific to the Cuban school with those of international contemporary and postmodern dance.

Compañia Otro Lado.

Noel Bonilla Chongo is also among the most determined advocates of new theoretical and practical solutions for the building of "in progress" paths for Cuban dance today. Through his work he clearly expresses the need to open and broaden horizons. These should include new "post-contemporary" dimensions, above all along the lines of theoretical and aesthetic developments from the French area.[135] As an anti-conservative, he created events such as Danza en Construcción and Focus Danza (2016). He referred precisely to France as a leader on the question of the body in performance. Chongo also launched the Bienales del Caribe as well as publications such as "Danzar.Cu". In line with his thinking, he created a Chair at the ISA for Dance Studies. In his aim to activate access to international contemporary dance today, he invited guests to Havana such as Spanish performer María La Ribot, and Jérôme Bel,[136] the French champion of "non dance". These initiatives offered new spaces for analysis and creativity.

The intermediate nuances between the various positions on the issue of tradition vs. innovation are many. The discussion is more than ever open, in books and magazines as well as online.

---

135. Cf. Laurence Louppe, *Danses tracées: dessins et notation des chorégraphes*, cat. Exhibition Dis-Voir, Paris 1991; *Poétique de la danse contemporaine*, Contredanse, Brussels 1997-2000; *Poétique de la danse contemporaine, la suite*, Contredanse, Brussels 2007; *Laurence Louppe, une pensée vivante*, L'Harmattan, Paris 2017.

136. See http://www.jeromebel.fr.

Carlos Acosta in *Apollo* by George Balanchine, Royal Ballet, 2013.

13.

ACOSTA DANZA

Carlos Acosta Quesada (Havana, 1973) has been a key figure in marking an impressive turning point in Cuban dance today, from its origins in the classical tradition at the ENB. Charismatic and virtuosic, he has been *primera figura* at the BNC, principal dancer at the Houston Ballet and English National Ballet, as well as esteemed guest with the American Ballet Theatre, Moscow's Bolshoi and the Opéra de Paris. In 1998, he was appointed principal dancer of the London Royal Ballet. He then turned his creativity to choreography, cinema and writing. Recently he has been the artistic director of Acosta Danza and since 2019, of the Birmingham Royal Ballet. Yet, though he has his family in London, Acosta has his heart in Cuba.

In Britain, he mastered the European contemporary dance styles and decided to form his own troupe in Cuba in 2016.[137] His aim was to "give back to my country what I had received", and to present Cuban and international quality choreographies, based upon academic dance in a contemporary style. This was organized with the support of the English company Valid Productions and London's Sadler's Wells. Carlos also began to create his own works. He cast dancers from the DCC for his first choreography work for the stage. It was an interweaving that also included autobiographical accents: *Tocororo, fábula cubana*. Carlos' nephew Yonah played the role of Acosta himself as a youth. There was even a real *almendrón*, that is, a very heavy American car from the fifties hoisted on stage at Havana's Gran Teatro.

He was a prodigy of the ENB, and at only sixteen years of age was awarded the Prix de Lausanne. He would be asked to be president of the jury of this same competition in 2019. In his youth, as the winner of the Prix, he was immediately asked to be guest dancer with the Bolshoi. He became an international star and winner of the Laurence Olivier Award. Yet, Carlos Acosta as a young pupil hated discipline. He was a boy from a poor neighborhood, the last of eleven children. He seemed

---

137. See http://www.acostadanza.com/.

13. ACOSTA DANZA

Carlos Acosta in a shot from *Memoria* by Miguel Altunaga.

legacy during the decades of her reign at the BNC. In this seemingly timeless Cuban landscape, the resourcefulness of Acosta Danza is indeed impressive. The company was formed with a base of twenty-five excellent dancers, mainly from the BNC and DCC. Dancers from these companies already had the flexibility to perform a range of different styles. Since 2017, a multidisciplinary academy organized with the support of sponsors is also based in the company's facilities at Calle Linea. It

uncontrollable and incapable of using his natural athletic gifts. Without a strict father and his demanding and intelligent teachers who were able to harness him and his talents, Carlos never would have made it.

The story of his life is told in his autobiography *No Way Home, a Cuban Dancer's Story*. He also authored the story *Pig's Foot*, on the themes of slavery, revolution, and identity, inspired by his people of *mezclada* Afro-Cuban origins.

Today Acosta has also acquired the assurance of his experience in the "*primer mundo*". He thus embodies a new frontier for Cuba without, of course, denying the patrimony of bravura that has been handed down by Alicia Alonso. The extraordinary "blind visionary" Alicia consolidated and transmitted this

Building of Acosta Danza at Calle Linea in Havana.

welcomes Cuban and foreign scholarship holders and offers studies in contemporary dance, Afro-Cuban modern dance, and academic ballet.

Acosta Danza on tour in Vienna, 2017.

Scholarship students of the Carlos Acosta Foundation.

event was organized by the Centro Nacional de Educación Sexual (CNESex) in the Avellaneda Hall of the Teatro Nacional. Yelda Leyva performed *Souls in Mirror*, a piece on the fluidity of identity. It was choreographed by Ely Regina Hernández who was also in the cast. Raúl Reinoso and Julio Léon danced *Silueta* to the music of Piazzolla.

Carlos, after brilliant performances in Ballanchine's American ballets, danced opposite super-étoiles such as Russian ballerina Natalia Osipova in the heroic *Spartacus*; Basilio in *Don Quixote*; and Albrecht in *Giselle*. This was the epitome of the "White ballet" that for so long seemed closed to a dancer of dark skin. In 2013, Acosta mounted a *Don Quixote* for the English Royal Ballet in which the performances of the male dancers were particularly applauded.

After Acosta left the company in

Doors have therefore opened onto horizons created by personal initiative. Of course, this was made possible as a result of personal global prestige which until then was unforeseen in the "a-capitalist" Caribbean.[138] Another indication of the company's openness was reflected in the participation of some of its dancers in the gala for the nineth year of the Jornadas Cubanas contra la Homofobia y la Transfobia in May 2016. The

Project by Norman Foster for the recovery of the complex for arts and dance at Cubanacán.

---
138. See https://carlosacostafoundation.org.

13. ACOSTA DANZA

Carlos Acosta in *Spartacus*, 2013.

2015, he was open to exploring new opportunities including neo-ballet (*Requiem* by Kenneth MacMillan) and contemporary dance. Dancers from Acosta Danza performed at the Ravello Festival in *Cubanía en el Ballet*. This brought together the island's "family" of dancers scattered over the entire planet[139] and who danced in a wonderful variety of works: from the glowing *Don Quixote* of the grand tradition with virtuoso Luis Valle,[140] to the plastic *Faun* by Sidi Larbi Cherkaoui, and *Anadromous* by Raúl Reinoso, a dancer from the troupe.

Yelda Leyva and Julio León in *Faun* by Sidi Larbi Cherkaoui, Ravello Festival 2016.

In addition to *Tocororo Suite* (the abbreviated title from the more complex *Tocororo, fábula cubana*), Acosta also staged his own version of *Carmen*, in coproduction with the Royal Opera House, the Texas Ballet Theater, and the

---

139. *Cubanía en el Ballet* is a special unpublished project of the Ravello Festival directed by Laura Valente, based on an idea by Elisa Guzzo Vaccarino with the collaboration of Alfio Agostini.
140. Luis Valle then joined the Ballet Nice-Méditerranée directed by Éric Vu-An.

Carlos Acosta with Natalia Osipova in *Giselle*, Royal Ballet, 2014.

Queensland Ballet. The international impact of the company was evident. Yet, the list of works presented by Acosta Danza also includes: *El cruce sobre el Niágara* by Marianela Boán; *De punta a cabo* by Alexis Fernández Maca, a Cuban artist previously with the DCC and today head of his own troupe (La Macana) in Galizia; *End of Time* (1984) by Ben Stevenson, director of the Houston Ballet, of which Acosta was also a member in the nineties. The protagonist couple of Stevenson's work – the last human beings on earth – was the inspiration for Stanley Kramer's post-apocalyptic film *On the Beach*. There are also two works in the company's portfolio by Spanish creator and AD resident choreographer Goyo Montero, director of the Staatstheater Ballett Nürnberg in Germany. The works are *Alrededor no hay nada*,

Faun by Sidi Larbi Cherkaoui, "Evolution" program, Acosta Danza, 2019.

with poems by Joaquín Sabina, and *Imponderable*, to the music by Silvio Rodríguez. Also of

13. ACOSTA DANZA

Imponderable by Goyo Montero,
AD resident choreographer, 2017.

Avium by Ely Regina Hernández,
AD, 2017.

note: *Derrumbe* ("Collapse", referring to buildings in Cuba) by Miguel Altunaga, a Cuban dancer with the company Rambert[141] (London, *Cubanía* evening, 2014); *Babbel* by Spanish choreographer María Rovira (2016); *Avium* by Ely Regina Fernández, to the music of the *Carnival of Animals* by Camille Saint-Saëns, orchestrated and performed at the piano by Pepe Gavilondo (José Victor Gavilongo Peón; Havana, 1989). In addition to these works, there was also *Twelve* by Jorge Crecis, the creator of an exciting game of graphic and mathematical permutations, halfway between athleticism and dance. This called for twelve dancers and countless plastic bottles of water. And then *Hokiri*, to rise from the ashes, by Mickael Marso Riviere. Born in France, active in England, Riviere was open to collaborations of all kinds, independently, with dancers from the Bolshoi to hip hoppers. In 2018, for the program Mitos, Acosta Danza presented Christopher Bruce's *Rooster* with music to eight songs of the Rolling Stones; *Impronta*, a solo on the goddess Yemayá of the *Yoruba* pantheon, and *El salto de Nijinsky*, based on the desperate life of the divo of Diaghilev (1890-1950). Both latter works were by María Rovira (1963). As mentioned previously, the Acosta Danza repertory featured the acclaimed *Faun* by Sidi Larbi Cherkaoui. This innovative Belgian-Moroccan choreographer was just as much at ease creating for the Ballets

---

141. Previously Rambert Ballet and Rambert Dance Company, see http://www.rambert.org.uk/about-us/our-history/. Cf. also Brigitte Kelly, 'Mim', A Personal Memoir of Marie Rambert, Dance Books, London 2009.

13. ACOSTA DANZA

Babbel by María Rovira, AD, 2017.

de Monte Carlo, the warriors of Shaolin, as for the tango dancers of Buenos Aires.[142] He also conceived and choreographed the work created especially for Acosta himself and Marta Ortega, *Mermaid*, to music by Satie. And then there is *Belles-Lettres* by very cool Justin Peck, resident choreographer for the New York City Ballet. Also performed by Acosta Danza as part of its repertory is *One Thousand Years After* by Saburo Teshigawara,[143] an artist of very fine formal elegance and a master of space, time, and the breath. The company also performs *Paysage, soudain, la*

Carlos Acosta and Pieter Symonds in *Derrumbe* di Miguel Altunaga, 2014.

Twelve by Jorge Grecis, AD, 2017.

nuit to music by Leo Brouwer and *Paisaje cubano con rumba*. Both of these works are by Swedish artist Pontus Lidberg.

There are also works created by talent within

---

142. Cf. Elisa Guzzo Vaccarino, *Danze Plurali, l'altrove qui*, Ephemeria, Macerata 2009.
143. *Ibidem*.

13. ACOSTA DANZA

144

145

Zeledy Crespo in *Impronta* by María Rovira, AD, 2020.

Carlos Acosta in *Rooster* by Christopher Bruce, AD, 2018.

the company. For example, young dancer Raúl Reinoso, once having joined Acosta Danza, was seized by – he says – a "choreographic restlessness". This was expressed not only through his work *Anadromous*, to music by Ezio Bosso and Yann Tiersen, but also the duo *Nosotros* created with Beatriz García to music by experimenter Pepe Gavilondo.[144] It also encouraged Raúl to explore the terrain of audio visuals. In 2018 he again presented *Satori* to music by Gavilondo.

The 2019 program of Acosta Danza was entitled *Rituales*. It presented works such as *Cor*, a creation by Marianela Boán, *Soledad* by Rafael Bonachela, and *Portal* by the Spanish choreographer Juanjo Arqués, the latter work to music by the Cuban-Iranian folk-electronic band Ariwo.

In 2020, Carlos Acosta danced the solo by Russel Maliphant, *Two*, previously performed by Sylvie Guillem.

The future for Carlos Acosta abounds in projects, and the calendar of the company grows busier and busier. There is a great desire for the project to expand Cubanacán. This is a space that should have been entirely renovated by 2019 for the occasion of the celebration of the five-hundred-year anniversary of Havana.

The success story of this great artist has inspired many films and documentaries. *Carlos Acosta: The Reluctant Ballet Dancer* (Great Britain, 2003), directed by Lucy Blakstad, draws a detailed portrait as it traces Carlos' life from his birthplace, his entire career, until his creation *Tocororo*. Acosta appeared in the romantic comedy *Day of the Flowers* (2012), directed by John Robert. He played the role of a dancer and tourist guide trying to cope with his two Scottish sisters, a fashion designer and a political activist. They adventurously decide to take their deceased father's ashes to Cuba. The bio-pic *Yuli* (2018)[145] – or Carlos as the son of the *Orisha* Ogún – was directed by Spanish filmmaker Iciar Bollain and was based on Acosta's autobiography (*No Way Home*). Eight fragments of contemporary dance from the repertory of his troupe come filtering through. There are multiple protagonist actors: Carlos as a boy played by Edison Manuel Olvera

---

144. **Link:** Video of *Nosotros*, Beatriz García and Raúl Reinoso, AD.

145. **Link:** trailer *Yuli*.

El salto de Nijinsky by María Rovira, 2018.

Paysage, soudain, la nuit by Pontus Lidberg, AD, 2018.

Anadromous by Raúl Reinoso, AD, 2017.

Belles-Lettres by Justin Peck, AD, 2017.

One Thousand Years After by Saburo Teshigawara, AD, 2018.

Núñez, who is a pupil at the ENB in real life; Carlos as a teenager played by Mario Sergio Elías; and Carlos as an adult played by Kevyn Martínez. The two latter are dancers with Acosta Danza. Carlos himself is the narrator of the film. The original choreographies, drawn from various moments in Carlos' biography are again by Rovira. In the role of the father deus ex machina, an extremely effective Santiago Alfonso;[146] and in the role of the teacher cum fairy godmother (in real life Ramona De Sáa), Laura De La Uz.

Carlos Acosta on the set of the biography film *Yuli* by Iciar Bollaín, with little Edison Manuel Olvera cast as Acosta as a child.

---

146. Cf. Elisa Guzzo Vaccarino, *Carlos Acosta, il biopic*, in "BallettoOggi/Ballet2000", n. 280, 2019.

14.

ISABEL BUSTOS AND RETAZOS

OTHER PATHS AND DESIRE FOR INDEPENDENCE

The organizational system of the arts in Cuba always bears the governmental seal. A desire for more autonomy is therefore constantly being expressed.

Isabel Bustos Romoleroux (Santiago del Cile, 1948) is an Ecuadorian who has lived in Cuba since 1963 where her parents were diplomats. She studied at the ENA – among her teachers were two of the "jewels" of Cuban ballet, Loipa Aráujo and Mirta Plá – and then trained in Paris on a UNESCO scholarship. She became a professor at the ISA, after a career as a modern dancer in Ecuador as well as with the Danza Nacional de Cuba directed by Ramiro Guerra.

In 1987, Isabel Bustos founded the troupe Retazos[147] ("remnants", "fragments", or "pieces of life") with a strongly theatrical and multidisciplinary vocation. The company regularly presents works by Isabel Bustos and her son, Miguel Azcue. The latter lives in Sweden where for the past fourteen years he has led the troupe Memory Wax with actress Johanna Jonasson (*Posible imposible*[148]). Retazos, a project "born at home in the living room", premiered with *Mujeres* before obtaining its own premises with a theater hall located on Calle Amargura.[149]

The center is called "Las Carolinas" after the trees that grow in its garden. Inside, there are many artistic activities organized for children as well. This is also where, since 1996, Isabel Bustos has directed *Danza en Paisajes Urbanos "Habana Vieja: Ciudad en Movimiento"* (initials CQD: Ciudades Que Danzan). The collection of posters of the various editions held in different venues in the city and

---

147. See http://www.danzateatroretazos.cu/.

148. See http://www.danzahoy.com/home/2014/03/la-tecnologia-se-pone-en-movimiento/cu-posibleimp2/.

149. **Link:** Video of *Encuentro* by Marco Lo Russo with the Danza Teatro Retazos.

14. OTHER PATHS AND DESIRE FOR INDEPENDENCE

Isabel Bustos with Retazos dancers.

Crisálida, Retazos and Memory Wax, 2015.

Posible imposible by Miguel Azcue, the company Retazos, 2014.

institutional sites is housed here. Since 1967, the Oficina del Historiador de la Ciudad de La Habana has been overseen with much dedication by Eusebio Leal Spengler (1942-2020). As the "savior" and guardian of La Habana Vieja, and as the soul of Editorial Boloña, he has offered his support to the choreographer-painter's proposals to have dance be promoted through

Retazos street dancing in Havana.

14. OTHER PATHS AND DESIRE FOR INDEPENDENCE

Poster by Isabel Bustos for the 2017 Street Dancing Festival.

Teatro Retazos building.

The Gigantería Habana.

14. OTHER PATHS AND DESIRE FOR INDEPENDENCE

house-museums and in the streets and squares of the city. This is also with Cuban participants such as Gigantería Habana as well as international entities. Since 1998, the project has been associated with the network *City Dance Network/ Red Ciudades que danzan*, with headquarters in Barcelona. Italian participants, with the support of the Turin festival Interplay, include the group Tecnologia Filosofica and Andrea Gallo Rosso.

Bustos' theater dance works have been nourished by her collaboration with musicians – among whom the Roman accordionist Marco Lo Russo for *Caminos* during the 2015 Italian Culture Week – and sculptors and filmmakers, as well as her interest in drawing from literary inspiration. Her works embrace emotions, feelings, reflections, experiences, dreams, metaphors, and the use of every image – and this is where it all begins, according to the choreographer – and every suggestion that urges creation while improvising. Thus, her works go beyond merely dancing from a technical point of view, to thus enter the expressive universe that springs from poetry. Just to mention only some of the many works that Retazos has presented over these years of steady commitment: *Esperame en el cielo*, named after the moving song by Antonio Machín; *Carmina Burana*; *Las lunas de Lorca*; the triptych *Andares*, *Destinos* and *Momentos*, performed at the Festival Oriente Occidente of Rovereto in 2012; and *El país de las sombras*.

Isabel Bustos likes to cite among her artistic guiding lights: film directors such as Stanislavski and Tarkovsky; writers and poets such as García Lorca and Lezama Lima, and painters such as Botero (*Naturaleza muerta con gallina blanca*). For the choreographer, the body is the paint brush and the canvas.

***Encuentro*, with Marco Lo Russo, Danza Teatro Retazos, 2014.**

Retazos in *Destinos*, for the company's 30th Anniversary, 2017.

14. OTHER PATHS AND DESIRE FOR INDEPENDENCE

Circunloquio, video dance by Laura Domingo Agüero, 2016.

Adolfo Izquierdo and Roxana de los Ríos.

VIDEODANCE

Among the many initiatives that have taken flight in the orbit of Retazos there are: DVDanza Habana, dedicated to videodance; Tecnologías que danzan; the organization Tránsitos Habana that arranges workshop exchanges with Sweden; and Impulsos-Encuentro de Jóvenes Coreógrafos.

In the field of videodance, the company performed in *Allí en el Olvido* and *Frágil*, directed by Javier García and Claudio Frola (2006). Here was a delicate vision poised between eros, solitude, and struggle, with the beautiful theme song *No puedo ser feliz* by singer Bola de Nieve – the romantic and legendary voice of Cuba – about an everyday situation of a woman desperately trying to wash her hair in a sink.

Media coverage of international dance in Cuba, and Cuban dance abroad, is an important stimulus for renewal and learning. "Dance and video have signed a pact to interweave their territories starting from different media: the body as a mobile object-subject, and a carrier of symbols, and the electronic technologies as an instrument to (re)produce the dynamics of variability of an act in a certain dimension, just as the introduction of graphic and sound elements contribute to language" thus wrote Andrés D. Abreu, esteemed exponent of the committee for the organization of Cuba's most important videodance festival, DVDanza Habana, led by Roxana de los Ríos.

Various spaces, among which the Lumière cinema and the FAC, have served as venues for many exemplary works from France, Belgium, Germany, Spain, the United States, and the MERCOSUR. Creative training courses have been held there, and also screenings of *Alicia* by Cuban director Victor Casaus, dedicated to the national ballerina Alicia Alonso, and a film tribute to Lorna Burdsall, leader of USA/Cuba modern dance.

The film *Inexistencia*, based on *Circumloquio* by Laura Domingo Agüero, was shot among the ruins of an abandoned hospital with dancers from the DCC, to music by Max Richter and Pedro Aznar. In 2018,[150] it was among the finalists of the competition *La danza in 1 minuto* (Italy-Canada).

Agüero also co-wrote the docu-film *Cuban Dancer* with director Roberto Salinas, about a young male dancer's story set in Havana and Miami.

---

150. See https://www.facebook.com/pg/DVDanza-Habana-1608636492691025/about/?ref=page_internal.

15.

BALLET, MODERN DANCE, AND EDUCATIONAL REVOLUTION

The revolutionary Cuban government had chosen to invest first of all in the creation of a school based on academic dance. With Alicia Alonso it activated an excellent program of ballet training that steadily developed over time, overcoming critical moments of shortages, conflict or rivalry.[151] However, seeking a "Cuban way" through the less clearly defined terrain of techniques, styles and works of modern and contemporary dance was a more complex challenge.

The founding of the multidisciplinary Escuela Nacional de Arte (ENA) goes back to 1962. It is located in the west of Havana, in the neighborhood of the Cubanacán, and crossed by the insidious Rio Quibú. In the past, the area was a country club "for Whites" a golf course for the "happy few", but the anti-elitist thinking of Castroism had it transformed into a Ciudad de las Artes, where ballet, music, theater, and the plastic arts could be brought together. In 1965, modern and folkloric dance programs also entered the ENA.

From 1976, the higher levels of study of the institution were given university equivalence and grouped under the name of the Instituto Superior de Arte (ISA). This covers a widespread system of all the schools brought under the general entity of the Centro Nacional de Escuelas de Arte (CNEART, 1989). In 1999, the original Havana base ENA/ISA became independent, under the direct jurisdiction of the Ministry of Culture. In the meantime, the sectors of circus arts, musical entertainment, and teaching methodologies were added to the list of areas of study and training.

The Circo Nacional de Cuba (CirCuba) sends an increasing number of excellent troupes abroad. They are admired for their top acrobatic training and the vibrant colors and rhythms of Cuban music and dance. They have a fixed tent in Havana, the Carpa Trompo Loco a Playa.

---

151. Cf. Isis Wirth, *La Ballerine & El Comandante*, *L'histoire secrète du Ballet de Cuba*, François Bourin Ed., Paris 2013.

15. BALLET, MODERN DANCE, AND EDUCATIONAL REVOLUTION

CirCuba.

The buildings of Cubanacán are among the most remarkable representatives of Cuban revolutionary architecture.[152] They were conceived for a great utopia, that is, based upon the ideal of the new man and the new artist during the burst of experimentation of the regime in its enthusiastic and daring beginnings. The structures are in brick and terracotta – locally produced building materials, since imported cement was impossible to obtain – and Catalan arches. The ENA structures were the work of several architects. Ricardo Porro designed the modern dance buildings in wedges around a central space, as if they were shattered glass. For the wing that would house the plastic arts, he based his circular plan and curved lines upon the model of

Escuela de Ballet, architect Vittorio Garatti, Cubanacán, 1961.

---

152. Cf. John Loomis, *Revolution of Forms - Cuba's Forgotten Art Schools*; Robert Wilson has created a theatrical work entitled *Revolution of Forms*.

15. BALLET, MODERN DANCE, AND EDUCATIONAL REVOLUTION

Escuela Nacional de Danza Moderna, architect Ricardo Porro, 1965.

Escuela de Ballet, interior, architect Vittorio Garatti, Cubanacán, 1961.

an African village. Roberto Gottardi conceived pavilions for the dramatic arts with random itineraries within a central space with an amphitheater. Finally, Vittorio Garatti designed the buildings for ballet with several entrances, great volumes, and cupolas. He built serpentine itineraries that wound their way throughout the entire structure to symbolize music. None of these projects however, was ever completed. The pavilions, besieged by the exuberant vegetation, were destined for a touch-and-go fate. Harshly criticized during the Soviet era of functionalism, they were then poorly maintained. In 2010, however, change was in the air and the complex was recognized as a National Monument.

Grand staircase at the ENB.

15. BALLET, MODERN DANCE, AND EDUCATIONAL REVOLUTION

THE ESCUELA NACIONAL DE BALLET: FROM CUBANACÁN (ENA) TO PRADO (ENB)

The beginnings of Cuba's present-day academic dance training may be traced back to 1931 with the ballet classes opened and led by Natalia Arostegui at the Sociedad Pro Arte Musical.[153] These classes were intended to bring a touch of grace to the education of young ladies. The circle Pro Arte was created in 1918 as an undertaking of certain ladies of Havana's high society. During the period from 1934-48 it was directed

Pupils at the ENB.

Pupils at the ENB.

ENB building.

by Laura Rayneri de Alonso. Anna (Ana) Leontieva (1919-1979) then took over the Society and she had more professional ambitions. She had studied at the Opéra de Paris and had also trained with Lubov Egorova, who had been Maurice Béjart's teacher. Leontieva had danced with one of the companies from Colonel de Basil's post-Diaghilev Ballets Russes. She came to Cuba with the company in 1941 and appeared in the revue *Congo Pantera* at the Tropicana. She then decided to open a school in Havana with her mother Eugenia Klemetskaya. Her mother had studied in Saint

---

153. Cf. Célida Parera Villalón, *Pro-Arte-Musical y su Divulgación de Cultura en Cuba, 1918-1967*, self-published/ Senda Nueva de Ediciones, New Jersey 1990; *Historia concisa del ballet en Cub*a, 1974. See also http://www.centropablo. cult.cu/wp-content/uploads/2017/05/sociedad_proarte.pdf. During the decade following the forming of Pro Arte, the Society opened its own auditorium, today named after Amedeo Roldán. Among Pro Arte perfoming guests: Jascha Heifetz, Martha Graham, Vladimir Horowitz, Arthur Rubinstein, Renata Tebaldi, Sergei Rachmaninoff, Pablo Casals, Victoria de los Angeles, Andrés Segovia, Sergei Prokofiev.

15. BALLET, MODERN DANCE, AND EDUCATIONAL REVOLUTION

Practicing a jump during a break at the ENB.

opened, there were 150 pupils and Fernando Alonso was appointed director. He was working on what would become the "Cuban Method" of ballet training: scientific, gradual, virgorous, and organic.

Ramona De Sáa, subsequently director of the ENB, was immediately part of the ENA faculty. It included many young and talented dancers among whom: her twin sister Margarita De Sáa; the "Four Jewels", as they were known (Aurora Bosch, Josefina Méndez,

Petersburg and had been a dancer in Diaghilev's Ballets Russes. Leontieva opened a Ballet Academy in 1943, and in 1955, her Ballet de Cáma. After the revolution, Leontieva's Escuela Provincial de Ballet in Havana played a crucial role in the training of new talent, with special focus on the male dancers among whom Pablo Moré (a.k.a. Moret or More), Raúl Barroso and Jorge Esquivel. Leontieva was also a choreographer for the Ballet Nacional de Cuba (*Exorcismo* and *Mascarada*, 1971, based on texts by Nicolás Guillén).

In 1961, the Escuela de Ballet Alejo Carpentier, which later became the Escuela Provincial Elemental de La Habana, was given the responsibility of the state-run educational program.

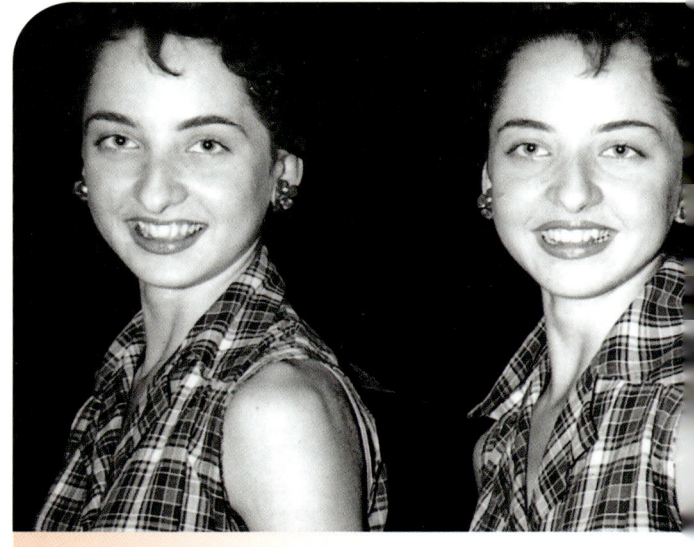

Ramona and Margarita De Sáa.

ENA – ESCUELA NACIONAL DE ARTE

In 1962, as a result of innovative post-revolutionary directions, a national ballet school was founded as part of the ENA. When the school

Mirta Plá, and Loipa Araújo – the latter today associate director of the English National Ballet); and Joaquín Banegas, a student at Pro Arte Musical who was destined to become a pedagogue and *maître*; and his wife, Silvia Marichal of Puerto Rican origin.

168

15. BALLET, MODERN DANCE, AND EDUCATIONAL REVOLUTION

In 1974, the school was organized on two levels, elementary and middle secondary. Those pupils who would become future dance teachers would also follow a course in a new subject: "Metodología de la técnica, didáctica y organización escolar".[154] But in the ENA project at Cubanacán, the ballet section lacked space, since construction of the structure had not been completed. The pupils were obliged to share the facilities of the modern dance students. Quite frequently, however, the students most suited for academic technique were recruited from the ranks of modern dance.

In 1984, the growing number of students made it necessary to transfer the Escuela de Ballet to Miramar where general education classes were held and where the students on scholarships were later housed. Other sites where courses were organized were the Ballet Nacional al Vedado, the Teatro Lírico de La Habana Vieja – for opera, operetta and *zarzuela*, the Spanish musical related to *opera buffa* – and a building on Calzada y 8. Lessons for practical training were organized at the Gran Teatro.

In 1992, the hardships due to the *periodo especial* caused a reduction of the space available at the Gran Teatro, and the postponement of projects for the expansion of the premises at Miramar and the Escuela Provincial Alejo Carpentier. Lessons were therefore held in certain primary and secondary schools, the multipurpose Ramón Fonst facility, which was usually a fencing school, and even on school buses.

ENB – ESCUELA NACIONAL DE BALLET

In 1998, work began on the second floor of the building where the school is presently located, on Prado between Trocadero and Colón. This site was originally destined for the Asociación de Dependientes del Comercio de La Habana (1907). The building was designed by the architect Arturo Amigó, and evoked the sixteenth-century Ca' Vendramin Calergi, where the Venice Casino is located. When the ballet school first moved into the building, the ground floor housed a cinema, and was also used for gymnastic demonstrations and fencing lessons. In 2000, finally all four floors of the structure were made available to the ENB, for a total of seven halls and three rooms, in addition to offices and workshops.

At the head of the ENB, Martha Ulloa Lamelas was succeeded by Ramona Elcira De Sáa Bello (Havana, 1939), whose nickname was "Cheri" – from the French *chérie* ("darling"), but Cubans pronounced "tchayree". She was married to a bodyguard of Fidel Castro and was mother of two daughters who were also both dance teachers: Niurka Naranjo, resident teacher at the Teatro Nuovo in Turin, and Margarita Naranjo, a dance teacher in Mexico, who was tragically murdered at the age of forty-one (2008) by her husband. Their mother Ramona graduated in 1976 from Metodóloga Nacional de la Dirección de Enseñanza Artística, today CNEART. She received a laurea honoris causa in 2000. Brilliant careers are indebted to her knowledge and masterful guidance,[155] such as those of Amparo Brito,

---

154. Cf. María del Carmen Mena Rodríguez, *El cuerpo creativo, taller cubano para la enseñanza de la composición coreográfica*, Colección Súlkary Cuba, Balletin Dance, Buenos Aires (Argentina) 2009.

155. **Link:** Video of the Escuela Nacional de Ballet, exemplary classes by Ramona De Sáa.

15. BALLET, MODERN DANCE, AND EDUCATIONAL REVOLUTION

Rosario Suárez, Tihui Gutiérrez (Mexico), Lorna Feijóo (USA), Alihaydé Carreño, Lázaro Carreño, and Carlos Acosta. Ramona De Sáa's twin sister, Margarita (1941-2017),[156] after her marriage to American dancer John White, previously a guest of the BNC, moved to the United States in 1964. She continued to dance and teach there and was closely involved with the Pennsylvania Ballet. She opened her own school, the Pennsylvania Academy of Ballet Society, with the help of

Mikhail Baryshnikov guest of honor at the ENB, 2007. With him, Fernando Alonso, Azari Plisetsky (in front), Ramona De Sáa, and Martha Iris Fernández Agüero, deputy director.

her daughter Melinda Pendleton. Margarita also appeared in several films, such as in the role of one of the swans in *Funny Girl* starring Barbra Streisand, or in *In Like Flint* with James Coburn. The De Sáa sisters, with détente between the U.S. and Cuba, could finally be reunited in Havana in 2004. They are protagonists in the beautiful documentary, *Mirror Dance* (PBS, 2005),[157] directed by Frances McElroy and María Teresa Rodríguez.

In 1994, the Escuela Nacional de Ballet organized Encuentro de Academias para la Enseñanza del Ballet with the important participation of Latin American countries, and also Spain, Italy, and the United States. In 1995, it also held the competition Concurso Internacional para Estudiantes, for young talents in three age groups. The ENB curriculum includes: ballet, repertory, pointe, folklore and historical dances, music education, fine arts, literature, French language, Spanish language, Cuban history, and also choreographic composition, pedagogy, teaching methodology, and stage professions. Classes begin at 7:00 a.m. depending on the dance studies above, and alongside this training, the student follows general scholastic subjects according to a program that occupies the entire day.

There are triplets among the graduates, a unique case anywhere in the ballet world: Marcos Abraham, Ángel Jesús, and César Josué Ramírez Castellanos. The *trillizos-triplet*s drew unanimous applause at the Premio Fondazione "Carla Fendi" held at Spoleto's Teatro Caio Melisso. The piece was presented by Quirino Conti, with the illusionist *Variación* by Dominican Yeira Genao to music by Lulli. It is only during the finale that the audience discovers that there

---

156. See https://www.dancemagazine.com/margarita-de-saa-white-cuban-ballerina-and-beloved-ballet-teacher-dies-2408556771.html.

157. See http://www.pbs.org/independentlens/mirrordance/film.html. **Link:** Video di *Mirror Dance*.

are actually three dancers and not just one.

In 2016, the first student from the United States was welcomed to the ENB. She was Catherine Conley from Chicago. This was arranged through an exchange program with the Ruth Page

However, going back to the history of the ENA, at the BNC, Alicia Alonso did not like the round layout of the building designed by Garatti. In Alicia Alonso's opinion it was in conflict with the rectilinear geometry that was precisely

The triplets Castellanos of the ENB, Spoleto, 2016.

School, directed by Cuban maestro Victor Alexander Ramírez. There was also another Cuban professor and critic, Ismael Albelo, who was a supporter of this initiative, successfully carried out under the presidency of Barack Obama. The ENB sent Cuban master teachers to the U.S. and received invitations and scholarships for Cuban students in the United States.

at the basis of her art form. The ballet company therefore did not move from its premises in Vedado. The school, however, went to settle in central Havana. It was preparing to become the largest school in the world, with its nearly 3,000 students who received their professional training all for free. Since 2014, the school bears the name "Fernando Alonso" and a huge image of him has been hoisted above the magnificent entrance staircase.

15. BALLET, MODERN DANCE, AND EDUCATIONAL REVOLUTION

At the ENB, under the guidance of Ramona De Sáa, the faculty knew they could count on Clara Carranco, Esther García, Adria Velázquez, Ana Julia Bermúdez, and Martha Iris Fernández Agüero. In addition, they could draw from the formidable experience of Mirta Hermid. She was ballet mistress of numerous Cuban stars whom she had trained during her career from 1966 until she passed away in 2012.

TRAINING IN MODERN DANCE

To teach Cuban modern dance, it was necessary to find a way to train future dancers from zero. If they lacked basic training, it was important to start from their spontaneous talents to then channel these into a structured program. The hips out of line with the axis, breaks of the torso, undulations of the spine, turns in contraction, bucklings, the circular movements of the head, shoulders and above all, the flexibility of the bust, have all become characteristics of modern Cuban *técnica*. The clean body lines, the precise extensions, the strong legs and feet have all marked the origins "*a lo cubano*".

Ramiro Guerra, Lorna Burdsall and Elena Noriega, in search of targeted, specific methods of training, therefore wisely combined their floorwork with Martha Graham's contraction and release work, Doris Humphrey's fall and recovery, and the fluidity of José Limón. Yet of equal importance was to integrate the flexibility of the torso and the strength of the legs that were typically Cuban.[158]

ISA – INSTITUTO SUPERIOR DE ARTE

Today at the Instituto Superior de Arte,[159] created in 1976, the training courses at the Faculdad de Arte Danzario offer three practical majors: Ballet, Contemporary Dance, and Folklore Dance. In addition, there is also an essentially theoretical preparation course to the Dance Sciences that has existed for some time.

The Ballet section is devoted to the study of academic dance, as it is understood universally. In Contemporary Dance, however, corporal practices are developed such as Cuban *técnica*, Graham *técnica* and *body contact* technique.

The section on Folklórica, already a Curso Regular para Trabajadores (CRT), focuses on dances of African heritage, in addition to those of French-Haitian, European, and Latin American origins.

The section on Dance Sciences prepares graduates to pursue studies to become historians, critics and theorists. They may deepen their knowledge of choreographic and aesthetic experience through numerous postgraduate research projects.

The most informed observers now look beyond the greatness of the results that have been achieved, to all that still remains to be accomplished in relation to what is occurring outside of the island nation.

---

158. **Link:** Lesson at the ISA.

159. See http://www.isa.cult.cu/; http://www.lajiribilla.cu/articulo/aportes-de-los-estudios-universitarios-a-la-escuela-cubana-de-ballet.

16.

YORUBA DANCES: CUBA BLANQUINEGRA

During the colonial period, Cuba was a wonderful place if you were wealthy and White.

But if you were Black, your fate would be a life of grueling work on the sugar and coffee plantations. You were only allowed rare breaks for rest and fun, mainly through music and dance. You were allowed to worship according to your particular religion during a few permitted moments. In Cuba, it was possible for Black enslaved people to buy their freedom. Yet they were always the ones to do the hard work in Cuba's three main sectors. There were the plantations of *azúcar* (owned by sugar magnate and financier Julio Lobo. His collection of Napoleonic memorabilia is today housed in Havana's Museo di Villa Dolce Dimora, charming villa in Florentine Renaissance style).[160] There was the production of *ron* (you would have worked for the Bacardi family, today based in Santiago).[161] There was *tabaco* (Fernández Rocha and Partagás were masters of *puro habano* cigars);[162] and *café* (you would have worked for José Antonio Gelabert). Coffee production in Cuba originated from seeds brought from Santo Domingo coupled with Haitian know how (Haiti is also where *tumba francesa* comes from).

The White population were the entrepreneurs. Their job was to exploit and enjoy the fruits of these activities. Their source of labor were enslaved people or workers paid next to nothing such as the Chinese "*Culíes*". Their treatment of these workers was arbitrary, depending upon the generosity of the masters or bosses.

A railway system – the first in Latin America – was already in service in Cuba by 1834. By 1889, there was electricity. Infrastructures such as these were needed for the production and transport particularly of sugar, coffee and tobacco. And, in

---

160. Cf. Joahn Paul Rathbone, *The Sugar King of Havana*, Penguin Book, London 2010.
161. Cf. Tom Gjelten, *Bacardi and the Long Fight for Cuba*, Penguin Books, New York 2008.
162. See http://www.conexioncubana.net/general/el-tabaco-cubano-2/4457-la-historia-del-tabaco-version-oficial and http://www.lahabana.com/guide/museo-del-tabaco/.

16. YORUBA DANCES: CUBA *BLANQUINEGRA*

Pierre Toussaint Frédéric Mialhe, a carriage ride, "Quitrin", 1855.

Slave traders, 1881.

Port of Havana, 1904.

Label for *cigarillos* of the brand Para Usted, 1850.

"*Sin azúcar no hay país*", "No sugar, no country".

16. **YORUBA** DANCES: CUBA *BLANQUINEGRA*

Gate to the *Barrio Chino*, Havana's Chinatown.

El Museo del Ron, Havana Club Rum Museum.

Tobacco production.

Chinese indentured laborers, "*Culíes*", 1860.

Harvesting coffee.

the city of Havana, people were riding in streetcars by 1859.

The discontinuity applied by the Castroist revolution greatly changed the social and economic face of the Isla Grande.

AFRO-CUBAN CULTURE: THE AFRICAN PATRIMONY

From the end of the sixteenth century, an oral culture that would be kept alive over centuries was brought to Cuba by the enslaved people of Africa.[163] To the present day, this vital culture affects every aspect – and every social class and milieu – of life in Cuba and has survived all political upheavals.

During the nineteenth century, more than half a million Black Africans were brought to the island. They were from various ethnic groups: Lucumí/Yoruba from West Africa; Bantù from the Congo (who settled particularly in the eastern part of the island and in Matanzas; Carabalì from Nigeria (Calabar) and Cameroon; Mandingo from Senegal, Upper Niger, Gambia; Macua from Mozambique; and then the Bambara, Diola/Jola, Ganga (there is disagreement as to their places of origin), Fon and Arará from Benin.[164]

Revolts, escapes, inter-racial unions,

Bracelets of the *Orishas*.

and new progressive ideas little by little created a varied fabric in the panoply of the population of color: enslaved people born in Africa who did not speak Spanish (*Bozales*), those who had

Ancient Batá drums of the *cabildo* Changó Tedún, Havana.

---

163. Cf. Fernando Ortiz, *Los negros esclavos*, Ciencias Sociales, Havana 1987; https://www.britannica.com/biography/Fernando-Ortiz#ref752631; José Antonio Piqueras, *La esclavitud en las Españas, un lazo transatlántico*, Los Libros de la Catarata, Madrid 2012.
164. For tables and details see http://www.hispanocubano.org/cas/cul1c1.pdf.

16. YORUBA DANCES: CUBA BLANQUINEGRA

Altar with Santa Barbara-Changó in the center.

learned the language of their masters (*Ladinos*), children of Black parents born in Cuba (*Criollos*), who were emancipated and liberated.

The religious practices of the enslaved people were referred to by the overall term "*Santería*".[165] Coming from a White person, the term could be condescending – in the same way as in Haiti "*Vudú*" was used, and in Brazil, "*Candomblé*".

These rites and rituals were tolerated and channeled to avoid dangerous unrest. The structure of the Spanish Roman Catholic confraternities of mutual assistance were the model. The various ethnic groups from Africa organized themselves into *cabildos*, each with its own music and dances.[166]

The *Bembé*, with its *Toques de Santo*, was also part of the celebrations of the Lucumí/Yoruba. This is an event every half century during which the divinities, the *Orishas*, are honored through singing and dance. Dances and chants open the *caminos* as an invocation to the *Orishas* to join the festivities. Every god is associated to a rhythm (*toque*) to be played on ritual drums called *batá*.

The *Ñáñigos*, or *Abakuá*, belong to Carabalí roots and are from southeastern Nigeria. They perform rites of initiation like a secret society and perform dances for the event when they wear masks of *íremes* or *diablito*.

The *Palo Monte* and *Regla Mayombe* systems of beliefs originate in the Congo-Angolian line. The *yuca*, a sinuous dance, yet during which couples never touch, are of Congo-Angolian origin just as the *makuta*, and the martial art and war dance *juego de maní* (or *bambosa*). The words *conga*, *bongo*, and *mambo* derive from the language of the Congolese ethnic group.

The syncretic *Yoruba* religion became

---

165. Cf. Raúl Canizares, *Cuban Santeria*, Destiny Books, Vermont 1993, Spanish tr. *Santería Cubana, El sendero de la noche*, Lasser Press, Mexico 2001; Katherine J. Hagedorn, *Divine Utterance, The Performance of Afro-Cuban Santería*, with CD, Smithsonian Institution Press, Washington, London 2001; Margarite Fernandez Olmos, Lizabeth Paravisini-Gerbert, *The Orisha Tradition in Cuba*, Chap. 2 and 3, in *Creole Religions of the Caribbean: An Introduction from Vodou and Santeria, to Obeah and Espiritismo*, New York University 2003; Yvonne Daniel, *Dancing Wisdom, Embodied Knowledge in Haitian Vodou, Cuban Yoruba and Bahian Candomlé*, University of Illinois Press, Champaign 2005; Alex Cuoco, *African Narratives of Orishas, Spirits and Other Deities – Stories from West Africa and the African Diaspora: A Journey Into the Realm of Deities*, SPI, Outskirts Press, Denver 2014.

166. For the bibliography by and on Lydia Cabrera, pioneer and authoritative scholar on the cultural and anthropological Afro-Cuban universe, see http://www.circulodeculturapanamericano.org/bibliografia_sub_pgs/LYDIACABRERA.html.

16. YORUBA DANCES: CUBA BLANQUINEGRA

absorbed by the religions of other populations of African origin living in Cuba. Today, synonymous with the universe of the *Santería* and its officiants, above all the *Babalawo* ("Father of the Mysteries") are: the *Ifá* priest who acts for Good and interprets the sacred scriptures; the 256 *Odu* signs – used for divination, obtained by throwing special shells; and the *Regla de Osha* (another name for *Santería*).[167] The latter oversees the practices of initiation for anyone who desires to "*pasar santo*". For this, the person must belong to an *Orisha*. To begin the process, he must dress only in white for a year (the color that symbolizes the principle of a new life). Terminology related to the *Santería* has entered the language and deeply influenced it. For example, "*montarse*", to be "*mounted*", "*subirse*" to "*endure*" are all terms that indicate when a *santero* is possessed by an *Orisha* (as in a religious trance); "*tener santo lavado*" or more imperatively, "*santo hecho*", means that a person has completed all the rituals of affiliation to his Saint. Even the common wish "*Aché*" refers to the *Yoruba* concept of vital force, power in life and through the songs.

Lázaro Ros.

RELIGION AND POLITICS

After the Cuban revolution, Catholicism and Afro-Cuban religions were considered an obstacle to the people's full adherence to the new ideology. Since it was secularized and egalitarian, these religions represented a threat, particularly during the period when Cuba relied on Soviet assistance. *Yoruba* rites were thus conducted in secret.

As relations with the country of 'real socialism' began to fail, in 1992 the Cuban constitution was amended with the addition of an article that prohibited discrimination on the basis of religious belief. An indication of this change was *¿Y qué tú quieres que te den?*, a popular song recorded precisely in 1992 by Orquesta Adalberto Álvarez y su Son, in which the syncretic saints are invoked.

The interest sparked by the universe of the *Santería* (or, more popularly, "*religión*") has also acquired commercial aspects (known as "*Santurismo*") in today's Cuba. A certain amount of money is needed, which can be quite considerable for non-Cubans, to follow the path that leads to the ceremony *coronación de santo*. To the delight of tourists, and despite being frowned

---

167. **Link:** Documentary *Planet Santería*.

16. YORUBA DANCES: CUBA BLANQUINEGRA

upon by purists, it is often possible to watch stylized dances of the *Orishas* on Havana's restored Plaza Vieja.

CONJUNTO FOKLÓRICO NACIONAL DE CUBA

The orthodoxy of Afro-Cuban cultures was studied by the Instituto Nacional de Etnología y Folklore, created in 1961. It was initially directed by Fernando Ortiz (1881-1969), and after him by Argeliers León (1918-1991). It gave the popular Afro-Cuban culture and its religious events and celebrations an official scientific and anthropological basis.

The Conjunto Foklórico Nacional de Cuba (CFNC) was created in 1962. Its purpose was to continue to promote popular culture and to preserve ethnographic authenticity. This was in response to the threat of exotic representations intended to appeal to tourists. The objective was to render this culture theatrical without falsifying it.[168] It intended to respect the original patrimony, yet also the demands of artistic creation.

The CFNC was asked to make the popular *rumba*, as well as expressions of rural *campesino* life and folklore into theatre entertainment. The CFNC held auditions and hundreds of singers, dancers and musicians flocked to the selection. There were 58 artists chosen to make their debut at the Teatro Mella.

Zenaida Armenteros.

Ballet Folklórico de Oriente in a *Tumba francesa*.

---

168. Cf. Ramiro Guerra, *op. cit.*, 1989.

16. *YORUBA* DANCES: CUBA *BLANQUINEGRA*

Asociación Yoruba de Cuba.

Reyes Cortés. They of course drew from the wealth of experience of artists such as Lázaro Ros (1925-2005) previously mentioned. Ros was self-taught and possessed a rich knowledge of the songs of the *Santería*. The dancer, singer, and actress Zenaida Armenteros (1931) was also an invaluable source. The CFNC company performed in Cuba and internationally. Yet it also organized workshops for foreigners to reveal the genuine "secrets" of *mambo*, *rumba*, *conga*, *cha-cha-cha*, *Mozambique*, and *pilón*.

The film *Historia de un ballet* directed by José

The repertory included *Yoruba* cycles (Eleguá, Changó, Ochún, Yemayá, Oggún), *palo congo*, *rumba*, Palo songs and dances, Maní, Yuka and Makuta, and *comparsa de los negros curros* (on freed slaves). These works remained in the troupe's repertory.

Experts such as Nieves Fresneda, Trinidad Torregrosa, Emilio O'Farrill, Isora Pedroso and Lázaro Ros helped to structure the approach to the material so that it would remain faithful to its most authentic core. This specific profile was originally traced by the Cuban "*griot*"[169] Rogelio Martínez Furé[170] (Matanzas, 1937), ethnologist, writer, and poet, and by the Mexican choreographer Rodolfo

"Casa de Africa", Havana.

Massip is based upon *Suite Yoruba*,[171] with cho-

---

169. "*Griot*" is the term for an African oral historian and storyteller.
170. Cf. Rogelio Martínez Furé, *Prismas de la memoria*, Editorial Letras Cubanas, Havana 2004.

171. **Link:** Nieves Fresneda-Yemayá in *Suite Yoruba* filmed by José Massip in *Historia de un ballet* (ICAIC, 1962) with the voice of Lázaro Ros.

16. *YORUBA* DANCES: CUBA *BLANQUINEGRA*

reographies by Ramiro Guerra. In the film, produced in 1962 by the Cuban national film institute, Istituto cubano dell'arte e dell'industria cinematografica (ICAIC), we see a young Lázaro Ros, then in his thirties; Nicolás Guillén, Cuban poet of the Négritude movement who recites verses from *Son número 6*; the *tamborero* Jesús Pérez; and singer Eugenio de la Rosa "*El yerbero*" (referring to a "vendor of medicinal herbs"), from the generation before Ros, and that was indisputably an inspiration. Lázaro Ros was later central to a documentary in posthumous homage to the legendary figure, as an *Ochún Niwé* (member of the *Santería*), *Akpwón Mayor* (singer of the *Santería*), and great singer-prophet of the Lucumí culture.

The active repertory of the CFNC today, with its dancers trained at the ENA, includes the works of the company's present director, Manolo Micler: *Coro y danza de apalencados*; *Obatereo*; *Dahomenyo*; *Oriki a Obatalá*; *Danza de canastas*, with baskets carried on their heads as they dance; and *Campesino*. Other works in the repertory, such as Ana Luisa Cáceres': *Bailes guajiros*, *Música popular*, and *Comparsa la jardinera*. And of course, numerous works by Lázaro Ros, Domingo Pau, Rodolfo Reyes, in addition to works by contemporary choreographers such as Santiago Alfonso, Lizt Alfonso, Isidro Rolando, Danny Villalonga, Pancho González, Alberto Méndez and Alexander Varona Marrero. The company has thus created, together with its basic permanent elements, a rich catalogue of works that represent Cuba's cultural roots

The CFNC also proposes performances of *zapateo*, *punto guajiro*, *toques de tumba francesa* and the Cabildo Carabalí Izuama, with its typical dances from Santiago and the eastern part of Cuba.

DANCE OF THE *ORISHAS*

The stories of events in which the *Orishas* are protagonists are called *patakín*. These are myths or apologues that unfold against a moral backdrop. The *patakín*, with their stories of loves, rivalries, escapes and disguises, are comparable to the epics of polytheistic mythology of ancient Greece. As Greek divinities, each *Orisha* has its own personality, symbols, and *collares*[172] of different colors. Every *Orisha* also has a corresponding figure from the Catholic religion (called syncretic saints). For example, Obatalá, the protectress of the world, is associated to the Virgen de la Merced. Her color is white. Orula, the god of divination, is linked to Saint Francis of Assisi and the colors yellow and green. In addition, every *Orisha*, to participate in the dances of the *Yoruba* pantheon, has its characteristic *toque*, colors, and gestures that refer to its distinctive features.[173]

ELEGUÁ – The divinity that opens the way, the messenger.
Syncretic saint: St. Anthony of Padua.
Colors: Red and black.
Gestures: With a branch of a *guayaba* (or guava) tree, the god opens the way.

OGGÚN – God of war.
Syncretic saint: St. Peter.
Colors: Indigo and green.
Gestures: He dances as a *herrero* ("blacksmith") as he strikes an anvil with a hammer or hits one

---
172. Cf. Lourdes S. Dominguez, *Los collares en la Santería cubana*, Editorial José Martí, Havana 2009.
173. **Link:** Video of *Fiesta de los Orishas* del CFNC.

16. YORUBA DANCES: CUBA BLANQUINEGRA

(from left to right, beginning from above) Eleguá, Oggún, Oyá, Changó, Ochún, Yemayá and Babalú Ayé.

hand against the other. He pretends to flail a sword in the air, or advances with back stooped and limping, as he drags a foot behind him. Otherwise, he may go through the motions of working in the fields and overturning the earth. Sometimes he may go hunting with bow and arrow.

CHANGÓ (Shangó) – God of fire and lightning.
Syncretic saint: St. Barbara with tower, chalice and sword.
Colors: Red and white.
Gestures: He dances with closed fists and mimes the throwing of meteorites (stones) taken from a bag. Otherwise, he majestically brandishes a double-edged hatchet.

16. YORUBA DANCES: CUBA BLANQUINEGRA

OYÁ (Oia) – Goddess of winds and storms.
Syncretic saint: Virgen de la Candelaria.
Color: Burgundy
Gestures: She moves a fly swatter made of horsehair and churns the air to create winds that will keep bad spirits away. She shakes her multicolored skirt at times creating swirls. She brandishes a sword of copper and turns like a top. The movement of her arms held up above her seems to be the summing up of all her characteristics. A virtuosic dance performed in time, or in syncopation with the beat of the drums.

OCHÚN (Oshún) – Goddess of beauty.
Syncretic saint: Virgen de la Caridad del Cobre, protectress of Cuba.
Color: Golden yellow.
Gestures: She moves her arms as if she were splashing water on her face from a river. She bathes her body with slow movements, looks in the mirror, combs her hair, and adorns herself as she exalts her femininity.

YEMAYÁ – Goddess of waters.
Syncretic saint: Nuestra Señora de la Regla.
Colors: Blue and white.
Gestures: She moves her blue skirt bordered with white to suggest the waves and foam of the sea. She swings her arms in the opposite direction from her legs, with undulating movements of the torso.

BABALÚ AYÉ – God of illness and poverty.
Syncretic saint: St. Lazarus, with his two dogs.
Color: Purple.
Gestures: He has a little brush with which he cleans his wounds. He is bent and moves like an old, infirm person with his hands stiff and gnarled.

The way the dancers move clearly reflects African roots:[174] the shoulders are bent forward, hips back, and knees bent. The feet are planted firmly on the ground as they respond to the divine call from the earth. These elements are also found in popular dance, though here, in addition, the arms and legs are pushed forward and away from the torso. There are stops and an oscillation and vibration of the shoulders and pelvis.

The Asociación Yoruba de Cuba is a religious institution that gathers and makes available information on Afro-Cuban rituals and worship. It has two conference rooms, the "Manolo Ibáñez", (founder of the Association), and the "Alberto Pedro" room, dedicated to the ethnologist and researcher.[175] There is a room for exhibitions called the "Merceditas Valdés" (1922-1996), in memory of the great singer of songs inspired by the *Yoruba* culture. The Museo de los Orishas houses a theme collection on Afro-Cuban divinities. The Association regularly publishes the "Letra del Año", with the predictions from the *Orishas* for followers.

The Casa de Africa is located in a seventeenth-century building on Calle Obrapia, in what was historically a snuff shop. Today it houses an exhibition of objects from various origins and African cultures such as sculptures, ritual masks, musical instruments, fabrics and clothing, as well as gifts received by Fidel Castro from the governments of various nations. The ground floor houses an exhibit of testimonies dating back to the era of slavery. The third floor displays a collection on the *Santería* that belonged to the anthropologist and essayist Fernando Ortiz.

---

174. Cf. Katina Genero Madrigal, *Tubab, una danzatrice sulla via dei tamburi*, con CD, Ananke, Turin 2000.
175. Cf. Alejandro de la Fuente, *Race, Inequality and Politics in Twentieth Century*, The University of North Carolina Press, Chapel Hill 2001.

Rumba at Calejón del Hamel, Havana.

17.

POPULAR DANCES: THE RHYTHMS OF CUBA

If nothing remains of the music of the *indios*, the Taínos[176] or Siboney, there is however a famous hit song, now become a great standard, entitled precisely *Siboney*. It is interesting to note how even the title of another famous song, *Sandunguera*, from the word "*sandunga*", encompasses the essence of several cultures. It is composed of "*sa*", the white salt of Andalusia, and "*ndungu*", the black pepper from the African continent. The contributions from Africa and those from the European patrimony are evident in the Cuban musical mix. There are the *jotas*, *soleá*, *tanguillos*, *gaditanos*, and *malagueñas* from Spain. From France, the minuets, *contradanse*, and *rigodon*. These have merged with the cultures from across the seas, from Africa, and together they have created the composite musical richness of the island. It is one that also resounds in its exalting rhythms that are as numerous as they are varied.

Africa introduced syncopated rhythm into Cuban music, and this element makes it unique. It is based upon the *clave*, the omnipresent measure of time consisting of four strong beats and four weak beats divided in two consecutive rhythmic cells. The beats that are stressed determine whether the rhythm is from the *clave blanca* in 3/2 time, the *rumba yambú* or the *son*, or the *clave negra* in 2/3 time of *rumba*. The *clave* is beaten out with two sticks (*palos*) that produce a quick soft sound like a *toc*. The left hand, that acts as a sound box, holds the "female" stick. It is struck with the "male" stick held in the right hand.

---

176. Cf. Daniel Torres Etayo, *Taínos, Mitos y realidades de un pueblo sin rostro*, Editorial Asesor Pedagógico, Mexico 2006. The Cuban performer and body artist Ana Mendieta (1948-1985) was a controversial and provocative figure. In 1981 she created a series of semi-abstract images carved in the soft rock of the quarries in Jaruco Park, on the outskirts of Havana. She gave them names of ancient goddesses worshipped by the indigenous peoples. See also https://www.castellodirivoli.org/wp-content/uploads/2012/12/giornale_ana_mendieta_definitivo.pdf. Similarly, in the nineties, Cuban performer Tania Bruguera (1968), staged the representation "El peso de la culpa", about the indigenous population who committed mass suicide by eating earth as resistance against the Spanish conquerors.

17. POPULAR DANCES: THE RHYTHMS OF CUBA

***Conga*, Santiago de Cuba.**

The *tumbao*, the basic pulsation of Cuban music, is an "innate" skill of rhythmic reactivity that is required of the dancers, too. This is executed in the bass, and its patterns are present even in the carnivalesque *conga* that, drawing also from *rumba*, adds to the sound of the *trompeta china* ("Chinese trumpet").

The *tumbao* is the exciting beat of what is called the Cuban *timba*. It is probably more generally known internationally as *salsa*.

The list of types of music that are also still related to a dance and the spontaneous creation of shared[177] popular dance[178] is broad and labyrinthine, with tangles and fusions of all kinds. Let us limit ourselves to the most frequent forms in this partial list:

Bolero	*Rumba*
Cha-cha-cha	*Salsa*
Conga	*Salsa gorda (or) brava*
Danzón	*(or) dura*
Danzonete	*Salsatón*
Guaracha	*Son*
Mambo	*Songo*
Mozambique	*Timba*
Pregón	*Trova – Nueva trova*
Pilón	*Reggaetón – Reguetón*
Punto guajiro	*– Cubatón – Traptón*

---

177. For famous Cuban dance couples see http://www.mariaargeliavizcaino.com/m-FamosasParejasdeBailePopularCubano.html.
178. **Link:** Video on Cuban popular dances.

17. POPULAR DANCES: THE RHYTHMS OF CUBA

ERAS AND GENRES

Whether composers, performers, or arrangers, Cuban music is spread by word of mouth, from musician to musician and singer to singer. The Cuban people know and love every song, every artist, every performance.

Generally speaking, the twenties and thirties were characterized by the *son*, *rumba* and *conga*. The golden years, the forties and fifties, were the era of the *cha-cha-cha* with the *charangas* (orchestras that played *son*, *danzón*, Creole and Hispano-Afro-Haitian music) and the *descargas* (jam sessions). The sixties were the years of the *pachanga*, a mixture of *son montuno* and the *merengue* dominicano, not far from the *cha-cha-cha*. The decade of the seventies saw the arrival of the *nueva timba* – *timbales* (kettledrums in pairs). These were played suggesting North American funk and eventually disco music. In the nineties the phenomenon of the Buena Vista Social Club exploded. It picked up the vein of the music of the Havana club of the same name at Calle 31 that had been closed during the forties. American guitarist Ry Cooder, with his long-standing musicians, revived the band in 1996. The group took the name of the club and recorded an album that was a huge hit in 1997. The band was destined to become the glorious protagonist of a documentary by Wim Wenders in 1999.

Rumba

Rumba, the mother of all Cuban popular dances[179] and "*orgullo del folclor urbano en Cuba*", was born as a dance of the outcast *negra* communities on the docks of the ports of Havana and Matanzas. There are three *rumba* genres: *yambú*, *guaguancó* and *columbia*.

The lyrics of *rumba* are improvised texts with a mixture of African and Latin influences that date back to the late 1800s (just as the tango on the Mar de la Plata). The songs may express the most disparate themes and its subjects can range from

Rumba yambú, Ireme de Asere Troupe.

mother to enemy, *Orishas* to historic moments, love to nature.

During the colonial period, *rumba* was considered with condescension, as an inferior form of expression that was to be left to the African population. Nevertheless, these same people were encouraged to perform "commercial" music for the enjoyment of the White population in specially designated places. Nevertheless, this discrimination was not enough to crush the *rumba*.

The *rumbera* couple are dressed all in white with a touch or two of red. This could be a red handkerchief for the man, and the red trimmings

---

179. **Link:** Documentary on the *rumberos*. See also: https://www.diariolasamericas.com/la-rumba-patrimonial-n4112016.

17. POPULAR DANCES: THE RHYTHMS OF CUBA

***Rumba guaguancó**, Niurka Aguero and Ariel Bridon.*

***Rumba columbia**, El Palenque Habana, Saturday Rumba.*

on the woman's wide skirt. Both dancers respond with their whole bodies to the rhythm set by the musicians. The man waves his handkerchief in the direction of the woman he is courting, as a provocation. The couple dance in the middle of the *músicos* (usually *claves*, *cajónes*, *congas*, and *catá* players) to the syncopated crescendo of the *tumbadoras* and to the song they accompany. The *rumba* might be a *yambú*, that originated in the western port, with its slow rhythm. In this dance, the couple moves together in mutual understanding without ever touching. *Rumba* could also be the style called *guaguancó*, from Havana, that mimes the motions of Eros in the thrusts of the hips, shaking and vibrating during stops, and dips of the pelvis towards the ground. The *vacuna* is a typical movement while dancing the *rumba guaguancó*. During this dance, the woman tries to anticipate the actions of the man and to protect herself from his advances. Yet, at the same time, she never stops provoking him. The man in the meantime tries to catch her off her guard to symbolically possess her with pelvic movements. He motions towards her belly with a handkerchief which is used like an erotic instrument of intrusion. This play is also comparable to the dances of milonga and tango. It is as if the two partners are playing a match: the man attacks to try to surprise the woman. She defends

"Palacio de la Rumba", Havana.

herself by wrapping her skirt around her legs, covering her pelvic area with her hand like a fig leaf, or pressing her knees together. The *rumba* of the genre *columbia*, however, is danced almost always by men. It originated in the farming areas in the central interior of the island. The *columbia* is characterized by very quick foot work, fluid movements of the shoulders, and sudden stops. The women *rumberas* have the role of seduction, with undulating, agile movements of the spine, and a very mobile pelvis.

There are many places and events today that cultivate and promote *rumba* on the island. The Palacio de la Rumba, that opened in 2009 in Cayo Hueso, in central Havana, hosts the International Timbalaye Festival. Callejón de Hame is also in the popular area of Cayo Hueso and is one of the centers of Afro-Cuban culture with giant murals and *rumba* dancing on Sundays. The neighborhood is named after Fernando Hamel, an arms trafficker and shrewd merchant who imposed his protection on the entire area. There is *rumba* dancing on Saturdays at the Centro Cultural el Gran Palenque, in Miramar. This is also where the Conjunto Folklórico Nacional is located.

TROVA AND BOLERO

Other fundamental elements at the soul of Cuban music are the *trova* and the *bolero*, that is, the invention of spontaneous storytelling and its expression through the singing of romantic ballads.

During the eighteenth century the *trovadores*, or wandering minstrels, mainly present in the eastern part of the island, made their living by impromptu singing as they composed on the guitar.

Pepe Sánchez (Santiago de Cuba 1856-1918) is known as the forefather of the *trova*. His first *bolero*, *Tristezas* (1885), is still a beloved, frequently performed song. Another enduring figure is the resourceful Sindo Garay. Illiterate until the age of sixteen, after participating in the war of independence, he travelled from Haiti to Paris with

"Casa de la Trova", Santiago de Cuba.

Cuban artist Rita Montaner. Garay was known as "The man who shook hands with José Martí and Fidel Castro". He was admired by Carlos Puebla, author of *Y en eso llegó Fidel* and *Hasta siempre Comandante – Che Guevara*. Puebla was one of the greatest exponents of the *nueva trova*. He was a specialist of *bolero* and songs with national themes and was thus known as *"El cantor de la revolución"*. Also among the most famous internationally acclaimed artists are Compay Segundo and the Trio Matamoros.

The guitar, the main instrument used in the *trova* and *bolero*, has undergone considerable technical development over the years. Eliades Ochoa, a maestro of the guitar and also the *trés* (the Cuban guitar with six strings divided into three couples

17. POPULAR DANCES: THE RHYTHMS OF CUBA

of two strings),[180] has conceived a mixed instrument of eight strings. Ochoa is one of the standard-bearers of innovation in our modern era.

These troubadours, with the gift of improvising on any given theme, are called *repentistas*. One of the most famous, the poet Orlando Laguardia, performs at the restaurant Bodeguita del Medio that was Ernest Hemingway's favorite

Danzón.

haunt during his famed stays in Cuba. It is today a necessary tourist stop.

During the forties and the fifties a genre emerged called *filin* (from the word *feeling*), and Pablo Milanés was one of its noted exponents. The style cultivated a romantic jazz feeling influenced by American crooners and legendary singers such as the magnificent Ella Fitzgerald, Nat King Cole, and Sarah Vaughan.

Danzón

The smooth, flowing and elegant *danzón* was very popular during the thirties. With its variations in tempo, turns, and changes of direction, it is danced not only in Cuba, but also in many Latin American countries where mass public events are held. *Danzón* is the dance that most closely resembles the tango from Rio de la Plata. Tango also enjoyed tremendous success in Cuba thanks to radio, and also singer Emilio Ramil, the "Cuban Gardel".

Son

According to veteran Ibrahim Ferrer (1927-2005), who was the musician, singer and legend of the Buena Vista Social Club, *son* is the veritable heart of Cuban music.

The Spanish-African origins and genres of the Cuban *son* are many: *son montuno*, *son oriental*, *son santiaguero* and *son habanero*.

The early styles of *son* were the *changüí*, accompanied by the typical *marimbula* – a *cajón* with holes so that it became a sound box with metal vibrating blades – the *nengón*, the *kiribá* and the *regina*, associated with the rural Afro-Cuban peoples of Bantù origin. They were present in the east of the island.[181]

The first recording of *son* dates back to 1917 and marked the emergence of a genre destined to grow. Over the years, increasingly more instruments were added to the music, including piano. This finally led to the creation of bands of six, such as the Sexteto Habanero of the twenties, and then seven musicians, such as the Septeto Na-

---

180. With its decisive yet gentle sound, the *trés* guitar is typical of the genre *punto guajiro*. With a spirit that Is rural and poetic, Its origins are both Spanish (*seguidilla*) and Cuban.

181. **Link:** Video *Son cubano, Una historia de la música cubana*.

17. POPULAR DANCES: THE RHYTHMS OF CUBA

cional Ignacio Piñeiro. In the forties and fifties, many more *conjuntos* appeared, and they included trumpets and drums in addition to the piano.

It was Piñeiro himself who brought to the *son* his *rumbera* sensitivity. This was the theme of his cult *Hechale salsita*, the song that in fact actually gave *salsa* its name. Celia Cuz, the famous *sonera* singer, claims that *salsa* does not really exist, but

Performing a *son* "tornillo" spin.

that *salsa* is *son*, the root of all the dances. Celia was the great *guarachera*, the *Diosa rumba*, the born *sonera*. She had sung every one of its songs, and in her early days the tango *Nostalgia* too. She was a backup singer for Radio Cadena before launching into a vertiginous career as a solo vocalist in Cuba and internationally.

Miguel Matamoros, admired for his *boleros*, brought the *trova* into *son* with his trio formed in 1925. He later expanded the trio into a *conjunto*, and made Beny Moré,[182] the mythic, divine, "greatest of all time" singers, the voice of the band from 1945 to 1947. Songs such as *Lágrimas negras* and *Son de la loma* ("They come from the hill"), were still beloved hits right up to the disbanding of the *conjunto* in 1961. And before his premature death, Beny Moré (1919-1963), "El Beny", "El barbaro del ritmo" with his hat and sacred-magic cane, marked the birth of a myth – *son*, *mambo*, *guaracha*, or *bolero*, he had made them all his signature.

The *son* came from the eastern mountains of Cuba accompanied by a guitar, a *clave* and a *güiro* (an oblong instrument, open and scored, to be scraped with a stick). Perhaps through soldiers, it won over Havana in the early 1900s and from there embarked for New York. During the seventies the *son* became known as *salsa*. It began to rival with the nascent hip hop sound and put excitement into Latin Jazz. In the meantime in Cuba, it evolved into styles such as the quick and striking *songo* and *timba*. *Salsa* thus became an all-encompassing word, a blanket term that spread throughout Latin America and was adopted by the North American *Latinos*. *Salsa*, in fact, consisted of Cuban and Puerto Rican music, as well as *fusion* and *free style*. It is interesting to note that when a couple is dancing, it is the woman partner who at times offers support to the man. An example would be the dance movement called *tornillo*. The woman spins the man on the floor as he rests on one leg bent at an angle under a buttock. The rest of the man's body lays parallel to the floor while finally – the last finishing touch – he flips his cap through the air and catches it over his free foot.[183]

---

182. Cf. Raúl Martínez Rodríguez, *Benny Moré*, Música Cubana/Letras Cubanas, Havana 1994, 1999.

183. **Link:** Video of a *son* at Caribedanza festival 2009.

17. POPULAR DANCES: THE RHYTHMS OF CUBA

***Mambo* scene in the film *West Side Story*, 1961.**

Mambo

The word *mambo* is sometimes associated with the Haitian *mambo*, "voodoo priestess", or with the Kilongo African idiom that means "conversation with the gods". With the dance's vitality and its syncopated beat and pauses, it held its own even with pop music and won the hearts of Americans. And the *cha-cha-cha*, with its onomatopoeic reference to three-time, also contributed to this success. With its energetic steps, *mambo*[184] is danced with quick support from the tips of the toes, and short jumps and kicks. It emerged in 1937, as remembers Israel López, "Cachao" (1918-2008), the double bass player, composer, and rhythm king. *Mambo* first began as *son-mambo*, in a romantic mood, then started to gain popularity in Mexico and the United States. The call "*dale mambo*" is often heard during *salsa* dancing as if to draw attention to the natural relationship between the two rhythms.

As flautist and conductor Antonio Arcaño (1911-1994) remembered, orchestras were aware of the dancers' desire to always improvise and create new steps. From the traditional *danzón*,

Dámaso Pérez Prado.

they invented *mambo*, a "*danzón de nuevo ritmo*", in a supremely creative and intense dialogue between the dancers on the floor and the musicians in the band. This dialogue also occurred for the swing in the States during the twenties and

---

184. Cf. AA.VV., *El mambo*, Editorial Letras Cubanas, Havana 1993, with an essay by Gabriel García Márquez, *Mambo en Nueva York*, and a conversation with Pérez Prado.

17. POPULAR DANCES: THE RHYTHMS OF CUBA

thirties, remarked choreographer Frankie Manning[185], who had witnessed the evolution of the historic Savoy's most creative dance. Manning had created choreographies for cinema, for Alvin Ailey's company, and for the show *Black and Blue* conceived by Argentinians Héctor Orezzoli and Claudio Segovia. The latter were brilliant writers and directors to whom we are indebted for the revival of the *porteño* world and tango through their 1983 musical stage production *Tango Argentino*, and the folklore of Spain in 1984 with *Flamenco puro*, a whirlwind of rhythms and dances. The duo's last work *Noche Tropical* (1992) was based on Cuban *son* and *rumba*, featuring the dancer Luís Tellez of the Tropicana. In 2005, Segovia created *Brazil brasileiro*, all in samba, capoeira, maxixe, and lambada.

"Rueda de casino", Club 1830, Havana.

Dámaso Pérez Prado (Matanzas, Cuba 1917 - Mexico City 1989) had conservatory training before he became the artist to make *mambo* the universal dance all the world knows today. With his gift for coaxing rare dissonances from the piano, he not only composed hits such as *Patricia* or *Cerezo rosa*, but also more complex works: *Voodoo Suite* (1954), *Concierto para bongó* (1955), and *Suite de las Américas* (1967).

Mambo became multi-ethnic and triumphed into the sixties. It appeared in the sophisticated musical *West Side Story* (1957) by Leonard Bernstein and Jerome Robbins, in a scene in which a "White" street gang and Puerto Rican youths clash over an impossible mixed-race love. Italians, Latin Americans, Blacks, or Jews, each group would do its part in the Big Apple to make the rhythms of the Caribbean a universal phenomenon. The *arreglos* ("settling of accounts"), in the urban New York world, when compared to the classic *son* in Cuba, appeared *más agresivos*.

In the meantime in Havana, bass player, arranger and composer Juan Formell (1942-2014) and his band Los Van Van ("go for it") marked a turn for the new. After a *Mozambique* period with a variation of *conga* and other Afro-Cuban rhythms, and a music-to-dance-by stage, they created a Cuban-Afro-Hispanic-Jazz neo-mix. This had an electronic sound too, and innovative percussions, with the addition of an electric guitar and trombone.

LATIN MUSIC TODAY

"Bailar salsa" in Cuba became "bailar casino". The "rueda de casino" dissolved and recomposed couples at will in a group circle. Formations and steps were set and called by dance leaders. "Somos salseros", "somos soneros" proudly declared the musicians of the Isla Grande who had overcome their initial reticence to use the blanket term

---
185. Cf. Frankie Manning, Cynthia R. Millman, *Frankie Manning: ambasciatore del Lindy Hop*, Derive/Approdi, Rome 2014.

17. Popular dances: the rhythms of Cuba

A record night of 980 couples dancing in a giant "rueda de casino" on the Malecón, Havana, 2015.

salsa[186] for all the different dances. They realized it was difficult to distinguish between the types of rhythms, even for Cubans themselves. The simplified label *salsa* kept their Cuban roots from being drowned out on the extremely competitive global scene. This included Africa too, with its sexy *kizomba*, an umbrella mix of *salsa* and tango. The planetary success of *Despacito* (2017) by Puerto Rican singer Luis Fonsi (1978) and his ultra-Latin sensuous dancing goes to prove it.

Frequently the lead singer in a band dialogues with a second voice and a chorus that acts as a responsory. And invocations to the divinities are customary, with cries such as: "*mano pa' arriba*" ("raise your hands") asking the public to raise their hands to the sky; "*agua*" ("water"), the purifying and inspiring element – alcohol too for the *fiesta* – or "*candle*" to indicate a situation that is *caliente*; and "*dale mambo*" or "*dale rumba*", to drive the energy level up even further. These are all expressions that are typically part of the singers' exhortations. "*Dale cintura*", or more vulgarly "*meneate*", is the call for the women to wiggle their hips to the delight of the men. And "*dale palo*", to give the sexual initiative back to the male partner again. These cues characterize the "scandalous" *reggaetón*. *Caribeño* corporal freedom allows for the legitimization of erotic gestures.

Rumba is part of *son*, *salsa*, *reggaetón*, and all Cuban music where the call of the earth is powerful and danced rooted into the ground, with the bust bent towards the floor. *Yoruba* belief, at the source of Afro-Cuban culture, still remains present, just as much today as yesterday. For example, consider El Chacal, the divo of *reggaetón* (or *reguetón*) and *cubatón*. He got his start as a *rapero* ("rapper"), and deftly embraces many different musical genres of the Caribbean. In his clip he sings *Changó* while dressed all in white as if "*pasando santo*" ("being reborn"). In this *salsa*, he invokes the god of the song's title as he holds a double-edged axe. He appeals to all the other *Yoruba* divinities too, as bystanders dance for joy. *Reggaetón* also often purposely vehicles "sexy porn" macho songs. This was to such a degree that the Ministry of Culture banned the performance of some songs in public venues. It was felt that they degraded the image of women who were represented as objects, lewd teasers, prey and hunters of the intoxicated *macho*, who the next morning does not even remember a girl's name (as in *Que clase de rumba*, meaning "What a great time", by Farruko/Balvin).

The *cubatón* street look very closely resembles the African American rapper 'brothers' dress: big gold chain necklaces, dark glasses, tattoos for the men. For the girls, silicone breasts, bikinis, shorts, or micro-miniskirts, and the obligatory hairstyle in long wavy curls. And then locations for the video clips are invariably street scenes, discos, the beach, or on luxury yachts, in flashy

---

186. **Link:** Video of *The Black Roots of Salsa: the Emancipation of Cuban Rumba* (2004-2016).

cars, by a shimmering pool, where there are always parties in full swing and fancy cocktails for all. These images reflect "how rich White people lived" before Castro, and how they do in Miami, the ultimate dream. Yet *cubatón* is now also being performed by musicians trained at the Escuela de Arte, ennobling this umpteenth musical evolution. In the meantime, the bolder songs of Los Aldeanos, an independent *cubatón* band that challenges the government with its social protest and "impolite" language circulate under the counter.

was chosen by Bizet for his *Carmen*. It also became a theme song in Argentinian tango. Her compositions *Veinte años* and the *bolero* and *son, Sólo pienso en ti*, are also magnificent examples of her talent. They are all enduring successes.

Orquesta Anacaona, year 2000.

WOMEN IN CUBAN MUSIC

There are fewer women on the Cuban music scene than men. They are usually singers, or part of a backing chorus. At best there may be some flautists, guitarists, or musicians in piano bar ensembles that perform in cafés and hotel lobbies. There are more courageous women who *tocan rumba*, encouraged by the commitment of recent cultural projects. They mark an important turning point in the overcoming of the limits of a universe that until now has been all male.[187] A notable example is the historic Orquesta Anacaona[188] that even since 1932 has been able to count on several generations of female musicians. There is also Las Hermanas Márquez, brought back to the stage by musician and composer Paquito d'Rivera in 2002.

The singer María Teresa Vera was also a guitarist and composer. Her *habanera*[189] — a type of country dance to a slow rhythm — took hold in Cuba and

Las hermanas Márquez.

María Teresa Vera.

---

187. See http://www.somosjovenes.cu/articulo/mujeres-rumba.
188. Cf. A. Castro, *Queens of Havana*, Grove Press, New York 2007.
189. The most famous *habanera* is the dance Georges Bizet introduced in *Carmen*, *L'amour est un oiseau rebelle*, inspired by the theme *El arreglito* by Spanish composer Sebastián Iradier.

"Mulatas de fuego".

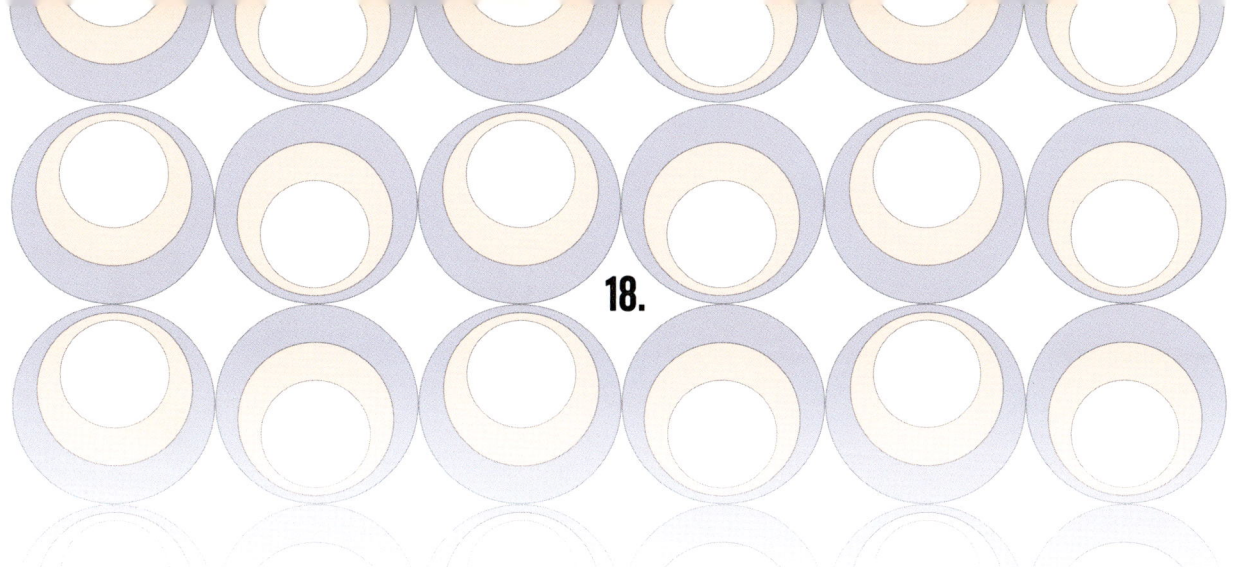

18. THE TROPICANA

Before the advent of Fidel Castro, Havana aspired to be the ideal Monte Carlo of the Caribbean. It would cater to the world's most rich and beautiful, offering them the most enticing and extravagant entertainment anywhere. Havana would be on a par with Las Vegas for its spectacular hotels, exciting shows and thrilling casinos. This was the grand project of the Italian-American mafia,[190] to make Cuba virtually its own State of hotels and night clubs.[191] The meeting of all the crime families, arranged by Lucky Luciano at the Hotel Nacional in 1946, remains mythical. In Cuba, you could do anything, just a few miles from the puritanical and segregationist United States under Prohibition. There were bars and clubs of all kinds, with alcohol, cigars, music, striptease and burlesque *extravagancias*, dancing with *Mulatas*,[192] gay propositions, and "taxi dancers", all to the delight of visitors looking for transgression in pre-revolutionary Havana. Here was Sin City devoted to *derroche*, to the *vie bohémienne*, a place to *rumbiar*, *faranduliar*, and *despelotarse* with no holds barred.

On top of the list of the prestige *lugares* there was the cabaret Tropicana in the town of Marianao. It was known as "*Un paraíso bajo las estrellas*"[193] ("A paradise under the stars") for its unique stage built amidst a lush tropical forest of royal palms, mango trees and cedars. A dream world created

---

190. Cf. T. J. (Thomas Joseph) English, *Havana Nocturne*, Harper, New York 2007; Enrique Cirules, *The Mafia in Havana*, Ocean Press, New York-Melbourne 2010; Luis Báez, Pedro de la Hoz, *Hotel Nacional de Cuba, Revelaciones de una leyenda*, Editorial Capitán San Luis, Panama 2014.
191. Cf. Basil Woon, *When it's Cocktail Time in Cuba*, Horace Liveright, New York 1928; Mark Kurlansky, *Havana, A Subtropical Delirium*, Bloomsbury (USA) 2017; It. trans. *L'Avana, un delirio subtropicale*, Bompiani, Milan 2018, also in ebook.
192. Cf. Melissa Blanco Borelli, *She is Cuba, A Genealogy of the Mulata Body*, Oxford University Press, New York 2016, Chap. 2; Tomás Fernández Robaina, *Recuerdos secretos de dos mujeres públicas*, Letras Cubanas, La Habana 1983; Rosendo Rosell, *Vida y Milagros de la Farándula en Cuba*, Taller, Santo Domingo 1990, Ediciones Univeral, Miami 1994, in 5 volumes; Rosa Miriam Elizalde, *Jineteros en La Habana*, in "Contracorriente", Havana 1995.
193. Cf. Rafael Lam, *Tropicana: un paraíso bajo las estrellas*, Editorial José Martí, Havana 1997

18. THE TROPICANA

The gaming room at the Hotel Riviera owned by mobster Meyer Lansky, 1957.

by the Italian-Latin American impresario Victor de Correa D'Costa, manager of the nightclub Edén Concert. A little spot happily far enough away

Tropicana, "Paradise Under the Stars", in the fifties.

from the tragedies of WWII, from which Cuba had benefited with its exportation of sugar at vertiginous global prices. Those were the "fat years" to such a degree that a show was staged at the Teatro Alhambra with the now proverbial title *La Danza de los Millones*.

The Tropicana was the Seventh Heaven where you could spend intoxicating nights with the Orquesta di Alfredo Brito, creator of the *bolero-son* entitled precisely, *Tropicana*. Or you could admire the sensuous shows of the most voluptuous *muchachas* ever, with their wasp waists and firm bodies splendidly exposed. The dances were created by Cuban choreographer Sergio Orta. With his experience working in Hollywood, he came back to Cuba intent upon imitating the dazzling shows with their lineups of beautiful girls such as in *Ziegfeld Girl* (1941). Orta staged *Siboney*, a revue set in a pre-colonial Cuban *Indio*s village, and choreographed the dances in the film *Tam Tam* or *El origen de la rumba* (1938). These were performed by dancers from the Edén Concert with music by the orchestra Sonora Matancera. The protagonist was Argentinian actress Chela Castro (María Celia Ovejero Martínez), star of the silver screen in Cuba and Mexico during its golden age from 1936 to 1959.

De Correa adopted a tone of high-class chic from Europe, above all from Paris, along the lines of the Lido, the Moulin Rouge, and the Folies Bergère. In 1941, he convinced his associates to invite Colonel de Basil's Ballet Russe to be their guests. The company came to Cuba and performed at the Sociedad Pro Arte Musical, but afterwards found itself virtually marooned in Cuba without the means to return to Europe. The impresario had simply slashed their fees. In exchange for board and the money for their return home, they had no choice but to perform for months in the revue *Congo Pantera*. The protago-

18. THE TROPICANA

Tatiana Leskova in *Graduation Ball*, 1948.

nist of the show was "classical" Tatiana Leskova. It was authored by David Lichine[194] and choreographed by Julio Richard, for years partner of star dancer Carmita Ortiz, famous for her bath in a mega champagne coupe. There was even Chano Pozo,[195] one of the founders of Latin Jazz,[196] in the part of a hunter. Mongo Santamaría and Silvestro Méndez played percussions under the trees, accompanied by appetizing *rumberas girls*. They also played the great favorites of "*La Única*", Rita Montaner. The Jesuits who lived in the neighborhood sued the nightclub for disturbance of the peace but lost the case to the advantage of the employees of the show.

Chano Pozo and Dizzy Gillespie, in the forties.

Martin Fox, "*El guajiro*" ("the peasant"), was the king of the *bolita*, a widely popular illegal lottery. He bought the Tropicana property from de Correa with ambitious plans for its lavish restoration with much more class. He called upon architect Max Borges (1918-2009) who, in 1952, designed and personally tested the spectacular

---

194. David Lichine (Rostov, 1910 - Los Angeles, 1972), dancer, ballet master, choreographer. Among his works was *Graduation Ball* (1940) to music by Strauss. The dance is still performed today with great success particularly in the famous ballet schools.
195. Chano Pozo (Havana, 1915), was murdered in a bar in New York's Harlem in 1948. A follower of *Santería*, he emigrated to the U.S. where he joined the company Jack Cole Dancers. Pozo influenced greats such as Dizzy Gillespie and was the first Latin percussionist to be hired In Dizzy Gillespie's band. **Link:** Video of *Manteca* with Chano Pozo and Dizzy Gillespie. The figure of Pozo is recognizable in the charming and touching animated film *Chico y Rita* (2010) directed by Fernando Trueba, Javier Mariscal, and Tono Errando, with music score by Bebo Valdés; Cf. Mats Lundahl, *Bebo de Cuba: Bebo Valdés y su mundo*, Rba Libros, Barcelona 2008.
196. Cf. Isabelle Leymare, *Cuban Fire, The Story of Salsa*

---

and Latin Jazz, Continuum, London-New York 1997-2002; Leonardo Acosta, *Raíces del jazz latino: Un siglo de jazz latino en Cuba*, La Iguana Ciega, Barranquilla 2001; *Cubano Be Cubano Bop: One Hundred Years of Jazz in Cuba*, Smithsonian Books, Washington 2003.

18. THE TROPICANA

parabolic "Arcos de Cristal", crystal arches that sweep over the main hall. Now artists could perform outdoors too, either on a central stage or on suspended catwalks between the illuminated trees. The comical parody of the operetta *La viuda alegre* (*The Merry Widow*) premiered here starring the tremendously popular Rosita Fornés.

"*El bárbaro del ritmo*" Benny Moré, the legendary singer and bandleader of *son*, "*El sonero mayor*", gave brilliant performances at the Tropicana all through 1958. The management had hesitated to engage him, afraid that his well-known bouts with alcoholism would make him unreliable. But the *maudit* champion of the *habaneras* music scene with his Banda Gigante did not let his bosses down at the Tropicana. Moré also performed at the cabaret Montmartre with Rita Montaner, in the super-production *El solar* (the term for a typical Cuban semi-detached house)

Rosita Fornés in *La viuda alegre*, 1962.

under director of choreography Alberto Alonso.

Among the featured artists at the Tropicana were Josephine Baker and Carmen Miranda in the Brazilian-inspired *Bahiondo*. And there was an impressive succession of singers: Bola de Nieve ("Snowball"), that is, the popular chubby, ebony star Ignacio Jacinto Villa Fernández; Nat King Cole, with his "all sold out" fifteen days of concerts in 1956; Sarah Vaughan; Frank Sinatra, in controversial dealings with mafiosi; Eartha Kitt; Mercedita Valdés; and Celia Cruz. And then, there were Omara Portuondo (1930), the voice of the Buena Vista Social Club;[197] Argentinian star Libertad Lamarque, and pianist Bebo Valdés. Also to be remembered were Elena Burke, the "*Señora sentimiento*"; Tito Puente (1923-2000), born in New York's Hispanic Harlem, "*El Rey de los timbales*" and maestro of *mambo*[198] and Latin Jazz; the Hispanic-American violinist and arranger Xavier Cugat (1900-1990), who had once even accompanied mythic Italian tenor Enrico Caruso. Cugat's first wife was Rita Montaner, his second spouse Tropicana star Carmen Castillo.

---

197. *Buena Vista Social Club*, a documentary directed by Wim Wenders (1999) on the musicians of Cuba's golden age. Guitarist Ry Cooder brings them back together to play again and they perform a repertory of Cuba's most famous songs.
198. Tito Puente appears in *The Mambo Kings* (1992), a film by Arne Glimcher. It recounts the adventurous and tragic story of the brothers Cesar and Nestor Castillo, played by Armand Assante and Antonio Banderas when the musicians leave Cuba for New York. Puente was also one of the irreverent characters in the TV series *The Simpsons*.

18. THE TROPICANA

Alberto Alonso (right), with Benny Moré, and actor Guillermo Alvarez Guedes, in the fifties.

Finally, he married a third time to Abbe Lane.[199] There were also performers Isaac Delgado, singer and revolutionary of the *timba* style (the band NG La Banda); and the presence of extravagant pianist, singer and actor (Valentino) Liberace. Indeed, in 1956, an immense winding gala table in the form of a keyboard was made especially for him decorated with black and white piano keys. Great stars of the artistic firmament all guests in this mythic setting.

The memoires of Ofelia Fox,[200] the wife of

---

199. Abbe Lane, American actress and singer (New York, 1932), was known as "*The swingiest sexpot in show business*". She created a sensation as Italian TV's super-sexy star during the sixties. Another sex bomb of cinema and TV in Italy was the fascinating Chelo Alonso, from Camagüey (1933). She was known for her swaying hips in exotic dances, including the belly dance.

200. Cf. Rosa Lowinger, Ofelia Fox, *Tropicana Nights: The Life*

18. THE TROPICANA

Josephine Baker in Cuba, in the fifties.

Xavier Cugat and Abbe Lane, in the fifties.

Tropicana owner Martin Fox and First Lady of the "infinite party" of *habanera* nightlife, reflect all the glamour of the times. Tropicana guest celebrities included Ava Gardner, Tyrone Power, Ernest Hemingway, Marlon Brando – who asked to buy a *tumbadora* from the orchestra to try his hand at the exciting Cuban rhythms himself. There was also Edith Piaf, Joan Crawford, Humphrey Bogart, Lauren Bacall, Errol Flynn, Marilyn Monroe, Marlene Dietrich, Gary Cooper, Maurice Chevalier, Anthony Quinn, Judy Garland, Ingrid Bergman, and Sammy Davis Jr.

Style was everything for a nightclub that claimed the sky was the limit. And the works of art chosen to worthily adorn the venue speak for themselves: the *Fuente de las Musas* by Italian sculptor Aldo Gamba (born in Acqualagna in 1881, he died in 1944 in a Nazi concentration camp) graces the main entrance to this temple of voluptuous pleasure. Yet even more famous is the marble ballerina en pointe also near the entrance. The elegant Art Deco work by Cuban sculptor Rita Longa (1912-2000) has acted as the emblem and calling card of the venue since 1949. It exalts Tropicana's dedication to dance as it draws inspiration from the ballerina played by Moira Shearer, as related by choreographer Léonide Massine,[201] in the film by Michael Powell

---

and Times of the Legendary Cuban Nightclub, Houghton Mifflin Harcourt, Boston 2007; Coco Fusco, edited by, *Corpus Delecti, Performance Art of the Americas*, Routledge, London 2000.
201. Cf. Léonide Massine, *My Life in Ballet*, Macmillan. London 1968, It. trans. *La mia vita nel balletto*, edited by Lorena Coppola, Fondazione Léonide Massine, Naples 1995.

18. THE TROPICANA

Liberace at the Tropicana, 1954.

Rodney "*El Mago*", apparently got his start in the *solo para hombres* risqué shows in the Chinatown Teatro Shanghai del Barrio Chino.²⁰² These were renowned for their penchant for live sex pantomime comedy.²⁰³ Former dancer Rodney turned out to be brilliant at exalting the local beauties, his *"Mulatas de fuego"*, all in feathers, fringe and sequins, beads and lamé, gigantic jewelry, crowns, candles and turbans, highlighting their generously exposed radiant dark-skinned bodies. The Tropicana became synonymous with the triumph of the provocative *Mulata* in her inimitable undulating spine that "spoke" with the beat of the music. Rodney succumbed to leprosy in 1960, but before he died, he had created a least 75 productions for the Tropicana. The decors and sets were of the most impressive quality, made with the finest materials he could find in the U.S. and France. Just some of the countless shows that

Fuente de la Musas at the Tropicana, a work by Aldo Gamba.

"Ballerina", a sculpture by Rita Longa, for the Tropicana.

and Emeric Pressburger *The Red Shoes* (1948).

In 1952, Fox asked Roderico Neyra to choreograph Tropicana's dances, luring him away from the rival nightclub Sans Souci. Neyra, alias

---

202. For Mitch Moxley, *Superman of Havana*, photos by Michael Magers, see http://roadsandkingdoms.com/2015/superman-of-havana/.
203. See http://yolandafarr.blogspot.it/2012/02/el-shanghai-un-teatro-muy-especial.html.

18. THE TROPICANA

Menu of the Cabaret Sans Souci, Havana, during the fifties.

The Tropicana Rodney Girls, in the fifties.

marked his production were: *Vudu ritual*, in a Haitian mood; *Carabalí*, on Afro-Cuban themes; *Mayombe*, with its masked *íremes* of the religious initiatory Abakuá society, and the bonus of eclec-

Rodney during an interview with Tropicana artists, in the fifties.

tic star Celia Cruz; *Carnaval carioca*; *Copacabana*; *Tambó* with the great dance couple Gladys and Freddy; *Canciones para besar*; *Rumbo al Waldorf*; and last but not least, *Noches del Trópico*.

Even the circus had a place on Rodney's stage, with acrobatic acts to give variety to the show. One of his most popular ideas, kept in all the shows afterwards, was the breathless leap into the void of a ballerina who plunged from the top of a tower to the waiting arms of the male dance corps below. The Mayoral (Foreman) who had caused the girl's fatal leap,[204] is then executed to the delight of onlookers. Every three months Rodney invented new attractions inspired by everything from Italian light opera, to Mexican folklore, Brazilian samba, or a Japanese tea ceremony.

During the era of Martin Fox, round-trip all-inclusive tickets were organized from Miami to Havana. For about thirty dollars these special flights offered American tourists drinks and a show on the plane. From the moment they took off for Cuba, they could already get a first taste of

---

204. **Link:** Leap from the tower of the Tropicana.

the delights awaiting them at the Tropicana. Their program consisted of departure for Cuba in the afternoon, a big night out on the island, gambling at the casino, short rest at the hotel, and return flight home the next day. And the ferry boats of those days brought *carros americanos* to the island where there was no car industry. The cars that grew old on the island were either repaired in the most impossible ways just to keep going, or else admirably preserved to become the many vintage cars on the road visitors found so charming.

Fox managed his business in agreement with the shrewdest of the American mafiosi, Meyer Lansky (1902-1983). Born in Belarus, his family was of Polish Jewish descent and had fled the pogroms by migrating to the U.S. Lansky was known as "The Mob's Accountant" and was the brain behind the casino businesses in Florida and New Orleans as well. The president of Cuba at the time, Fulgencio Batista (from 1940 to 1944, and then from 1952 to 1959), "*El mulato lindo*", had no objections to the presence of Lansky who was ready to turn over a sizeable part of the earnings to him. Similarly, Lansky paid the appropriate incentives to police chiefs to turn a blind eye to his lucrative interests. References to the Lansky era emerge in the HBO TV series *Boardwalk Empire* and in *Godfather Part II* (1974). Francis Ford Coppola's film co-written with Mario Puzo and starring Al Pacino and Robert De Niro in the roles of the Corleones, refers to Havana's wild nightlife. The protagonists mock the gestures of the incredible "Superman" in one of the shows they have seen with the super-endowed male shamelessly using his sexual weapon. The scene with Superman on stage is a famous pivotal moment of the film.

The mafia was not seriously concerned about the disorders or protests of opposers of the Batista government, even after a bomb was planted in the bar of the Tropicana. Though other mafiosi thought these disturbances could be suffocated, Lansky, remembering events in Russia, was convinced communism was just around the corner. Some wanted, hoped, or feared that the Americans would intervene.[205] Nothing happened, though, and when Fidel Castro seized power in 1959, he made the bosses and betting business-

Celia Cruz, 1957.

es in Havana leave, and had the gambling houses with their imported slot machines from Chicago destroyed. These were all "enemies of the people" that only meant heaps of money for the Batista family.

---

205. Cf. Ruby Hart Phillips, *Cuba: Island of Paradox*, McDowell, Obolensky, New York 1959, ACLS Humanities E-Book 2009. Phillips, first as the wife of a correspondent, and then as a correspondent herself for The New York Times, investigated events In Cuba under presidents Gerardo Machado and Fulgencio Batista, and during the early years after the advent of Fidel Castro.

18. THE TROPICANA

The famous leap from the tower of the Tropicana.

When Castro came to power, everything in Cuba changed. Yet the Tropicana could never stop celebrating its "*Diosas de carne*", goddesses of the flesh, without penalizing the many workers of the club. "*Diosas de carne*" was the title of one of its shows in 1958 based upon the Greek goddesses of Antiquity. After the revolution, however, the shows staged had more popular themes, such as *Tropicana alrededor del Mundo* (1960), with one of Cuba's greatest voices, Esther Borja (1913-2013). She was known as "*La damisela encantadora*" ("Lovely Lady"), as the melodic song by Ernesto Lecuona, *Pachanga en Tropicana* declared. And then there was *Salsa, sazón y ritmo* ("Salsa, spice and rhythm", 1962); *Tu música en Tropicana* (1965) with the Meme Solís quartet; *Brindis por Tropicana* (1967); and *Carnaval de Lecuona* (1967) by Santiago Alfonso and Fernando Valdés.[206] Nevertheless, in the late sixties the legendary cabaret was forced to close.

The Tropicana only reopened in 1970 with works such as *Pelea de gallos* starring twins Alberto and Armando Pérez. Most striking however was *Los romanos eran así* (1972), with camels and lions on stage. The production was directed by Joaquín Miguel Condall (1923-2010). Since the fifties Condall had conceived many popular TV shows and for about twenty years he was artistic director of the Tropicana.

The choreographic movements of the dancers of the glorious venue are in fact today prepared in a strict, specialized school directed precisely by Fernando Valdés. The standard of training of the pre-selected pupils, with a background in dance

Lottery in Havana.

of various genres, is becoming increasingly more demanding. There are regular controls[207] to produce "*bailarines de espectaculo*", entertainment dancers, of a certain quality. Anyone who has stage presence and talent, a good body, and engaging smile may apply for entrance, but iron discipline is a prerequisite for the training and

---

206. For the complete list of productions and shows, see http://ramondiazarticulos.blogspot.it/2010/03/tropicana-centro-nocturno-que-esta.html.

207. See *Tropicana*, a film by Thomas Wallner and Jochen Beckmann, Xenophile Media, Zdf/ARTE 2008

18. THE TROPICANA

Celia Cruz, Isidro Camara and Esther Borja, Cuban television, in the fifties.

work ahead. The mandatory age requirement for the girls is from seventeen to twenty years of age. The physical requirements are just as precise concerning height: 1.65m for female dancers and 1.75 for male dancers and *modelos*. Models do not limit themselves to the fashion show runways but are expected to also show an aptitude for dance. Until the fifties, Tropicana showgirls were not to have complexions that were too dark, and they were to have hourglass figures and appeal to the eyes of a clientele that was preferably White. Or they were to be pleasing to some nonwhite guests of honor such as François "Papa Doc" Duvalier. The Haitian dictator was invited with his wife to the premiere of *Vudú Ritual*, a production Rodney staged in 1958.

One of the shows that ran for the longest time, from 1996 to 2005, was *Tropicana: la gloria eres tu*, conceived and directed by Santiago Alfonso. After the Rodney era, for fifteen years it was precisely a director-choreographer such as multitasking Santiago Alfonso (1939) to show-case what the Tropicana had always been famous for in all the world. That is, dancing beauties with pom-poms in just the right places of their scanty costumes, accentuated by gloves, high heels and ruffles strategically highlighting their sexy curves, all to Cuba's irresistible pulsating rhythms. The male dance partners of the *chicas* are all charming, deft, muscular and suave, in their thong costumes or fluttering shirts. Allusions to ceremonies, celebrations, and dances from the Afro-Cuban cultural *mezcla* abound, in the *trance*, the men's quickness in the *columbia*, and their virtuoso *tornillo* spins.[208]

Among the many unforgettable shows, *Tambores en concierto* (2006) was truly exceptional. It was created by Tomás Morales to be a panorama of all the exciting rhythms of Cuba. In 2014, it was this show chosen to celebrate the Tropicana's 75th Anniversary. The general manager was David Varela Mateo de Acosta and artistic director,

Tropicana "modelos".

---

208. **Link:** Video of the *son* in *Siboney* performed by Estela and René, the famous Cuban couple that in 1939 went to Hollywood and appeared in several films in Mexico.

Mulatas of the Tropicana.

18. THE TROPICANA

Twins Alberto and Armando Pérez with twins Mary and Kathy Salazar at the Tropicana, in the seventies.

Armando Pérez Sánchez. An extravaganza *conga* finale even had the audience get up and dance.

Armando, former dancer, and his twin brother Alberto, choreographer, formed one of the twin dance couples – there were five twin couples in all – who brought polished artistry to the Tropicana dances. Another of the twin couples were the sisters nicknamed "Odette and Odile", the white swan and black swan of *Swan Lake*.

The choreographers of the Tropicana were almost always former dancers of the venue. Pedro Armenteros was one of them, and among the *maîtres de ballet* there were notably Henry Boyer and Eduardo Perovani. They were principal dancers who brought finesse to the corps and guaranteed a high level of excellence.[209]

As for the music, among those who offered the exalting rhythms to the Tropicana shows, Armando Romeu was a key figure. Victor de Correa asked him to be musical director and create an orchestra for the club. He later asked Romeu to be the percussionist in his uncle's ensemble. Nat King Cole recorded in Spanish with the band. Important contributors to Tropicana's sound were also the Grenet brothers: Ernesto, percussionist and director, and composers Eliseo and Emilio (Neno). Also of note was Chuchito Valdés, the son of Chucho Valdés (1941), who was in turn the son of Bebo Valdés (Havana, 1918 - Stockholm, 2013). Chuchito was one of Tropicana's most successful music arrangers and was particularly known for his arrangements for the famous singer Rita Montaner.

Leonela González, the *primerisima bailarina* star of the Tropicana, next to her statue created by Tony López, 1956.

---

209. See http://www.lahabana.com/content/on-diamonds-razzle-and-goddesses-of-the-flesh.

18. THE TROPICANA

BEAUTIES OF THE TROPICANA

There are so many names of Tropicana beauties, an infinite list, and it is not always easy to find out about their lives or careers. An interesting dictionary exists edited by Cuban researcher María Argelia Vizcaíno. The editor has lived in the United States since 1980 and has a website where she posts biographies and photos.

From 1955 to 1957, the reigning beauty of the Tropicana was Leonela González. She was photographed in a shimmering wasp-corset tutu – and en pointe, to suggest her qualities as a true ballerina.

After the revolution, the *modelo* Alicia Figueroa was officially appointed to receive Russian astronaut Gagarin. Then it was *modelos* Sandra Taylor and Olga González, Olga Chaviano, Nora Osorio, and Zita Coalla, as emblematic figures, to demonstrate how the taste for curvaceous figures was so powerfully ingrained in male fantasies.

Among the many dance couples, the annals cite above all spicy Ana Gloria (Varona) and Rolando Garcia. The couple also regularly danced aboard the famous Miami-Havana round-trip flights. For years they were the shining couple at the center of Tropicana's dance corps, just as were Marta Castillo and Miguelito Chekis.

The Cuban-Mexican film *Yambaó*[210] (1957), with choreographies by Rodney, boasted tropical-style beauty. Here popular dance, with its ties to the religious roots of *Santería*, and cabaret dance meet. The encounter comes through the story of a young woman, played by Ninón Sevilla. Her dances ignite men's fantasies as she falls dangerously in love with the White plantation master. In the film, Xiomara Alfaro sings "The Nightingale Song". She was singing at the Tropicana when she was noticed by Katherine Dunham[211] (1909-2006), the dancer, choreographer, and African American anthropologist known as "the Matriarch and Queen Mother of Black Dance". Alfaro also sang in the film *Mambo* (1954), starring Silvana Mangano and Vittorio Gassman, in which Dunham's company was also cast.

The audacious, brazen beauties of the Tropicana were featured on the covers of magazines such as "Show". In one article, the showgirls were an appetizing "*Ensalada de pollos*" (Chicken or "chick" salad). Each girl was described with all the deserved admiration for her specific endowments. The words for the occasion were red hot, but always wonderfully flattering *piropos*.

Tropicana has also been on tour and its image is worldwide. Among events and television appearances, the company performed at the Christopher Columbus celebrations at the 1992 Expo in Genoa.

The migration of people and documentation makes research into this past also an interweaving of myth and glowing personal stories through the memories of its protagonists. Yet it is certain that the Tropicana, under the sign of its famous undulating signature, will keep its ambition in the new millennium of being the greatest temple of Eros of the Caribbean.

---

210. **Link:** *Yambaó* with Ninón Sevilla.

211. Cf. James Haskins, *Katherine Dunham*, Coward, McCann, & Geoghegan, New York 1982; Barbara O'Connor, *Katherine Dunham: Pioneer of Black Dance*, Carolrhoda Books, Minneapolis 2000; Joyce Aschenbrenner, *Katherine Dunham: Dancing a Life*, University of Illinois Press, Champaign 2002.

Poster for the film *Yambaó* (1957).

BIBLIOGRAPHY

ALICIA ALONSO, THE BNC, FOUNDERS, DANCERS, THE SCHOOL AND FESTIVALS

AA.VV., *Alicia Alonso esta noche baila aquí*, cat. exhibition Museo Nacional de Bellas Artes, Havana 2008.

Albelo S., Ismael, *... Y hablando de danza*, Ruth Casa Editorial, Panama 2015.

Alonso, Alicia, *Diálogos con la danza*, Editorial Letras Cubanas, La Habana 1986; ed. Editorial Galerna, Buenos Aires 1988; ed. Editorial Complutense, Madrid 1993, text for the Alicia Alonso Chair of the Universidad Complutense; ed. Editora Politica, Havana 2000; ed. Ediciones Oceano, Mexico 2004; ed. Editorial Letras Cubanas, Havana 2010; Eng. ed. *Dialogues with the Dance*, Editorial José Martí, Havana 2018.

Álvarez, M.C., and Blanco, S., *Appreciación y Práctica en torno a la Escuela Cubana de Ballet*, Ediciones Cumbre, Madrid 2015.

Bernier-Grand, Carmen, *Alicia Alonso, Prima Ballerina*, Two Lions, New York 2011.

Bustamante Fontes, Mayda, *Alicia Alonso en Carmen, Mito y leyenda*, Ediciones Cumbres, Madrid 2014.

Bustamante Fontes, Mayda, *Alicia Alonso o la Eternidad de Giselle*, Ediciones Cumbres, Cuba-España 2013.

Cannatello, Alfredo, *Alicia, una mujer, un sueño*, Ballet Nacional de Cuba, Havana 2007.

Céspedes, Garzón, *Construir, siempre construir* (interview), Editorial Cumbres, Madrid 2013.

Cabrera, Miguel, *Ballet Nacional de Cuba, Medio siglo de gloria*, Ediciones Cuba en el Ballet, Havana 1998;

Cabrera, Miguel, *Alicia Alonso, La realidad y el mito*, Ediciones Cuba en el Ballet, Havana 2000.

Cabrera, Miguel, *Festival Internacional de Ballet de La Habana, Una cita de arte y amistad (1960-2004)*, Letras Cubanas, Havana 2006.

Cabrera, Miguel, *Orbita del Ballet Nacional de Cuba 1948-1978*, Orbe, Havana 1978.

Cabrera, Miguel, *El Ballet en Cuba, Apuntes Históricos*, Ediciones Cúpulas, Havana 2011.

Cabrera, Miguel, *El Ballet en Cuba, Nacimiento de una Escuela en le siglo XX*, Ediciones Balletin Dance, Buenos Aires 2011.

Chryssoulis, Dominique, *L'Assoluta de Cuba*, L'Échappée Belle, Paris 2018.

Dávalos, Gabriel *Viengsay Valdés, Soy lo que ves*, Ocean Sur, 2017.

Fina de Calderón, *Los pasos que no regresan*, Huerga & Fierro Editores, Madrid 2004.

de Gámez, Tana, *Alicia Alonso at home and abroad*, Citadela Press, New York 1970.

del Carmen Hechevarría, María, *Alicia Alonso, más allá de la técnica*, Universidad Politécnica de Valencia, Valencia 1998.

Deyá, Giselle, *Mirta Plá, una joya de la cultura cubana*, Ediciones Cumbres, Cuba-Spain, 2013.

Estrada Betancourt, José Luis, *De la semilla al fruto: la compañia*, Casa Editoria Abril, Havana 2008.

Estrada Betancourt, José Luis, *El mundo baila en La Habana*, Ediciones Cuba en el Ballet, Havana 2010.

García, Marta, *Danzar mi vida*, Ediciones Cumbre, Madrid 2014.

Guillén, Alfaro Yailín, *Danza en Cuba*, Ocean Sur, 2019.

Guillén, Alfaro Yailín, *Ballet Nacional de Cuba en tres tiempos/in three acts*, Ocean Sur, 2019.

Léon, Heras Eduardo, *Desde la platea*, Editorial José Martí, Havana 2010.

Llanes, Julio M., *Alicia el vuelo de la mariposa*, Colección Vidas, Editorial José Martí, Havana 2018.

Loomis, John, *Cuba's Forgotten Art Schools, Revolution of Forms*, Princeton Architectural Press, New York 1999

Martin Arnold, Sandra, *Alicia Alonso: First Lady of the Ballet*, Walker & Co., 1993.

Neyra, José Ramón, Alfaro Guillén, Yailín, *Alicia Alonso, Una mirada a su vida a través del lente*, Ocean Sur/Ocean Press, Victoria 2019.

Roca, Octavio, *Cuban Ballet*, Ed. Gibbs Smith, Leighton, Utah, 2010.

Salas, Roger, *Más allá del escenario: el ballet «Muerte de Narciso» de Alicia Alonso*, Ediciones Cumbres, Madrid 2012.

Salas, Roger, *Papelería sobre la danza (y el ballet)*, vols. I, II e III, Ediciones Cumbres, Madrid 2014, 2015, 2016.

Schwall, Elizabeth, *A Spectacular Embrace: Dance Dialogue between Cuba and the Soviet Union, 1959-1973*, published online, 2019.

Siegel, Beatrice, *Alicia Alonso: The Story of a Ballerina*, Warne, London 1979.

Simón, Pedro, *Giselle, historia y leyenda: Alicia Alonso - Vladimir Vasíliev*, Ediciones Niocia, third ed., Barcelona 2013.

Simón, Pedro, *El Ballet, una devoción, enfoques y precisiones*, Ediciones Cumbres, Madrid 2014.

Simón, Pedro, Neyra José Ramón, *Prosas cubanas por Alicia Alonso*, Ediciones Unión, Havana 2020.

Singer, Toba, *Fernando Alonso, The Father of Cuban Ballet*, University Press of Florida, 2013.

Tablada, Carlos, *De acero y Nube – Biografía de Viengsay Valdés*, Editorial Letras Cubanas, Havana 2017.

Terry, Walter, *Alicia and her Ballet Nacional de Cuba*, Anchor Books, New York 1981.

Triguero Tamayo, Ernesto Rafael, *Nikolai Yavorsky: un maestro ruso en la isla del ballet*, Ediciones Santiago, Santiago de Cuba, 2010.

Triguero Tamayo, Ernesto Rafael, *Estancia cubana del maestro Nicolai Yavorsky: sus aportes al desarrollo del ballet*, Editorial Universitaria, Havana 2018.

Wirth, Isis, *La ballerine & el Comandante, L'histoire secrète du Ballet de Cuba*, François Bourin Éditeur, Paris 2013.

Ballets Russes

Anderson, Jack, *The One and Only: The Ballet Russe de Monte Carlo*, Dance Horizons, Trenton (NJ) 1981; ed. Dance Books, London 2010.

Chazin-Bennahum, Judith, *René Blum and The Ballets Russes: In Search of a Lost Life*, Oxford University Press, 2011.

Garafola, Lynn, *Diaghilev's Ballets Russes*, Oxford University Press, New York 1989.

García-Marquez, Vicente, *The Ballets Russes: Colonel de Basil's Ballets Russes de Monte Carlo 1932-1952*, Knopf, New York 1990.

Vinay, Gianfranco, and Veroli, Patrizia, *I Ballet Russes di Diaghilev tra storia e mito*, Accademia Nazionale di Santa Cecilia, Rome 2013.

Modern and Contemporary Dance

Aguilar, Alejandro, *Boán, La Danza*, Editorial Tablas-Alarcos, Havana 2017.

Burdsall, Lorna, *Más que una nota al pie*, Ediciones Unión, Havana 2012.

del Carmen Mena Rodrígues, María, *El cuerpo creativo: Taller cubano per la Enseñanza de la composición coreográfica*, Editorial Adagio, Havana 2007.

Garcetti, Gil, *Dance in Cuba*, Princeton Architectural Press, New York 2005.

Guerra, Ramiro, *Teatralización del Folklore*, Editorial Letra Cubanas, Havana 1989.

Guerra, Ramiro, *Una metodología para la enseñanza de la danza*, Havana 1989.

Guerra, Ramiro, *Coordenadas danzarias*, Ediciones Union, Havana 1999.

Guerra, Ramiro, *Eros baila*, Editorial Letras Cubanas, Havana 2000.

Guerra, Ramiro, *De la narradividad al abstraccionismo en la danza*, Centro de Investigación y Desarrollo de la Cultura Cubana "Juan Marinello", Havana 2003.

Guerra, Ramiro, *El síndrome del placer*, Editorial Capiro, Santa Clara de Cuba 2003.

Guerra, Ramiro, *Calibán danzante*, Editorial Letras Cubanas, Havana 2008

Guerra, Ramiro, *Siempre la danza, su paso breve...*, Ediciones Alarcos, Havana 2010.

Guerra, Ramiro, *Develando la danza*, ICAIC, Havana 2013.

Guillermoprieto, Alma, *Dancing with Cuba*, Vintage Books/Random House, New York 2005.

John, Suki, *Contemporary Dance in Cuba, Técnica Cubana as Revolutionary Movement*, McFarland & Company Publishers, Jefferson, North Carolina 2012.

Mahler, E., Guerra, R., and Limón, J., *Fundamentos de la danza*, Editorial Pueblo y Educación, Havana 1978-1982.

Marquéz Romero, Guillermo, *Danza Moderna y Contemporánea*, Editorial Pueblo y Educación, Havana 1980.

Pajares Santiesteban, Fidel, *Ramiro Guerra y la danza en Cuba*, Editorial Casa de la Cultura, Quito 1993.

Pajares Santiesteban, Fidel, *Danza moderna en Cuba. La cargada como una forma más del movimiento*, FEDUPEL, Caracas 1998.

BIBLIOGRAPHY

Pajares Santiesteban, Fidel, *La danza moderna cubana y su estética*, Editorial Union, Havana 2005.
Pajares Santiesteban, Fidel, *Danza contemporánea cubana* (Multimedia), Editorial Cubarte, Havana 2005.
Pajares Santiesteban, Fidel, *Dramaturgia de la danza en Cuba*, Editorial Adagio, Havana 2010.
Pajares Santiesteban, Fidel, *Escuela cubana de danza moderna*, Editorial Adagio, Havana, 2011.
Pajares Santiesteban, Fidel, *La danza moderna y la crítica de la danza en Cuba*, Editorial Tablas-Alarcos, Havana
Pajares Santiesteban, Fidel, in AA. VV., *La danza postmoderna en Cuba*, in «Cúpulas», n. 9, year III, Aprile 1998.
AA.VV, "Danzar.Cu", n 1, 2017.

Africa-Cuba-Caribbean-USA

AA.VV. *L'isola magica Haiti*, Ticordi/Mi-To, 2011.
Cabrera, Lydia, *Cuentos negros de Cuba*, Ediciones Nuevo Mundo, Havana 1961.
Chakravorty Spivak, Gayatri, *Critica della ragione post-coloniale, verso una storia del presente in dissolvenza*, Meltemi, Rome 2004, first ed. Harvard University Press, Cambridge 1999.
Canizares, Raúl, *Cuban Santeria*, Destiny Books, Vermont 1993, Spanish ed. *Santería Cubana, El sendero de la noche*, Lasser Press, Mexico 2001.
Cuoco, Alex, *African Narratives of Orishas, Spirits and Other Deities - Stories from West Africa and the African Diaspora: A Journey into the Realm of Deities*, SPI, Outskirts Press, Denver 2014.
Daniel, Yvonne, *Dancing Wisdom, Embodied Knowledge in Haitian Vodou, Cuban Yoruba and Bahian Candomlé*, University of Illinois Press, Champaign 2005.
del Carmen Mestas, María, *Pasión de rumbero*, Editorial Pablo de la Toriente, Havana 2014.
Feliu Herrera, Virtudes, *Fiestas y tradiciones cubanas*, Centro de Investigación y Desarrollo de la Cultura Cubana Juan Marinello, Havana 2003.
Franco, Susanne, *Danzare la nazione all'epoca delle post-colonie: il caso del Kenya*, and respective general bibliography, in "Danza e Ricerca" n. 9, December 2017.
Genero Madrigal, Katina, *Tubab, una danzatrice sulla via dei tamburi*, con CD, Ananke, Turin 2000.
Giancotti Patrizia, *Bahía de todos los Santos*, Garzanti, 1994.
Guzzo Vaccarino, Elisa, *Africa danza*, in "Balletto Oggi/Ballet2000" n 272; in It., Fr., Eng.

Hagedorn, K.J., *Divine Utterance, The Performance of Afro-Cuban Santería*, with CD, Smithsonian Institution Press, Washington, London 2001, with CD.
Long, Richard A., *The Black Tradition in American Dance*, Smithmark Publications, New York 1995.
Ortiz, Fernando, *Los bailes y el teatro de los negros en el folklore de Cuba*, Editorial Letras Cubanas, Havana 1951-1981.
Ortiz, Fernando, *Africanía de la música folklórica de Cuba*, Editorial Universitaria, Havana 1965.
Ortiz, Fernando, *Glosario de afronegrismo*, Editorial de Ciencias Sociales, Havana 1990.
Ortiz, Fernando, *Los negros brujos*, Ciencias Sociales, Havana 1995-2001-2007, with a prologue-letter of praise addressed to the author by Cesare Lombroso.
Santos Gracia, C., and Armas Rigal, N., *Danzas Populares Tradicionales Cubanas*, Centro de Investigación y Desarrollo de la Cultura Cubana Juan Marinello, Havana 2002.
Rivero Glean, Manuel, *Deidades cubanas de origen africano*, Casa Editora Abril, Havana 2011.
Shay, Anthony, *Dancing Across Borders, The American Fascination with Exotic Dance Forms*, McFarland & Company, North Carolina 2008.
Sanou, Salia, *Afrique danse contemporaine*, Éditions Cercle d'Art/Centre National de la Danse, Paris 2008.
Sloat, Susanna, editor, *Making Caribbean Dance*, University Press of Florida, 2010.
Taylor, P.C., *Black is Beautiful: A Philosophy of Black Aesthetics* (Foundations of the Philosophy of the Arts), Wiley-Blackwell, New Jersey 2016.
Carol Beckwith, Angela Fisher, *African Twilight: The Vanishing Rituals and Ceremonies of the African Continent*, Rizzoli, USA 2018.

Ramiro Guerra as Translator

Ramiro Guerra translated the following texts on dance into Spanish, with his own introductions. They were works by authors and founders from the United States.

De Mille, Agnes, *Dance to the Piper*, Little Brown, Boston 1952.
Hawkins, Alma, *Creating through Dance*, Princeton Book Company, Trenton 1988.
Horst, Luis, *Pre-classic Dance Forms*, Princeton Book Company, Trenton 1987.
Horst, L., and Russell, C., *Modern Dance Forms in*

Relation to other Modern Arts, Dance Horizons/Princeton Book Company, Trenton 1969.

Ballet in Dance Ediciones/Súlkary Cuba, Buenos Aires 2009, list the following translations:

Horst, Luis, *Danzas preclásicas* di Louis Horst, musical director for Ruth Saint Denis at the Denishawn School and for Martha Graham; *La danza* by Agnes De Mille, choreographer and niece of filmmaker Cecil B. De Mille; *La creatividad en la danza* di Alma Hawkins, methodologist of dance as an academic discipline and founder of the Chair of Dance at UCLA Los Angeles; *La danza moderna en relación con las otras artes contemporáneas* by Louis Horst and Carroll Russell, eminent patron of modern dance, often in support of Martha Graham.

DANCES, ENTERTAINMENT, CUSTOMS

Aguilar Cabello, Juan Carlos, *Tropicana de Cuba*, Visual America, Havana 1996.

Beck, Henrik, *Salsa*, Systime, Aarhus 2002.

Blanco Borelli, Melissa, *She is Cuba, A Genealogy of the Mulata Body*, Oxford University Press, New York 2016.

English, T.J., *Havana Nocturne*, Harper, New York 2007.

Fabrizi, Mimmo, Martínez Furé, Rogelio, Chao, Graciela, Vinueza, María Elena, *Cuba canta y baila*, Arcari, Mogliano Veneto 2003.

Fernández, María Antonia, *Bailes Populares Cubanos*, Editorial Pueblo y Educación, Havana 1981-1985.

Fernández Robaina, Tomás, *Recuerdos secretos de dos mujeres públicas*, Letras Cubanas, Havana 1983.

Lam, Rafael, *Tropicana: Un paraíso bajo las estrellas*, Editorial José Martí, Havana, 1997.

Lowinger, Rosa, Fox, Ofelia, *Tropicana Nights: The Life and Times of the Legendary Cuban Nightclub*, Houghton Mifflin Harcourt, Boston 2007.

Rosell, Rosendo, *Vida y milagros de la farandula de Cuba*, Editora Taller, Santo Domino, 1990.

Sierra Madero, Abel, *Del otro lado del Espejo, La sexualidad en la construcción de la nación cubana*, Casa de las Américas, Havana 2006.

Woon, Basil *When it's Cocktail Time in Cuba*, Horace Liveright, New York 1928.

MUSIC, LITERATURE, POETRY, CINEMA

Blanco Borelli, Melissa, edited by, *The Oxford Handbook of Dance and the Popular Screen*, Oxford University Press 2014.

Carpentier, Alejo, *Écue-Yambaó*, Havana 1927-1933, It. trans. Lindau, Turin 2015.

Contreras, Félix, *La música, una cuestión personal*, Ediciones Unión, Havana 1999.

Daniel, Yvonne, *Rumba, Dance and Social Change in Contemporary Cuba*, Indiana University Press 1995.

de Léon, Carmela, *Ernesto Lecuona*, Letras Cubanas, Havana 1996.

Delannoy, Luc, *¡Caliente!, Une histoire du Latin Jazz*, Denoël X-Trème, Paris 2000.

Diccionario Enciclopédico de la Música en Cuba, Instituto Cubano del Libro, Editorial Letras Cubanas, Havana 2009.

Leal Spengler, Eusebio, *La luz sobre el espejo*, Ediciones Boloña, Havana 1996.

Howe, Linda S., *Cuban writers and artists after the revolution*, The University of Wisconsin Press, Madison 2004.

Leymare, Isabelle, *Cuban Fire: Musiques populaires d'expression Cubaine*, Outre mesure, Paris 1997-2002.

Leymare, Isabelle, *Cuban Fire, The Story of Salsa and Latin Jazz*, ed Eng. Continuum, London 2002.

Linares, María Teresa, *La música y el pueblo*, Editorial Pueblo y Educación, Instituto Cubano del Libro, Havana 1974.

Manera, Danilo a cura di, *L'isola che canta, Giovani poeti cubani*, Universale Economica Feltrinelli, Milan 1998;

Manera, Danilo, *Canzoni dei Caraibi*, Stampa Alternativa, Rome 2000.

Martínez Rodríguez, Raúl, *Benny Moré*, Editorial Letras Cubanas, Havana 1994-2007.

Orovio, Helio, *Diccionario de la música cubana, Biográfico y técnico*, Letras Cubanas, Havana 1981.

Orovio, Helio, *El bolero Latino*, Letras Cubanas, Havana 2003.

Orovio, Helio, *El Carnaval Habanero*, Ediciones Extramuros, Havana 2005.

Orovio, Helio, *Música por el Caribe*, Editorial Oriente, Santiago de Cuba 2007.

Sandretto Carolina, *Cines de Cuba*, Skira, Milan 2019.

Soublette, Ned, *Cuba and Its Music: From the First Drums to the Mambo*, Chicago Review Press, Chicago 2007.

Ziff, John, *Cuban Music, Dance, and Celebration*, Mason Crest, Broomhall 2017.

BIBLIOGRAPHY

Vaughan, Umi, Aldama, Carlos, *Life in Batá, Cuba, Diaspora and the Drum*, Indiana University Press, Bloomington 2012.

POLITICS

Andreini, F., and Romano, P., *Che Guevara, tu y todos*, exhibition cat. Skira, Milano 2017, and respective bibliography.

Castro, Fidel, *La storia mi assolverà*, Demetra/L'Espresso, Rome 1996.

Castro, Fidel, *Io e il Che*, Mondadori, Milan 2007.

Castro, Fidel, and Ramonet, Ignacio, *Biografia a due voci*, Mondadori, Milan 2008.
Cannataro, Italia Maria, *L'America di José Martí. Razza e identità*, Rubbettino Università, Catanzaro 2010.

Garafola Lynn, edited by, https://www.academia.edu/37692386/Dancing_the_Cold_War_An_International_Symposium, 2017.

Gilroy, Paul, *The Black Atlantic, Modernity and Double-Consciousness*, Harvard University Press, Cambridge (Massachusetts) 1995.

Guevara, Ernesto Che, *Diario della Rivoluzione cubana*, Newton Compton, Roma 1996. Guevara, Ernesto Che, *I diari della motocicletta*, Mondadori, Milan 2013.

Hart Phillips, Ruby, *Cuba: Island of Paradox*, McDowell, Obolensky, New York, 1959.

Johnson, Patrick, *Appropriating Blackness: Performance and the Politics of Authenticity*, Duke University Press, Durham 2003.

Lee Anderson, Jon, *Che Guevara*, Fandango Libri, Roma 2009, and respective bibliography.

Lupi, Giordano, *Fidel Castro. Biografia non autorizzata*, A. CAR., Chiari BS, 2011.

Sánchez Guevara, Canek, *33 révolutions*, Metailié, Paris 2016; It. trans. *Il disco rotto. 33 Rivoluzioni*, and/or, Rome 2016.

Sánchez, Yoani, *In attesa della primavera*, edited by Giordano Lupi, Edizioni a nordest, Lancenigo TV, 2013.

https://www.minimumfax.com/autore/fidel-castro-1850.

West, Alan, *Tropics of History, Cuba imagined*, Bergin & Garvey, Westport/London 1997.

Zanatta, Loris, *Fidel Castro, l'ultimo "re cattolico"*, Salerno Editore, Rome 2020

GENERAL BIBLIOGRAPHY

Alonso, N., and Yáñez, M., *Damas de Social, Intelectuales Cubanas en la revista Social*, Ediciones Boloña, Havana 2014.

Alvarado, Percy, *Le confessioni dell'agente Fraile, una storia vera di terrorismo*, Editorial Capitán San Luis, Havana 2005.

Cirules, Enrique, *The Mafia in Havana*, Ocean Press, New York-Melbourne 2010.

Coyula, Mario, *La Habana que va conmigo*, Letras Cubanas, 2002.

del Carmen Mestas, María, *Mujeres*, Havana 2006.

del Ojo de la Cruz, Yaneli Leal *Los Jardines de la Tropical*, Ediciones Boloña, Havana 2014.

Depestre, Leonardo, *Cien mujeres célebres en La Habana*, Editorial José Martí, Havana 2014.

Kurlansky, Mark, *Havana, A Subtropical Delirium*, Bloomsbury USA, 2017; It. trans. *L'Avana, un delirio subtropicale*, Bompiani, 2018, also ebook.

Moruzzi, Peter, *Havana before Castro, When Cuba was a Tropical Playground*, Gibbs Smith, Layton 2008.

Reifenscheid, Beate, *Cuba Libre, Contemporary Art in Cuba since Peter Ludwig*, Silvana Editoriale, Milan 2016.

WRITINGS BY THE AUTHOR ON BALLET AND DANCE IN CUBA

Ballet Nacional de Cuba, theater program for *Giselle* and *Don Chisciotte*, Teatro Regio di Torino, 2014.

Danza – Alicia Alonso (edited by Elisa Guzzo Vaccarino), Rai 5 of 19 January 2014.

Il Museo Nazionale della Danza a Cuba, Wikiradio RAI of 6 November 2017, https://www.raiplayradio.it/audio/2017/10/Il-Museo-Nazionale-della-Danza-di-Cuba---Wikiradio-del-6112017-e78a6598-310c-4095-b24e-2c3dca619c76.html

La magia della danza, theater program for performances of the Ballet Nacional de Cuba in fragments from *Giselle*, *La bella addormentata*, *Lo Schiaccianoci*, *Coppelia*, *Don Chisciotte*, *Il Lago dei cigni*, *Sinfonia di Gottschalk*, choreographies by Alicia Alonso, Ravenna Festival, 2017.

Ritratto di Alicia Alonso, in theater program for *Lo Schiaccianoci* of the Ballet Nacional de Cuba, Teatro La Fenice di Venezia, 1999.

VIDEOS AND FILMS

DVD

A tribute to Alvin Ailey, DVD, Kultur 2000.
An Evening with the Alvin Ailey American Dance Theater, DVD Image Entertainment-Arthaus, 2001.
An Evening with Katherine Dunham, DVD Insight Media, 2007.
Don Quijote, with Viengsay Valdés and Romel Frómeta, Ballet Nacional de Cuba, BelAir, 2008.
Dance of My Heart, with Alberto Alonso, Sonia Calero, Maya Plisetskaya, directed by Ricardo Acosta, Daphne Stacey/Santa Fe College Foundation, 2009.
Giselle (film), with Alicia Alonso and Vladimir Vassiliev, Ballet Nacional de Cuba, VAI, 1980.
Giselle (film), with Carla Fracci and Erik Bruhn, American Ballet Theatre, Deutsche Grammophon, 2005.
Mambo, film with Katherine Dunham, Golem Video, DVD 2017.

On Carlos Acosta

Coppelia, with Carlos Acosta, Royal Opera House, 2002.
Don Quixote, with Carlos Acosta and Marianela Nuñez, Royal Opera House, 2014.
Giselle, with Carlos Acosta and Natalia Osipova, Royal Ballet, 2014.
La Bayadère by Natalia Makarova, with Carlos Acosta, Tamara Rojo and Marianela Nuñez, Royal Opera House, 2010.
La fille mal gardée, with Carlos Acosta and Marianela Nuñez, Royal Opera House, 2012.
Manon, with Tamara Rojo and Carlos Acosta, The Royal Ballet, Universal Music, 2009.
Romeo and Juliet, with Carlos Acosta and Tamara Rojo, The Royal Ballet, 2009.
Spartacus, with Carlos Acosta, Bolshoi Ballet, Universal Music, 2008.
Yuli, film by Icíar Bollaín, 2018.

Documentaries on Alicia Alonso, Fernando Alonso and the Ballet Nacional de Cuba

Alicia Alonso, la "prima ballerina" de Cuba, y su relación con los Castro, CNN documentary, https://www.youtube.com/watch?v=etu15mWkt2I.
Alicia Alonso: Órbita de una leyenda, directed by José Ramón Neyra, Museo Nacional de la Danza, 2010.
El despertar de un sueño, Alicia Alonso, directed by Luis Ernesto Doñas, 2009, https://www.youtube.com/watch?v=r36-PtDML1Q&feature=emb_logo
Espiral, Alicia Alonso Prima ballerina assoluta, directed by Miriam Talavera, texts by Zoe Valdés, ICAIC, 1991.
Fernando Alonso, un maestro de la danza, directed by Senobio Faget, Estudios Cinematográficos del Instituto Cubano de Radio y Televisión, 1985.
Imprescindibles – Alicia Alonso. Para que Giselle no muriera, directed by Nico García, rtve, 2010.
La Bella Cubana (Cuatro Joyas) directed by Idania D'Valle, CINED, 2004.
ParAlicia (video-arte), directed by Fernando Pérez, with Alicia Alonso, Viengsay Valdés and Frank Fernández, choreography by Tania Vergara, 2015.
Rostros Cubanos – Fernando Alonso, maestro de maestros, directed by Idania D'Valle, 2005.

ACKNOWLEDGMENTS

CUBA
Alicia Alonso

Andrés D. Abreu
Raquel Agüero Mercado
Ismael Albelo
Rosa Elena Álvarez
Carolina Balmaseda
Norge Cedeño Raffo
Noel Bonilla Chongo
María del Carmen Borroto, Centro Danza Prado
Jorge Brooks, Danza Contemporánea de Cuba
Isabel Bustos Romoleroux, compagnia Retazos
Martha Castellano Bosch
Graciela Chao Carbonero
Roxana De los Ríos
Ramona De Sáa, Escuela Nacional de Ballet, and her Staff
Laura Domingo Agüero
Luis Ernesto Doñas
Martha Iris Fernández Agüero
Guido Gali
José Ernesto González Mosquera, Danza Contemporánea de Cuba
Helson Hernández
Marcos Madrigal
Yamilet Núñez Valdés and Alfredo Cannatello
Luisa M. Olivares Navarro
Ahmed Piñeiro – *La Danza eterna*, program Cuban TV educational channel
José Ramón Rodríguez Neyra
Abel Rojo
Fidel Pajares Santiesteban
Digna Rosa Pérez, Conjunto Folklórico Nacional
Armando Pérez Sánchez, Tropicana, and all the Staff
Iliana Polo
Sandra Ramy Aparicio
Nancy Reyes
Fernando Sáez, Malpaso
Nelson Ramírez Arellano Conde
María Rovira

Aurélie Sampeur and Candelario, LASA
Lourdes Ulacia
Marisela Verdú García, Faculdad de Arte Danzario
Lester Vila Pereira, Acosta Danza
The management and staff of the Biennale d'Arte, of the Biennale del Teatro, of the Fototeca de Cuba and the Fábrica de Arte Cubano dell'Avana.

Special thanks to:
Pedro Simón – Museum of Dance and "Cuba en el Ballet"
Heriberto Cabezas, Ballet Nacional de Cuba
Miguel Cabrera, Historiador Ballet Nacional de Cuba
Mauricio Abreu, Prensa Ballet Nacional de Cuba
Martha Espinosa, BNC
Tancredi Francese, Embassy of Italy in Cuba
Samuele Fazzi, Embassy of Italy in Cuba
Giulio del Federico, Embassy of Italy in Cuba

MIAMI
Pedro Pablo Peña
Eriberto Jiménez

LATIN AMERICA
Gloria Castro - Cali, Colombia
Augustina Llumá, "Balletin Dance" - Argentina
Alicia Sanguineti - Argentina

ITALY
Enrico Giacovelli
Patrizia Giancotti
Chiara Giordano
Pietro Guarini, Centro Studi Italia Cuba
Paolo Cantù, Matteo Negrin, Piemonte dal Vivo and Staff
Daniele Ninarello
Paolo Mohovich - Teatro Piemonte Europa (TPE)
Pompea Santoro - Eko International Dance Project
Laura Valente, Ravello Festival
Gennaro Cimmino, Körper Centro Danza, Naples, and Staff
Quirino Conti

ACKNOWLEDGMENTS

Fondazione Carla Fendi and Staff
Loredana Furno, Viola Scaglione - Balletto Teatro di Torino (BTT)
Lavanderia a Vapore di Collegno and all the Staff
Torino Danza and Staff
Rete Anticorpi XL
Teatro alla Scala, Milan, Photographic Archives

Special thanks to:
Lisset Argüelles
Anna Cremonini
Angelo Bellotti
Franco Bolletta
Natalia Casorati
Franco Cis
Gigi Cristoforetti
Rino De Pace
Emanuele Enria
Katina Genero
Bruno Genero
Cristina Golin
Roberto Grano
Pino Izzo
Marco Lo Russo
Enrica Palmieri
Roger Salas, Madrid-Rome
Mayda Bustamante, Madrid
Francesco Scavetta, Salerno - Norway/Sweden
Simona Soledad Rinaldo, Brussels
Davide Tosolini
Matteo Vinti
Stefano Zenni
Yetart Videomakers

Special thanks to Alfio Agostini, "Balletto Oggi/Ballet2000"

The Author wishes to thank her colleagues, the journalists in Turin, Naples, and Havana, for their interest in following the projects that she has organized on ballet and Cuban and Italian-Cuban dance.

She expresses her admiration for the dancers and choreographers, men and women, students and professionals, whom she was able to follow during classes, rehearsals, and on stage, and for their tireless momentum, dedication and enthusiasm. In Cuba. And also in Italy.

The Author thanks the International Festival that has had her as a regular guest in Havana for so many years. It has truly been a school, a very concrete, direct way to learning and understanding Cuban dance and all dance. She expresses her gratitude above all to the incomparable Alicia Alonso so close to all.

The Author's many thanks to the Festival Callejero, directed by the generous and warmhearted artist Isabel Bustos, for being the catalyst to living and breathing the air of the island. At the home of her troupe, Retazos, the welcome was an incredible stimulus.

Nicolas Emmanuel and his mother Sylvia, dance teachers at the school Lys, were essential in helping the Author to grasp the history and memory of popular dances and tango in Cuba and how they are practiced today. With Leonardo Rodríguez, she experienced *tango negrero y blanquizado* in the Casa de África. And Julio Álvarez, in welcoming the Author to the Casa del Tango, in Havana, opened the doors wide for her to the world and passion of dance.

A special dedication is expressed by the Author to all of the Cuban friends who helped her for any question, everyday or professional. They were so many: Yaigsa and family, Yoandry and family, Luisito, Francys, Fernando and Mairobys, who introduced her to the complex life of Havana and the secrets of Cuban nightlife.

To Carlo Majer, Fabio Soto and Carlo Montanella with whom the Author shared precious cultural experiences in Havana and in Italy.

To Laura Domingo and Sandra Ramy, particularly, who opened so many doors, brought contacts, acquaintances, shared information, ideas, writings, images, and projects, always with such affection, generosity, and warmth.

The Author's heartfelt thanks to all.

PHOTO CREDITS

p. 14: © Detroit Photographic Company (top)
p. 16: © DM Archives
p. 19: © Timelife (top)
p. 20: © National Library of Australia (left)
pp. 25-25: © Jacques Moatti
pp. 28-29: © Irving Penn
p. 32: © Arch. C.V. (bottom)
p. 36: © Maurice Seymour
p. 39: © Nancy Reyes (bottom)
p. 44: © Archivio BNC (bottom)
p. 47: © Fabrizio Ferri (top)
p. 48: © World Dance Agency (bottom left)
p. 49: © Robb Aaron Gordon
p. 50: © Eliccer Quijada
p. 53: © Lelli e Masotti
p. 54: © Rosellina Garbo (top)
p. 56: © Pino Izzo
p. 58: © Angel Valentin (top)
p. 59: © Foteini Christofilopoulou (bottom)
p. 62: © Jackie Gleason (top);
© Rosalie O'Connor (center)
p. 63: © Pino Izzo
p. 68: © Nancy Reyes (bottom)
p. 72: © Archivio BNC (top);
© Armand (bottom)
p. 73: © Maurice Seymour
p. 74: © Nancy Reyes
p. 75: © Osiel Gouneo (bottom)
p. 77: © Nancy Reyes
p. 79: © Yuris Nórido
p. 81: © Jack Devant
p. 83: © Museo Casa Roig
p. 104: © Eric Politzer (bottom left);
© Luca Fiaccavento (bottom right)
p. 106: © Yander Zamora (bottom left)
p. 107: © Alejandro Rojas (center)
p. 108: © Carlos Mera (top);
© Ana León (bottom left)
p. 109: © Carlos Mera
p. 111: © Andrea Mohin (top)
p. 112: © Anja Beutler (top);
© Judy Ondrey (bottom left)

p. 113: © Roberto Grano
p. 114: © Johannes Hjorth (bottom)
p. 116: © Carlos Quezada (top);
© Roberto Salinas (bottom)
p. 118: © Anne-Sylvie Bonnet (top)
p. 121: © Aquino
p. 123: © Andrew W. Lang
p. 126: © Josep Aznar (left.);
© Gabriel Guerra Bianchini (right)
p. 128: © Rosario Cárdenas
p. 129: © Aquino (left)
p. 131: © Edgar Ariel
p. 134: © Andrew W. Lang
p. 137 © Gabriel Guerra Bianchini (bottom)
pp. 138-139: © Pino Izzo
p. 140: © Roberto Grano (top);
© Pino Izzo (bottom)
p. 141: © Beppe Giardino (top left)
p. 143: © Kyra Sama (bottom)
p. 146: © Johan Persson
p. 149: © Raúl Reinoso (center)
p. 150: © Michel Lidvac (top);
© Pino Izzo (bottom)
p. 151: © Bill Cooper (top);
© Johan Persson (bottom)
p. 154: © Manuel Vason (top)
p. 164: © Unulaunu
p. 191: © Ramiro Nogal
p. 198: © Peter Moruzzi (top)

The Publisher has made all efforts possible to locate the names of the people who have taken the photos that appear in this book and indicate them to the reader. If this has not been possible in all cases, please excuse any possible errors or omissions. The Publisher is prepared to complete any missing details in future new editions of this book. The Publisher is also prepared to recognize rights as per Article 70 of the 1941 law 633.

Other dance books in the
"Performing Arts" series:

Flavia Pappacena
The Language of Classical Ballet
Guide to the Interpretation of Iconographic Sources

M.E. García – M. Plevin – P. Macagno
Creative Movement and Dance
The García-Plevin Method

Roger Tully
The Song Sings the Bird
A Manual on the Teaching of Classical Dance

Agrippina Vaganova
Foundations of Classical Ballet
New, complete and unabridged translation of the 3rd editon